WOBURN PLACE

GOWER STREET

RUSSELL SQUARE

SOUTHAMPTON ROW

RUSSELL ST.

COURT ROAD

GREAT

Regent Sound

White Tower

British Museum

Indica Bookshop

CBS

THEOBALDS RD.

Conway Hall

GRAY'S INN ROAD

CLERKENWELL ROAD

Farringdo

Sadler's Wells

VENUE

FARRINGDON ROAD

Chancery Lane

100 Club

Wimpy Bar

Dominion

Immediate

BLOOMSBURY WAY

NEW OXFORD STREET

HIGH HOLBORN

Holborn

HOLBORN VIADUCT

Smit

Daily Mirror

Penny-Farthing Print Room

FARRINGDON ST

SOHO SQUARE

Edelweiss Indiacraft

Better Books

AVENUE

Saville

KINGSWAY

CHANCERY LANE

Lincoln's Inn

NEW FETTER LANE

Dr. Johnson's House

SHOE LANE

Foyle's Bookshop

Cousins Le Kilt One Act One Scene One 2 "I's"

Wheeler's

DRURY LANE

La Terrazza

CHARING CROSS RD.

Theatre Royal

Royal Opera House

Middle Earth

Covent Garden

FLEET STREET

Wimpy Bar

B

SHAFTESBURY

Whisky A'GoGo & Pink Flamingo

Studio 51

Mecca Dancing

ALDWYCH

BBC Bush House

Waldorf

Temple

Aldwych

Somerset House

LEICESTER SQ.

Tiffany's

Odeon

GREAT NEWPORT ST.

Pickwick

Vaudeville

La Discotheque

Adelphi

Chez Solange

St. Martin-in-the-Fields

STRAND

Talk of the Town

Prince of Wales

National Gallery

Q.

AYMARKET

Her

ESTY's

BBC Playhouse Theatre

TRAFALGAR SQ.

Charing Cross

WHITEHALL

VICTORIA EMBANKMENT

Savoy

WATERLOO BRIDGE

National Film Theatre

Royal Festival Hall

Queen Elizabeth Hall

YORK RD.

AMES'S PARK

WESTMINSTER

London County Hall

D0630812

THEATRES (for pop concerts musicals)

STAR SPOTS (Discotheques and Only clubs)

POP CLUBS (Beat, folk, psyched with "live" groups)

STAR NOSHES (Restaurants stars eat)

CHEAP EATS (Eateries for pe visitors!)

HAPPENINGS (Tourist's "musts

CLOBBER (Up-to-the-minutest ge and fellas)

CINEMAS (latest releases)

TUBES (London's underground m

SOUNDS (Studios of recording, ra companies)

BOOK SHOPS (Centres of where well-informed hippies!)

HOTELS (Good for American pop

THE
BRITISH
INVASION

George Harrison

Ringo Starr

Jane Asher

Jardine

Danish Gall

Michael

Dennis Wilson

Paul Peterson

Carl Wilson

Hayley Mills

Mike Love

Patty Duke

Brian Wilson

Peter Asher

Gene Pitney

Michael Burns   Eric Burdon   Gordon Wal

Bill Wyman

Keith

Richard   Chad Stuart   Brian Jones

Jerry Clyde   Dick Jagg

Charlie Watts

Bill Black   Tom   Keith Richard

THE
BRITISH
INVASION

BARRY MILES

STERLING

New York / London
www.sterlingpublishing.com

STERLING and the distinctive Sterling logo are registered trademarks of
Sterling Publishing Co., Inc.

10 9 8 7 6 5 4 3 2 1

Published by Sterling Publishing Co., Inc.
387 Park Avenue South, New York, NY 10016

© 2009 Essential Works Limited

Distributed in Canada by Sterling Publishing
c/o Canadian Manda Group, 165 Dufferin Street
Toronto, Ontario, Canada M6K 3H6

Distributed in the United Kingdom by GMC Distribution Services
Castle Place, 166 High Street, Lewes, East Sussex, England BN7 1XU
Distributed in Australia by Capricorn Link (Australia) Pty. Ltd.
P.O. Box 704, Windsor, NSW 2756, Australia

Produced for Sterling Publishing by Essential Works
www.essentialworks.co.uk
Publishing Director: Mal Peachey
Managing Director: John Conway
Editors: Fiona Screen, Ross Plotkin, Howard Watson, Dipli Saikia, Jennifer Eiss
Designers: Michael Gray, Kate Ward, scanning by Jessica Cash

Printed in China
All rights reserved

Sterling ISBN 978-1-4027-6976-4

For information about custom editions, special sales, premium
and corporate purchases, please contact Sterling Special Sales
Department at 800-805-5489 or specialsales@sterlingpublishing.com

CONTENTS

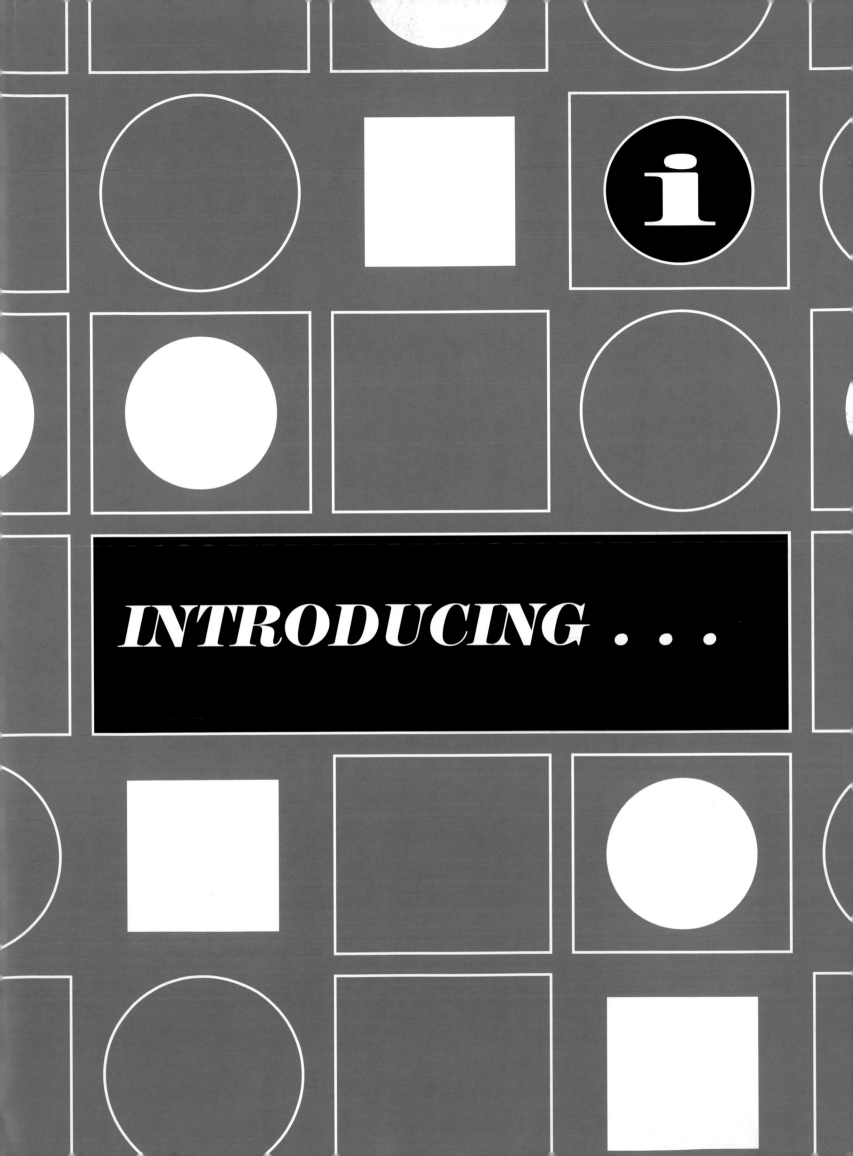

INTRODUCING . . .

TO SURVEY THE SCENE MORE THAN 45 YEARS DISTANT *from the Beatles landing in America is to see a truly astounding spectacle. Looking back at the effect that four barely intelligible, shaggy-haired musicians from Liverpool had on the mighty popular culture of America compounds that astonishment. For five years from 1964 to 1969 the American pop, fashion, and film scenes were inundated and almost overpowered by British acts, designers, and actors. Pop acts who barely registered in the British charts in that time were scoring top 10 hits Stateside (Chad & Jeremy immediately spring to mind);* Time *magazine, that international clarion of all things American, put Swinging London on its cover; Oscars went to a string of British actors, directors, and films; hems across the nation drew up as Mary Quant, Twiggy, and Jean Shrimpton were paraded in chain clothes stores from coast to coast. The Monkees, the only American-grown pop act to rival the Brits in the charts, were created in Hollywood in the image of the Beatles and had a cute British singer (Davy Jones).*

This was astounding. But why and how did it happen? There have been several theories put forward, including the idea that the Beatles were cheering up a nation still in mourning for John F. Kennedy. Of course, it wasn't as simple as that, even if there was a hint of truth in it. It is just as likely that, since American pop music and teen culture hadn't progressed much since Elvis was drafted, a generation born too late to jive to Elvis eight years earlier wanted something that they could call their own.

Frankie Avalon, Fabian, and Ricky Nelson were too clean-cut, too similar and bland to provoke the kind of hysterical reaction in teen girls (and some boys) created by the Fab Four. The Everly Brothers and Roy Orbison were fine enough, but they were fifties artists. The Beatles sounded newer, fresher, and more immediate. Their songs had a pace and passion that was missing in mainstream American pop music. Plus, there hadn't been a band of four musicians who played their own instruments, wrote their own songs, and appeared to be democratic in their lineup so far in the history of rock 'n' roll. Rock 'n' roll had always been about the lead singer, even if there was a band behind him. The Crickets had to put Buddy Holly in front; the Blue Caps had to push Gene Vincent; and doo-wop was only ever about interchangeable vocal groups.

The Beatles were Elvis to the power of four.

Their songs owed something to American music of the same era as Elvis, a lot to Little Richard, and an equal measure to American teen culture of the early fifties and the girl groups of Phil Spector and to the Berry Gordy sound of the early sixties. The Beatles were new, but familiarly so.

They and all the groups who followed them across the Atlantic were playing music that had been born in the U.S.A., and they were so excited to be in the States that their enthusiasm for America reflected back to the audience. If the death of their young, modern President had shown Americans anything, it was that they should live now, while they had a chance and the money to do so. The British Invasion gave them a soundtrack of their own to dance to, one which hadn't been sanctioned by their parents or older siblings.

American parents were indulgent of the Beatles and their ilk, though, perhaps because they were British. As World War II had shown, the British were honorable, upstanding, defiant, and, most importantly, on their side back then, as they were in the fight against the cold wind blowing from the East. Plus, of course, apart from the funny haircuts and accents, the Beatles arrived in New York wearing matching suits, praising America, and singing songs of love that were familiar, even if they were performed in a different manner.

ATOM MAN VS.
SUPERMAN
Based on the SUPERMAN adventure feature appearing in SUPERMAN and ACTION COMICS magazines and in daily and Sunday newspapers coast to coast. Adapted from the SUPERMAN radio program.
Copyright 1950,
National Comics Publications, Inc.
with
SUPERMAN
KIRK ALYN · LYLE TALBOT
NOEL NEILL · TOMMY BOND

Love Me Do

To discover how the Beatles got to JFK airport on February 9, 1964, you have to go back in time to the end of WWII. In 1945 Britain was in a perilous condition. Schools and hospitals operated from Nissen huts and emergency prefabricated buildings designed for temporary accommodation (many of which were still in use 15 years later). Roads were potholed, bridges were closed. Almost four million houses had been destroyed by bombing and those that remained were often damaged and hastily patched up; cracks ran across ceilings, floors sloped alarmingly, wooden buttresses held up walls and there were weed-covered bomb sites everywhere. It was a time of shortages, with food and fuel rationed. The generation born in Britain during the war—which produced the Beatles, the Stones, Pink Floyd, and the Who among others—grew up in a drab, gray environment.

In the United States, things could not have been more different. The economy was booming and, by 1947, America had the world's highest standard of living. The American influence in Britain during this time was significant—there were over 100 American military bases in the UK and servicemen were everywhere handing out chewing gum and comics. British comics were thin, black-and-white affairs, often reprints of American material but lacking the color; American comics had 52 pages of full color. There were *Adventure Comics*, *Detective Comics*, *Superman*, *Batman*, *Little Lulu*, *Archie*, *Tales From the Crypt*, bloodthirsty war comics, and horror comics. They carried ads for almost mythic products, not sold in Britain: Tootsie Rolls, Popsicles, Wrigley's "Double Bubble" chewing gum, children's bicycles with extra fat wheels and frames, hula hoops, and "BB" guns! (Brits didn't know the latter were the same as the air rifles available in the UK.)

Brits soon became acquainted with more Americana via Saturday morning flicks, which saw theaters screen a morning matinee main feature, sometimes British but usually from Hollywood, as well as a short and a serial. *Flash Gordon* was popular even if the spaceships moved so slowly it was impossible to see how they could stay up; *Batman* was popular, and so was *Superman* (though people always jeered when, just as he was about to burst through a door, an outline of holes appeared on it so that he could smash through, leaving a clear outline of his body). There were a bunch of cartoons, too, which were always American: *Tom & Jerry*, *Popeye*, *Bugs Bunny*, *Mighty Mouse*, *Pluto*, and so on. The British war generation grew up with American kiddie-culture.

It was the same on television. Britain did not produce enough programs to fill the time so more than half of all T.V. programming came from America. *Maverick*, *Rawhide*, *Wagon Train*, *Cheyenne*, *The Life and Legend of Wyatt Earp*, *Lassie*, *Have Gun—Will Travel*, *Bonanza*, *Laramie*, *Hopalong Cassidy*, *Gunsmoke*, *Tales of Wells Fargo*, *The Lone Ranger*, and all westerns were followed avidly by adults and kids alike on their predominantly black and white television sets; *Tales of the Texas Rangers*, *The Untouchables*, *Dragnet*, *Highway Patrol*, *Naked City*, and other cop shows were big, too; and there were never enough of shows like *I Love Lucy*, *The Phil Silvers Show* or *77 Sunset Strip* (Edd "Kookie" Byrnes was a definite role model to young British boys in the 1950s), despite much of the humor in those shows being distinctly American. Sometimes, no one had even bothered to edit out American ads from the cans of film delivered to UK broadcasters, and so mid-program Bob Hope might pop up, selling Buick cars (which were never for sale in the UK). This was simply seen as a cheap way of filling airtime, but to teenagers in Britain used to their near-deserted highways, it was a view of paradise, a million miles from the grim reality of everyday life.

American comics, like everything else American, were bigger, more colorful, more desirable than their British equivalents of the 1950s.

Rock Around the Clock

Bill Haley's version of Shake, Rattle and Roll reached number 4 in the British charts in December 1954. The bowdlerized version of Jesse Stone's original lyrics for Big Joe Turner transfixed Britain's youth. Some people sought out the uncensored cut, which was much raunchier. Ignored by the B.B.C., the only legally sanctioned radio station in Britain, rock 'n' roll was heard mostly across the crackling airwaves transmitted from Radio Luxembourg or on shows like Alan Freed's hour-long American Forces Network program from Frankfurt. Most people heard rock 'n' roll music from the records themselves, and would gather in each other's bedrooms for record parties. The news that someone had a desirable disc was cause to take long bus rides across town in order to hear it.

Ten months later Bill Haley was back in the charts with Rock Around the Clock. It was 1955 and things were beginning to change. The song was used for the opening credits of the Richard Brooks film *Blackboard Jungle*, starring Glenn Ford and Sidney Poitier, a schoolroom drama about an idealistic black teacher in a white high school filled with cynical teenagers. The song was an instant classic in the States and was the first rock 'n' roll record to reach number 1. In Britain it reached number 1 in January 1956 on the strength of the film's release there. Stories of American teenagers rioting and smashing up movie theaters when the song was played had reached British tabloid newspapers; Britain's newly emergent Teddy Boys—a sort of equivalent to New York's juvenile delinquents, whose name derives from their clothing inspired by the Edwardian era—took this to heart and did the same, provoking fury from the authorities unused to any youth dissent and, of course, encouraging the same thing to happen across the country wherever the film opened. Back in the States, Columbia Pictures jumped on the bandwagon and quickly hired Bill Haley and His Comets as the stars of two quickly slapped together exploitation movies: *Rock Around the Clock*, which roughly tells the (brief) history of rock 'n' roll, followed shortly after by a loose sequel called *Don't Knock the Rock*.

Rock Around the Clock was released in Britain in September 1956, driving the Teddy Boys wild. They sprayed fire hoses, slashed the theater seats, and danced in the aisles and in the streets outside. Policemen's helmets went flying and municipal flowerbeds were trampled. The film was quickly banned by town watch committees across the country, even though the Queen had requested a private screening of it in Buckingham Palace.

Bill Haley, in a British Teddy Boy-inspired jacket, meets Elvis to pass on the rock 'n' roll baton. Haley made several tours of the UK; Elvis never appeared there at all.

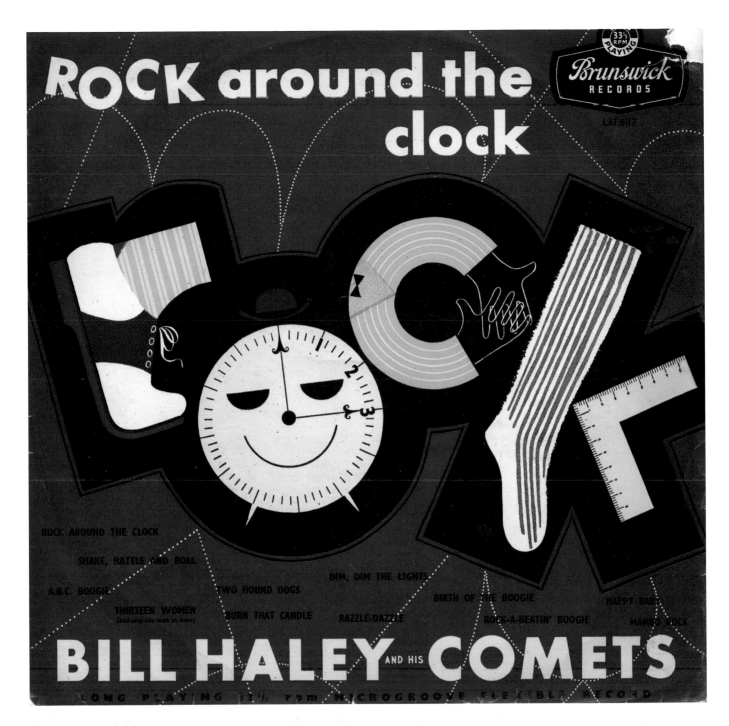

ROCK around the clock

Brunswick
RECORDS

33⅓ RPM
PLAYING

LAT 8117

ROCK AROUND THE CLOCK

SHAKE, RATTLE AND ROLL

A.B.C. BOOGIE   TWO HOUND DOGS   DIM, DIM THE LIGHTS   BIRTH OF THE BOOGIE   HAPPY BABY

THIRTEEN WOMEN   BURN THAT CANDLE   RAZZLE-DAZZLE   ROCK-A-BEATIN' BOOGIE   MAMBO ROCK
(And only one man in town)

BILL HALEY AND HIS **COMETS**

LONG PLAYING 12" rpm MICROGROOVE FLEXIBLE RECORD

But Bill Haley was only the beginning. In May 1956, Elvis Presley's Heartbreak Hotel had reached number 2 in the UK charts, to be quickly followed by six other singles before the year was out. This was someone the Teddy Boys could actually relate to: with his long, dyed black hair and his sneer, here was a real role model. Teenagers across Britain saw someone they could identify with; unlike most of the entertainers in the charts and on the television variety shows, Elvis was not far off their own age. Suddenly, the charts were flooded with Elvis songs: that same year saw Blue Suede Shoes, I Want You, I Need You, I Love You, the amazing double A-side: Hound Dog/Don't Be Cruel, Blue Moon, and, from his first film, Love Me Tender. In Britain, the wartime generation could barely understand many of his lyrics: what was a "penitentiary"? What did it mean when he asked a girl to "Wear my ring around your neck"? Despite so much American television, the mating rituals of American middle-class white teenagers were at that time virtually unknown in Britain.

This innocuous-looking record was regarded as deeply subversive by the church, family groups, and the establishment despite its dance party sleeve.

13

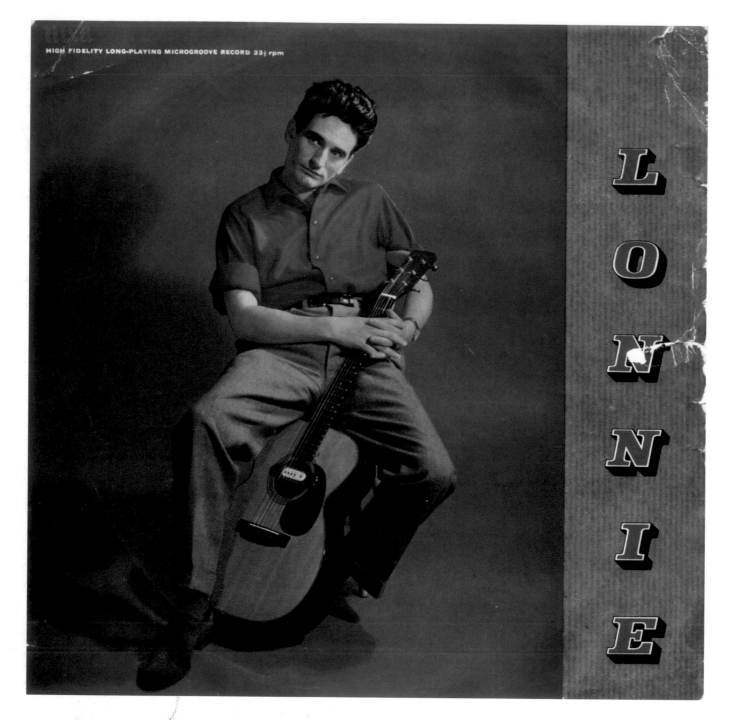

HIGH FIDELITY LONG-PLAYING MICROGROOVE RECORD 33⅓ rpm

L O N N I E

Rock Island Line

At around the same time Britain enjoyed another new musical phenomenon, this time a home grown one, if of American descent. Skiffle originated around 1900 in New Orleans as a term for pick-up bands using improvised instruments such as washboards and a broom-handle bass at rent parties. By the 1950s it was really only remembered by jazz and blues aficionados. The so-called father of English skiffle was guitarist Lonnie Donegan, a member of Ken Colyer's Jazzmen, a traditional New Orleans-style band. In 1953, in order to give the rest of the lineup a break, during live performances Donegan, Chris Barber, and Monty Sunshine began playing a pared-down, three-piece, mid-set interlude. Ken Colyer named the trio the Breakdown Band before his older brother Bill, who knew his jazz history, informed him they were actually playing skiffle. Bill Colyer worked at Collett's famous jazz and folk record shop in London's New Oxford Street and among the records he imported from the States was one by

Lonnie Donegan, the father of British skiffle, and a huge influence on virtually every British Invasion band from the Beatles to Van Morrison.

I always thought I was singing American folk music.

LONNIE DONEGAN

Dan Burley & His Skiffle Boys. Ken Colyer relented and began introducing the Breakdown Band as a skiffle group.

Traditional jazz was very popular in Britain, and many other bands also had a mid-set interlude. Bands were employed at dances and most promoters could not afford to hire two acts. The New Crane River Jazz Band had no name for their interlude act so they were introduced as the St. Louis Trio skiffle group. Good time traditional jazz was much closer to popular music than the jazz of the bebop era. It needed a lot of energy to keep up the momentum so the mid-set break was a welcome innovation that began to be featured by all the traditional bands playing at the time. At first, skiffle groups relied on numbers for volume as none of the instruments—washboard, tea-chest bass, acoustic guitar—was amplified. It was not unknown for a group to have as many as six acoustic guitars. Lonnie Donegan changed all this by the introduction of Denny Wright's electric guitar to his lineup. Promoters and club owners began to wonder if they could just hire the skiffle group and forget about the trombones and clarinets.

In 1954 Ken Colyer left and the band became the Chris Barber's Jazz Band. They released a 10-inch album *New Orleans Joys*, which, thanks to Donegan's skiffle cover versions of Rock Island Line and John Henry, sold an astonishing 50,000 copies. The record company, Decca, released Rock Island Line as a single in 1956 and it over a million copies worldwide, reaching number 8 in the American charts. Donegan had received only a $100 session fee for the song, but he signed to the Pye Nixa label as a solo artist and his Lost John record reached number 2 in the UK charts in April 1956. Skiffle was with us. In the next six years Donegan was to have 34 hits and to influence a whole generation of British musicians: Van Morrison's first band, the Sputniks, had a lineup of Van on vocals, accompanied by washboard, kazoo, tea-chest bass, and guitar; Ronnie Wood (of the Faces and Rolling Stones) first played live with the Candy Bison Skiffle Group; Graham Nash and Alan Clarke of the Hollies began as a skiffle group called the Two Teens; Mick Jagger played with the Barber-Colyer Skiffle Group in the early sixties; John Lennon's skiffle group, the Quarrymen, featured washboard and tea-chest bass, and the first song they rehearsed when Paul McCartney joined the band was Don't You Rock Me Daddy-O. Before joining the Beatles, George Harrison was in the Rebels, playing guitar to the backing of a tea-chest bass and mouth organ. The British had taken an American musical idiom and made it their own.

The Beatles went on to take a different American musical style further, with infinitely more success, beginning on *The Ed Sullivan Show* on national American television.

Below: The Helen Shapiro tour brought the Beatles to national prominence in the UK. Their first single, Love Me Do, reached number 17 in the British charts.

Following pages: Life magazine ran an 8-page feature on The Beatles in the week before they arrived in the U.S.A.

LIFE
Vol. 56, No. 5   Jan. 31, 1964

Four Screaming Mopheads
Break Up England

HERE COME THOSE BEATLES

First England fell, victim of a million girlish screams. Then, last week, Paris surrendered. Now the U.S. must brace itself. The Beatles are coming and already teen-age Americans are as keyed up as the days, only a dim decade ago, when Elvis first came twisting on.

The Beatles? They are the four shrewdly goofy-looking lads at left. Fifteen months ago they were singing their songs in a smoky Liverpool jazz cellar. A talent scout took them and their haircuts to London. Today their records have sold five million copies in England and they are a national institution, seemingly as solid as Big Ben and a lot louder. Their musical style embellished standard rock 'n' roll with a jackhammer beat and high screams that would do a steam calliope proud.

Princess Margaret is a devoted Beatle fan, and the Queen Mother summoned them to her regal presence and enthusiastically asked, "When is your next performance?" Field Marshal Montgomery said he would invite them down for a country weekend. Oh, a few old fogies have been grumbling in Parliament about the thousands of pounds of overtime pay given Bobbies to protect the Beatles from their teen-age admirers and prevent full-scale riots. But Beatlemania has become a British way of life.

They come here Feb. 7 for three Ed Sullivan TV appearances, two Carnegie Hall dates, and they should find Americans easy pickings. In the past week their record of *I Want To Hold Your Hand* has jumped to No. 1 in the U.S. —as two million ear-sore parents will testify.

**Photographed for LIFE
by TERENCE SPENCER**

HAIL BEATLEMANIA! English girls go screeching down the streets after the four Beatles (*left to right*), Paul McCartney, 21, George Harrison, 21, John Lennon, 23, and Ringo Starr, 23.

25

PACKING T...
even the hug...
lo above. Th...

BILLIONAIRE BEA...
ty, "world's richest
tle wig at party in h...

BEATLING BARB...
pay $1.85 for a Be...
20,000 Beatle wigs...

THEY ROCK 'N' ROLL IN A HAIL OF JELLY BABIES

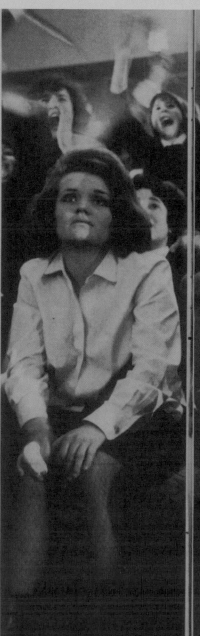

STICKY STAGE. Skipping among scattered jelly babies (jelly beans) hurled by fans, John, George and Paul sing. Ringo is on drums.

ADORATION. Some girls scream, "Please marry me." Others shout, "Beatles forever!" And others sit quietly, nursing their hopeless love.

SE. The Beatles always fill [theaters], like Manchester's Apollo [aud]itory consists of songs two of them, John and Paul, have written. None can read music, even the two composers. They get the name Beatle from their insistent, four-four beat.

RAISING THE ROOF. Fans explode in pandemonium, subsiding only briefly when a Beatle shouts "shurrup" from the stage. British parents do not mind their offspring's mania because Beatles' lyrics are clean and happy. As one critic observed, "Their hair is long and shaggy, but well scrubbed."

PROTECTING THE IDOLS. Battery of Bobbies stands guard where the Beatles are to exit. "If those girls caught those ruddy lads," commented one officer, "they'd tear them to pieces." At one theater a hundred girls battled police for four hours outside when they couldn't buy tickets.

Paul Get-[ ] Bea-[ ]sh castle.

THEY CROWN THEIR COUNTRY WITH A BOWL-SHAPED HAIRDO

LONDON

Success has made life wonderful for the Beatles—but not safe. A Beatle who ventures out unguarded into the streets runs the very real peril of being dismembered or crushed to death by his fans.

In some English cities where the Beatles perform the police have ruled that the Beatles must be inside the theater by midafternoon, half an hour before school lets out. Otherwise the police will not be responsible for the consequences. Where early arrival is not possible, getting into the theater often turns into a major tactical problem. When the Beatles arrived one afternoon at the London Palladium, their chauffeur-driven limousine was stopped dead and besieged by screaming girls. They tore off the wing mirror before the terrified driver stepped on the gas and fled with the Beatles still locked inside. The four finally made it by disguising themselves as floor mats in a couple of taxis that cruised up to the Palladium with "for hire" signs lighted. At Birmingham the Beatles were smuggled to a performance disguised in police coats and helmets, and at Portsmouth they escaped from the theater through a tunnel. At Manchester, to the undoubted delight of the local underworld, the city had to deploy half its police force around the theater to prevent a riot.

Once in the theater, there are still problems. Most Beatle performances take place with a wall of cops lining the stage to keep back frantic girls.

"I don't think they'll ever get us," says Beatle John with a show of bravado. Police are not so sure. "I nearly got my ruddy shoulder dislocated trying to stop three girls dashing under a bus," grumbled one London police sergeant. "These girls are like eels—through your legs and after the Beatles before you know where you are."

Anyone who actually wants to listen to the Beatles had best do so on his own hi-fi. Though loud they be, the live performances are rarely audible above the bedlam they touch off. Girls wave, lash about and screech. They hurl Teddy bears, Beatle idols,

BEATLE'S GOSPEL. The Salvation Army's Joystrings combo rocks gospel tunes Beatle-style to "keep up."

[ ]sh boys [ ]rcut and [ ]en sold.

jelly babies and love letters. Through it all girls faint by the platoon. Burly policemen carry them out like sacks of coal until the foyer is strewn with bodies.

The biggest problem during shows is those flying jelly babies. Ever since the Beatles confided that this was their favorite candy, jelly babies have pelted them like a hail storm.

"They can make as much row as they like," says John. "All I wish is they wouldn't throw jelly babies." "Have you ever tried walking on jelly babies?" asks Paul. "They're one of the most adhesive substances known to man. Sometimes kids think I'm trying out new little dance steps when I'm really trying to get my foot up off the floor."

A few weeks ago the Beatles tried to end the menace. "We did like jelly babies once," Paul shouted into a mike, "but now we've had enough. Now we like peppermint creams and chocolate caramels." They have come to regret this almost as much as the stage managers all across the country who have to clean up the chocolatey, minty mess.

On the whole the Beatles have adjusted well to their madcap life and manage to keep their good humor under the constant threat of butchery. Asked to explain their funny haircuts, John replied, "What funny haircuts, old man? What exactly do you mean, funny?" When Ringo Starr was asked why he wore four rings on his fingers, he responded innocently, "Because I can't fit them all through my nose."

Even at the Royal Command Variety Performance with the royal family in the minked and tiaraed audience, their humor was uncurbed. Stepping to the microphone, John growled a request: "Would people in cheaper seats please clap their hands? The rest of you can rattle your jewelry."

Not everyone has been amused by the Beatle cult and some grump at the widespread way the quartet's style of grooming is copied by adolescent England. Snapped the executive officer of the carrier *Bulwark*, "I note with alarm an increasing number of peculiar haircuts affected by teen-age members of the ship's company, attributable, I understand, to the Beatles. . . . Get deBeatled now."

The headmaster of a boys' school in Guildford declared a ban on Beatle cuts. "This ridiculous style brings out the worst in boys," he said. "It makes them look like morons." I found such

THE BRITISH ARE COMING!

FOR JOHN LENNON, *Paul McCartney, Mick Jagger, Keith Richards, and all their British pals, May 1956 was a turning point in their lives. See You Later Alligator was still in the British pop charts (and the B.B.C. was actually playing it), when suddenly Elvis Presley burst on the scene with Heartbreak Hotel and changed everything. A week later he was joined by Carl Perkins singing his own composition Blue Suede Shoes; the week after that Elvis' version also debuted on the charts. Elvis went to number 9 with Carl Perkins' song, but Perkins' original version was only one place lower in the charts (and it was his version that Lennon and McCartney went for).*

In July, Frankie Lymon's high falsetto trilling of Why Do Fools Fall in Love was also in the UK charts, and Gene Vincent's Be Bop a Lula entered in August. The top 20 in Britain was at last beginning to look and sound good.

All over Britain those teenagers at school who would make up the first wave of British bands to reach the States in the mid-sixties were absorbing this new music: the rock 'n' roll triplets, the chord changes, the harmonies and techniques. They examined photographs of their heroes, noting the makes and models of their guitars and amps, studying which chords they were playing, wondering how they achieved those special effects, their echoes, and bent notes. They quickly sorted out the quality from the dross and rejected the cover versions to seek out the originals.

A good example of the British kids' discriminatory powers was demonstrated in the success of Little Darlin' by a white Canadian group called the Diamonds, who specialized in cover versions of songs by black musicians. It peaked at number 2 and spent eight weeks in the U.S.A. *Billboard* chart in 1957 and reached number 3 in the UK charts in May that year. The original version, written by Maurice Williams, was by the Gladiolas and made number 11 on the U.S.A. R&B charts (but as mainstream white radio stations would not play black music in the U.S.A., it was the white cover group who had the hit). The Diamonds' version may have become a hit in Britain, but the aficionados of rock 'n' roll tried to get the original version. Everyone in Liverpool knew someone who worked on the boats that made the regular crossings to the States, so they put in requests to their older brothers, their cousins, and their uncles to bring back Little Darlin' or, for that matter, anything by the Gladiolas. Eager to earn a few extra shillings for so little work, sailors readily and illegally imported 45s from America into Britain as asked. In 1959, the Gladiolas became Maurice Williams and the Zodiacs, whose 1960 record Stay was the shortest ever U.S.A. number 1, lasting just 1 minute 39 seconds. It was later a UK hit for the Hollies.

It was a matter of honor among the hip teens in Britain to never buy any recording by Pat Boone, whose white bread, emasculated covers of Little Richard, Fats Domino, and Chuck Berry did well among the mainstream British record-buyers just as they did in the States.

At the time, it seemed most of the music that really counted to those hip teens like Lennon, McCartney, Jagger, and Richards was by African-American artists: the ecstatic shrieks of Little Richard, the rolling piano of Fats Domino, the guitar virtuosity of Bo Diddley, the high falsetto of Frankie Lymon, and the celebratory teen lyrics of Chuck Berry appealed most to them. In 1956 Elvis was the only white performer to carry equal weight among Brit hipsters since there was no denying the authenticity of his delivery or his vocal range. That year, as mentioned, he dominated the British charts, releasing seven singles in eight months, all with brilliant B-sides and all showing that real, hip-swinging, finger-clicking, down and dirty rock 'n' roll could appeal to everyone.

Right: Although plenty of white cover versions of hit records were released in the UK, young British musicians sought out the original black versions and later, when touring in the U.S.A., made a point of including their heroes in their shows.

Below: A string of movies carried the music of America's early rock 'n' rollers to Britain. Jamboree helped Charlie Gracie score his first hit over there.

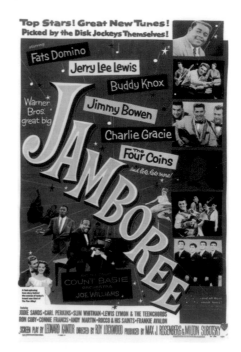

Left: Buddy Holly had a tremendous influence on young British rockers. It was through him that the British developed their love of high vocal harmonies. They could relate to his nerdy image. John Lennon: "He made it OK to wear glasses. I was Buddy Holly."

Below right: Guitarist for British instrumentalists The Shadows, Hank Marvin took his physical resemblance to Buddy Holly as far as he could. He even played the same guitar, finished in the same color.

Not a Juvenile Delinquent

The first major American rock 'n' roller to actually tour Britain was Bill Haley and His Comets. Unfortunately, the great energy and thrill of Haley's Rock Around the Clock and See You Later Alligator had disguised the fact that the singer was a middle-aged, portly gentleman with a false cowlick kiss-curl who toured with his wife. Haley was no hip-swiveling juvenile delinquent, unlike the next big American rocker to tour the UK.

Frankie Lymon arrived in Britain on April 1, 1957 for a 12-week tour, during which he cut an LP for Gee Records called *Frankie Lymon at the London Palladium*. He enjoyed four big hits in Britain—Why Do Fools Fall In Love, I'm Not a Juvenile Delinquent, Baby Baby, and Goody Goody—and his unbroken pre-pubescent falsetto had considerable influence on British groups, who even now have a liking for high falsetto vocals. (He was also an influence on American girl groups.) His recordings were the extreme of rock 'n' roll which is why they were so popular; his voice was the highest, his bass singer sang the lowest, and the sax solo on Teenage Love (1957) was the longest sustained note anyone had ever heard in rock 'n' roll.

Philadelphian rocker Charlie Gracie had three top 20 hits in the UK in 1957: Butterfly, Fabulous, and I Love You So Much It Hurts. He became the first American solo act to tour Britain (Haley had toured with his band) and had tremendous influence on teenage British musicians: George Harrison, in a *Billboard* interview, cited Gracie's guitar playing as a seminal influence on his own; Van Morrison said that seeing Gracie prompted him to start playing guitar; Graham Nash of the Hollies, and later Crosby, Stills and Nash, was an even bigger fan. At a Gracie gig years later, Nash, by now famous, approached the guitarist and showed him a box containing one of Gracie's old Camel cigarette butts.

Gracie recalled that, "Graham had saved it all these years. And then he thanked me for getting him to play music. Wow, it just made me feel good!"

Probably the most influential American performer to tour Britain in the late fifties, though, was Buddy Holly, who arrived in March 1958 with the Crickets on the strength of only two singles: Peggy Sue and Listen to Me. Brian Poole of the Tremeloes recalled:

Buddy Holly and the Crickets were the loudest thing we'd ever heard. It was a small band but they made such a crack when they came on and it was very, very exciting. We were doing Buddy Holly songs for the next five years. At one stage there was nothing in our act that wasn't a Buddy Holly song. We were so much into Buddy Holly that I had hair and glasses just like him.

Charlie Gracie may have started Graham Nash on the road to rock, but it was Buddy Holly he named his band after: the Hollies (although this is disputed, as some people claim it was named after the tree).

However, it was the Beatles who were perhaps the most affected. That'll Be the Day was the first song that John Lennon learned to play, taught to him by his mother Julia on the banjo. Lennon remembered her "endless patience until I managed to work out all the chords. She was a perfectionist. She made me go right through it over and over again until I had it right. I remember her slowing down the record so that I could scribble out the words. First hearing Buddy absolutely knocked me for a loop."

The Beatles' early songs such as She Loves You and I Want to Hold Your Hand showed Holly's enormous influence on their songwriting. Their early live sets in Hamburg and Liverpool featured a string of Holly songs such as Peggy Sue, That'll Be the Day, It's So Easy, Maybe Baby, Crying, Waiting, Hoping, Think It Over, and Mailman, Bring Me No More Blues, while they included Words of Love on their December 1964 *Beatles for Sale* album. Ringo Starr noted how Jerry Allison's percussion sound on Buddy Holly's Not Fade Away was made by lightly tapping a cardboard box and how he just slapped his knees on Everyday, giving Ringo the freedom to innovate and experiment with the Beatles. When McCartney decided to move into music publishing the first catalog he bought was the songs of Buddy Holly. Buddy enjoyed himself so much during his four-week tour that he was making plans to open a studio in London at the time of his death.

Frankie Lymon and the Teenagers were enormously popular in Britain where they were seen as an exotic novelty act: they sang higher and lower than any other group.

Following pages: U.S. teen magazines such as 16 quickly took to the Fab Four in 1964 and ran as much as they could on them.

I saw Frankie Lymon and said if he can do that, I can do that.

REUBEN BLADES

AN EARLY TRIUMPH FOR THE BEATLES. This was the happy evening of the presentation of an award by northwest England's own pop publication, "Mersey Beat." The Beatles topped that paper's annual popularity poll in 1961 and 1962.

LITTLE RICHARD AMONG THE LIVERPOPLIANS.
He loved the vocal wildness of The Beatles; he exploded with glee when he found acceptance among the Beatle people.

A-Wop-Bop-a-Loo-Bop-a-Lop-Bam-Boom

Little Richard was another particular British favorite: his delivery was frantic, manic, and no one had heard anything like it before. Each new single seemed even faster and more energetic than the one before: Rip It Up, Long Tall Sally, Tutti Frutti, and She's Got It were big hits. Despite no one in Britain knowing what he was talking about half the time, they knew it was the real thing. If adults could not understand the lyrics that was even better. For a time, Little Richard was the personification of rock 'n' roll itself in Britain, with the chorus of Tutti Frutti—"A-wop-bop-a-loo-bop-a-lop-bam-boom!"—becoming a rock 'n' roll catch phrase across the country.

Richard sang the title song of the 1956 film *The Girl Can't Help It*, starring Jayne Mansfield, which is possibly the greatest rock 'n' roll film ever made. It was enormously popular in Britain, maybe more so than in the U.S.A. Paul McCartney did a particularly good imitation of Little Richard singing Long Tall Sally, complete with shrieks and screams, hand gestures, and head nods, all copied from Little Richard's performance of the song in the film *Don't Knock the Rock*, which was released in Britain in February 1957 (Little Richard also performed Tutti Frutti in the same film). All these songs would feature in the early repertoires of the Beatles and other British bands when they performed live.

After becoming an evangelist in 1957, claiming that rock 'n' roll was the music of the devil and that he could not serve God and be a rocker at the same time, Little Richard retired from music. However, he soon changed his mind and in November 1962 played a residency at the Star Club in Hamburg on the same bill as the Beatles, which the Liverpudlians loved.

In 1963 Richard toured Britain with Bo Diddley and the Everly Brothers. They took with them the youthful Rolling Stones as their support group.

For sheer rock 'n' roll energy, no one compared to Little Richard and all the newly emerging British bands used his songs in their acts. The Beatles were particularly influenced by him.

Right: Released in 1964 just as he was beginning another rock 'n' roll comeback, this album contains only religious numbers from the Georgia Peach.

HERE'S LITTLE RICHARD

TIGER
SALUTES
CHUCK
BERRY

To Many, Including the
Beatles, His
Talent Is The
GREATEST in
the ROCK WORLD

IF THERE'S any one dynamic entertainer in today's wildly exciting music business, some believe it's Chuck Berry. But although he's at the peak of his talent, his records of late haven't been hitting the top of the charts.

"Whether he sells the most records or not isn't important," John Lennon said only recently. "Chuck Berry has had more to do with our style of music than most other performers. He's true rhythm and blues and has a sound that no one can duplicate."

Where some entertainers perform as if they've learned their skill, Chuck Berry lets everyone know when they hear him that his talent comes from deep within. He feels what he's singing and the sounds and rhythm come out stronger and clearer than any single entertainer.

Acts like the Righteous Brothers have gained ideas of interpretation from Berry for he represents the Best in his kind of music and his kind of music is the music of the Beatles, the Stones and all of today's other great groups. They, like Chuck, don't just perform. They feel each note . . . each beat . . . and they make their audiences feel it in much the same way.

Today, Chuck's 34 years old, but his talent keeps growing with the years. While still in high school he got his start as an entertainer working house parties and church affairs as a singer-guitarist. On his days off he worked as an assistant to his father who was a carpenter.

In 1952 he started his own small group and began appearing at clubs in and around St. Louis, Missouri. He was soon discovered by Chess Records and put under contract to this firm and in 1955 Chuck and Chess Records hit it big with his recording of **Maybellene**. He received the triple crown from The Billboard when his recording hit all three major rating charts in the No. 1 position.

Since then Chuck's been continually on the scene singing his heart out and writing his own songs that have inspired many of the other young song writers of today.

John Lennon and Paul McCartney are perhaps the finest song writers and performers on today's pop charts but they always have time to pay tribute to Chuck. "Without talent like Chuck Berry," Paul insists, "it's likely that today's sound would never exist. This man deserves every bit of respect and admiration the music world has to offer."

Paul, John, and all the other entertainers join TIGER in saluting CHUCK BERRY.

54

Come On

It is impossible to overstate the influence of Chuck Berry on British rock 'n' roll. The Beatles recorded Berry's Rock and Roll Music on *Beatles for Sale* and Roll Over Beethoven on *With the Beatles*, and played many more of his songs during their numerous B.B.C. radio appearances at the time. The Stones debut single was their version of Berry's Come On (with a B-side by Willie Dixon) and his songs also featured in the acts of most of the Liverpool bands as well as those of groups like the Animals over in Newcastle.

Chuck Berry attributed much of his success to his clear diction, which was deliberately designed to appeal to the white market as well as American R&B fans. The car, girl, and high-school dramas of his songs were also more likely to ring true to a white high-school audience, and his songs were the first R&B numbers to cross over into the white charts—his first record, Maybellene, reached number 5 in the American charts in August 1955. In Britain, where there was no such distinction made between artists and no separate R&B chart, it was his image as the bad boy of rock that appealed; much of the adolescent angst in his songs didn't really apply in Britain. Teenagers didn't own cars in the fifties and early sixties in Britain, and most of their parents didn't either. However, the British loved his rhythm and the way he kept just ahead of the beat. The future musicians noted his signature "duck walk," which he introduced into his act in 1956 at a concert in New York. (He said he did it in order to hide the wrinkles in his rayon suit. "It got an ovation," he recalled, "so I did it again and again.") It became one of the classic rock 'n' roll poses, often referenced by other artists. British kids found his early criminal background romantic and could not understand his 1959 arrest and imprisonment for the Mann Act offense of transporting a 14-year-old girl across a state line, not having any state lines to cross. For someone like Keith Richards, Berry was a life-long role model.

While the Stones showed a greater preference for R&B music of the late fifties, the Beatles mixed their R&B with rockabilly. When John Lennon first met Paul McCartney he was impressed by the fact that McCartney knew all the chords to Eddie Cochran's Twenty Flight Rock (which he still performs in

John Lennon: Whether or not he sells the most records or not isn't important. Chuck Berry has had more to do with our style of music than most other performers. He's true rhythm and blues and has a sound that no one can duplicate.

Without talent like Chuck Berry, it's likely that today's sound would never exist.

PAUL MCCARTNEY

concert to this day). The group took its name—in part—from Buddy Holly's Crickets, admired the slap bass sound of Gene Vincent, and imitated the high vocal harmonies of the Everly Brothers. Carl Perkins was a role model for George Harrison, and of all the Beatles Harrison was the one most drawn to rockabilly. He preferred that guitar sound over all others and in the late sixties actively disliked feedback and the psychedelic histrionics of Jimi Hendrix, provoking a number of arguments within the group at the time when it was felt that George was stuck in a rockabilly rut. Both George and Paul played Les Paul Gold Top guitars (among others), the model Perkins had used to record Blue Suede Shoes.

In May 1964, R&B and rockabilly made a combined assault on Britain when Carl Perkins and Chuck Berry toured together, backed by the newly formed Newcastle band the Animals, whose lead singer was Eric Burdon. At a party thrown for Perkins on the last day of the tour the American ended up sitting on the floor, strumming his guitar, and telling stories about the old days to the assembled guests, which included the Beatles. Ringo Starr, sitting next to him, asked if he could record Honey Don't for a new Beatles album. "Man," replied Perkins, "Go ahead, have at it." The Beatles also covered Perkins' Matchbox, which was one of McCartney's favorite songs, and Everybody's Trying to Be My Baby, which Perkins had adapted from a 1936 original by Rex Griffin.

Breathless

The piano player on Carl Perkins' Matchbox was an all-American country boy named Jerry Lee Lewis. The British loved his 1957 hits Whole Lotta Shakin' Goin' On, which reached number 8 in the British charts, and his UK number 1 hit Great Balls of Fire, with its infectious hook line. Lewis was the wild man of rock who played piano standing up, sometimes lifting his feet to play the chords with his heel; he stood on top of the instrument and raked his fingers up and down the keyboard. His hair was long for the period and swept back, but as he played it fell in front of his eyes, covered in sweat. Yet with a deft flick of his head, every hair would fall back into place. The Teddy Boys loved it: he looked dangerous and unpredictable, a bringer of chaos and rebellion.

Unfortunately, it was a visit to Britain that almost destroyed his career. When Lewis arrived for a tour in May 1958 he was accompanied by his then third wife, Myra. An airport news agency reporter thought she looked young and asked her age. When the news broke that she was only 13, and also his first cousin once removed, the British press erupted in prurient puritanical fury. His marriage may have been legal in Tennessee, but to the British newspapers it was outrageous (and a perfect news story). He only played three concerts before the tour was canceled. The uproar continued back in America and was used by the similarly middle-aged and reactionary American press to fuel an anti rock 'n' roll backlash. His concert fees dropped from $10,000 to $250 a night, Dick Clark wouldn't have him on his squeaky-clean show, and Sun Records stopped recording him. It took ten years for his career to recover. Of course, to people like John Lennon and Keith Richards, the 13-year-old bride only made Jerry Lee more interesting.

It is sometimes said that without Little Richard there could have been no Chuck Berry, and without Chuck Berry no Rolling Stones, but there was another strand to the history of rock 'n' roll: the R&B sound of Bo Diddley, and it had an equally big impact on British R&B in the early 1960s.

Thirteen-year-old Myra Lewis hugs her husband as they endure the storm of abuse which their marriage provoked on both sides of the Atlantic. (The marriage lasted 12 years.)

I'm a rompin', stompin', piano playing son of a bitch. A mean son of a bitch. But a great son of a bitch.

JERRY LEE LEWIS

BO DIDDLEY

With his infectious "shave and a haircut, two bits" rhythm and deceptively simple songs which often had no chord changes, he was another much-loved and imitated figure in Britain. Known as "The Originator", he brought a harder, more rhythmic guitar sound to rock. On that epochal British tour of 1963 with the Everly Brothers and Little Richard he so impressed bottom-of-the-bill Rolling Stones that they covered his I Need You Baby (Mona) on their first album and used his distinctive beat on a number of their songs including Please Go Home and I'm Alright. Buddy Holly used the same rhythm on Not Fade Away, which the Stones also covered. A founder member of the Stones, Dick Taylor, left the band and formed the Pretty Things with Phil May in 1963. They took their name and much of their early set from Bo Diddley.

Round and Round

More than anything, it was the raunchy, exuberant, free-for-all days of original rock 'n' roll that so impressed the British musicians who would go on to form bands in the early part of the next decade. They were given extra impetus because the original rockers were becoming more bland. When Elvis broke big around the world Broadway was packed out with musical arrangers and songwriting teams who, although astonished by the rise of rock 'n' roll, had been content to sit back and allow it to play itself out, confident that it was a passing fad like the hula hoop. But as Danny and the Juniors sang in March 1958, "Rock and Roll Is Here to Stay." If anything, it seemed to be growing. So the music industry—a very conservative business—made moves to control and sanitize, or simply erase, the rock 'n' roll artists and bands. As Bo Diddley, who had received nothing for his early hit recordings, said, "I am owed. I've never got paid. A dude with a pencil is worse than a cat with a machine gun."

Artists were encouraged to sing classics, to use string arrangements, and to make lame Hollywood movies. By 1960 Elvis was in the army; Eddie Cochran and Buddy Holly were dead, Little Richard had renounced rock 'n' roll, Jerry Lee Lewis was denounced and disgraced by the puritans, and Bill Haley turned out to be a charming middle-aged gentleman cowboy in a plaid shirt. Frankie Lymon went solo and lost his excitement.

When Dick Clark started hosting the *American Bandstand* television show in 1957 it began to broadcast clean-cut kids singing anodyne novelty records that

Bill Haley prepares for a comeback as Elvis Presley goes into the army.

FEBRUARY 1959

PHOTOPLAY

THE WORLD'S TOP FILM MAGAZINE

1/3

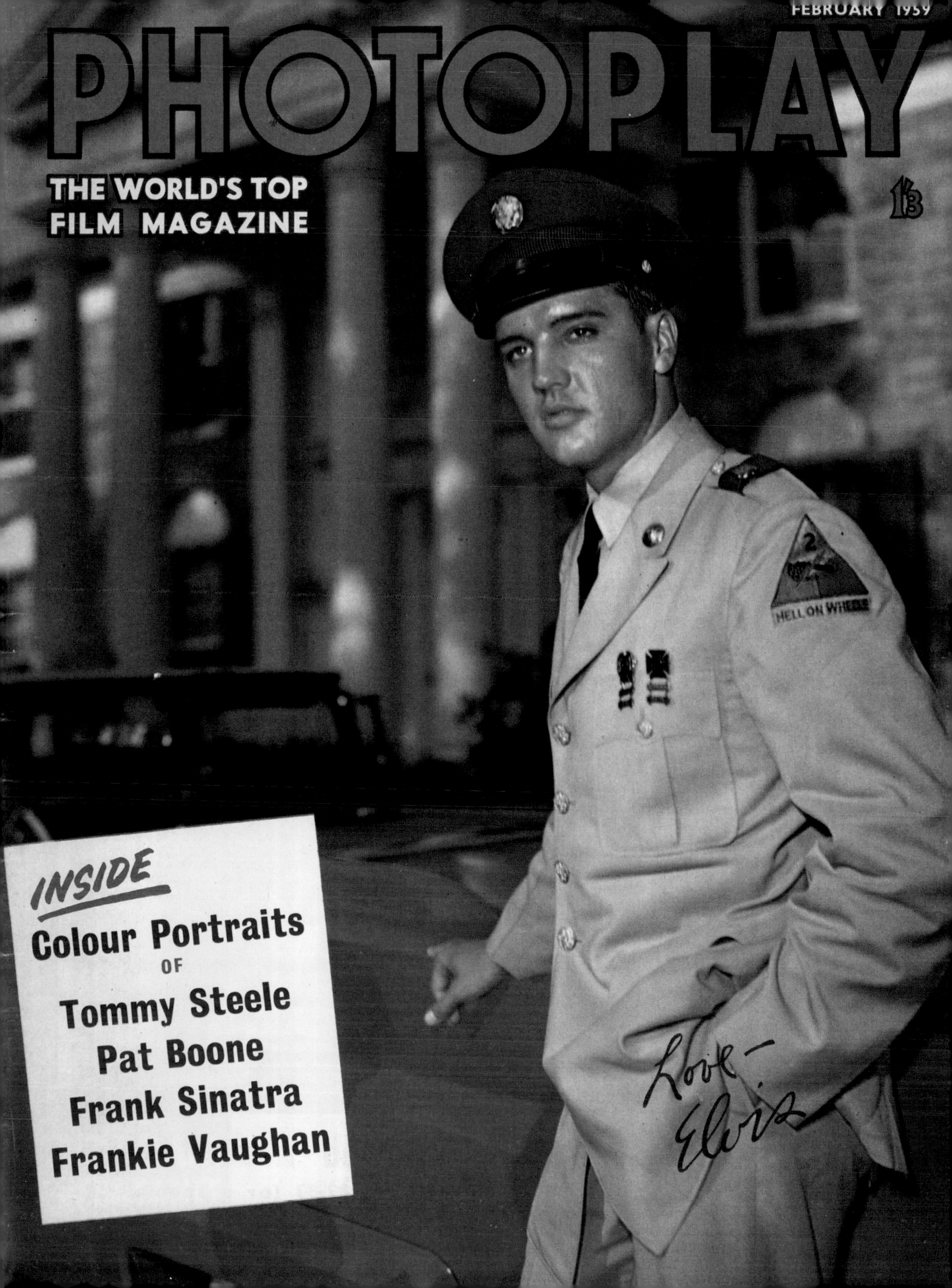

INSIDE
Colour Portraits
OF
Tommy Steele
Pat Boone
Frank Sinatra
Frankie Vaughan

HELL ON WHEELS

Love—
Elvis

I don't set trends.
I just find out what
they are and exploit
them.

DICK CLARK

would become typified by then 16-year old Brian Hyland's Itsy Bitsy Teenie Weenie Yellow Polka Dot Bikini in 1960. Instead of the original performers, American teenagers heard cover versions by people like Pat Boone and a series of wholesome teenage role-models like Frankie Avalon, Bobby Rydell, and Fabian. *American Bandstand* was not shown in Britain and none of these new white performers caught on there. The future British Invaders of America stuck to the original performers and found new ones like Ray Charles, Big Mama Thornton, Big Joe Turner, and Little Walter to listen to on the ever-so-desirable discs carried across the Atlantic by sailors and sold in the ports of Liverpool, Bristol, Dublin, and Southampton.

American servicemen doing their compulsory military service in the many army and air force bases across Britain found that they could make pals with British kids by playing them a few records from back home and the wilder the disk, the better the British liked it, or so it seemed. No homegrown British artists had been allowed to mature into fully fledged rock 'n' rollers because of the pernicious influence of their managers and the music establishment. Tommy Steele, Britain's first homegrown teen idol and rock 'n' roll star, released the raw, wild, Rock with the Caveman and the uncharted Doomsday Rock in 1956 but enjoyed real success with a cover of Guy Mitchell's Singing the Blues, which climbed to number one in December of that year. His management's reaction was to immediately stick him into pantomime. Steele recalled, "I had to dance, sing and do comedy routines and all of a sudden I was in a musical and loved it." Exit rock 'n' roller, enter the all-round entertainer. Cliff Richard, an English Elvis impersonator complete with sneer, quiff, and leg action, only made one great rock record—his first, Move It—before being co-opted to make novelty records like Living Doll. Managers like Larry Parnes groomed their singers from the beginning as variety artists.

In Liverpool, where there was Tin Pan Alley, things were changing and the locals remained true to their rock 'n' roll roots. When rock died a death in the U.S.A. in the late fifties, Liverpudlians particularly turned to the blues and R&B originals heard on those illicitly transported 45 rpm singles from the States. Among the singles coming over from across the pond were several on a new label, Philles. These had a whole new big and thrilling sound to them, a sound which caught on quick.

Dick Clark's American Bandstand turned rock 'n' roll into wholesome family entertainment. It took the arrival of the Beatles to revive it as a must-watch program for teens.

To Know Him Is to Love Him

John Lennon once told Phil Spector, "You kept rock 'n' roll alive while Elvis was in the army." Elvis went into the army with a leather-tooled guitar, black eyeliner, dyed hair, a sneering lip, and a swiveling hip. He came out an all-American boy singing a modern version of the old Neapolitan ballad O Sole Mio called It's Now or Never, and started his journey towards the Las Vegas nightclubs. Everyone had held great hopes for his return. When he released Hard Headed Woman, Paul McCartney said, "We thought 'great title, oh this is going to be great!' But there's a dreadful great big trombone right in the middle of it, and we thought, 'good God, what in hell has happened?' We were very disappointed about that." No more Jailhouse Rock—he didn't rock again until it was too late. So with Elvis down, it was all up to Phil and his new, big sound.

The British first encountered Spector without being aware of it when the Teddy Bears' To Know Him Is to Love Him was a hit there in 1958. Written and produced by Spector, it just seemed like a catchy group number with an engaging hook line. Then, beginning in January 1961, Spector had a series of minor hits in Britain, first with Ray Peterson's Corrina Corrina, which reached number 41, followed in the summer by Curtis Lee's Pretty Little Angel Eyes at number 47, which was enough to get his name known in music circles. Then in November 1962 came the Crystals' He's A Rebel, followed by Da Doo Ron Ron and Then He Kissed Me. It wasn't long before stories were beginning to spread about this eccentric recording genius. The legend was fixed by the release of Be My Baby and Baby, I Love You by the Ronettes and songs like Zip-A-Dee-Doo-Dah by Bob B. Soxx & the Blue Jeans.

It was an instantly recognizable, haunting sound, with memorable hooks and a massive driving rhythm section—it was the Phil Spector "Wall of Sound." It was known that many of the groups didn't really exist, that he used the same group of musicians and singers in different combinations to produce his self-styled "little symphonies for the kids." Bands like the Beatles loved Spector and they went on to have a long association with him. The Rolling Stones' manager, Andrew Loog Oldham, modeled his entire career on Spector: he based his record productions on those of Spector, formed his own Andrew Loog Oldham Orchestra in imitation of Spector's band of session musicians, and even imitated his personal style. When the Stones played their first British headline tour, Oldham made sure of success by co-headlining them with the Ronettes, who were accompanied on tour by the possessive and jealous Spector—who had become romantically attached to the Ronettes' teenaged lead singer, Veronica Bennett.

Spector found himself at the center of the British invasion before the groups had reached America, even attending the Rolling Stones' Not Fade Away recording session the month before the Beatles arrived in America. The Beatles played several of the songs Spector had written, arranged, and produced for his acts in their early live sets, even recording To Know Her Is to Love Her at the B.B.C.

Rather presciently, it seems Spector had always had an eye for British music that reinvented American songs. In 1956, at the age of 15, he made his first ever public performance playing Leadbelly's Rock Island Line at a talent show held at Fairfax High School in Los Angeles. The song had become an American hit in a version recorded by the British "skiffle" king Lonnie Donegan the previous year. Donegan was one of the first British artists to enter the American charts, and prompted Bobby Darin to record the same song as his first single in 1956. Spector would go on to produce the Beatles' final album release, *Let It Be* in 1970, while simultaneously producing George Harrison's *All Things Must Pass*.

Blues Inc.

The way that new young British bands fused the past with the present can be seen by looking at the set list of the Quarrymen just as they were about rename themselves the Beatles: Peggy Sue (Buddy Holly), All Shook Up (Elvis Presley), Bony Moronie (Larry Williams), Lucille (Little Richard), and Clarabella (the Jodimars). The presence of the 1956 Jodimars song—sung by Paul—shows the depth of knowledge of American music held by these groups. The Jodimars were ex-members of Bill Haley's Comets who recorded between 1955 and 1958 with no real success. The Quarrymen had a repertoire of over 100 songs, many of them taken from obscure single B-sides.

This in-depth knowledge was enhanced by the parallel development of blues and R&B bands in Britain alongside the more mainstream pop acts. Brian Jones, co-founder of the Rolling Stones, began as a blues fanatic with a pronounced disdain of pop. Musicians like Eric Clapton, Mick Fleetwood, John McVie, and Jeff Beck all began in the circle of blues players surrounding Alexis Korner and Cyril Davies, who first started their Blues and Barrelhouse club in London in 1955, which frequently featured visiting American blues musicians. They launched Blues Incorporated in 1961, an immensely influential group that over the years featured a stellar lineup of British musicians including Charlie Watts, Ginger Baker, Jack Bruce, Graham Bond, Dick Heckstall-Smith, Danny Thompson, and Long John Baldry. Others who jammed with them, did guest spots, or were part-time members included John Mayall, Jimmy Page, Brian Jones, Keith Richards, and Mick Jagger.

John Mayall also played a significant informal educational role on the scene. After he moved to London from Manchester in 1963 his flat became a magnet for young musicians. His father, Murray, had amassed a huge collection of southern blues and jazz records, and John brought many of them with him to London. Mayall's band, the Bluesbreakers, included many celebrated guitarists in its changing lineup throughout the 1960s, including Eric Clapton, Peter Green, and Mick Taylor. There were always people sitting around at John's house, playing music and records. It was a great place to go back to after the clubs had closed. Paul McCartney remembered:

> He was a blues DJ, fantastic collection. I think his dad had been into it and passed it on to his son. John would sit me down in a good position for the stereo, "Can I get you a glass of wine?" and you'd get cooled out there and sit back in the chair, and he literally would DJ it from his corner; banks of records. He first played me B.B. King . . . John would play you some great great blues; Buddy Guy he'd play a lot. It was a great education.

John Mayall was to become one of the long-term British Invaders. He was so taken with the Laurel Canyon music scene in Los Angeles that he recorded an album, *Blues from Laurel Canyon*, in 1968 when he moved there for good.

The British musicians had absorbed all they could from American music; now it was time for them to go there and show them what they knew. A number of the bands had made tentative advances but it was left to the Beatles to make the assault. They were apprehensive as no British stars had ever made a significant impact before. As Brian Epstein said: "We knew that America would make us or break us as world stars. In fact she made us." John Lennon was more confident: "I realized that kids everywhere go for the same stuff, and seeing as we'd done it in England, there's no reason why we couldn't do it in America too."

MURDE

ERS'

Nixa Jazz Today Series 45 rpm E

An anthology of Negro worksongs and country blues compiled by Alan Lomax

HOME

PART

TWO

BEATLE EAT

After years of playing the clubs of Hamburg and Liverpool together, the Beatles knew each other better than they knew their own families. They spent so much time together before they were famous—eating, sleeping, playing, working— that they were perfectly at ease in each other's company and this helped them to stay together as a band for as long as they did. They endured the rigors of fame as a unit, finding a kind of solace in their friendships amid the madness which fame in America brought them.

2

WE LOVE YOU,
YEAH YEAH YEAH!

WHY DID THE BEATLES TAKE BRITAIN BY STORM? *For all of the reasons outlined earlier—they were new, exciting, and playing to a new generation of British girls who hadn't previously had much to swoon over (Elvis never made any live appearances in the UK, remember). Being Liverpudlians, cheeky, cute, and full of great pop tunes they couldn't fail to win over a population just emerging from a prolonged era of post-WWII austerity into one of optimism and social revolution. Having had a decade of American pop music rule their social lives, they were ready for something homegrown.*

In America though, it seemed the opposite was true. The spirit of optimism that had existed since the early fifties had taken a severe downturn after the assassination of President Kennedy on November 22, 1963. John, Paul, George, and Ringo arrived less than three months after J.F.K.'s funeral and didn't know anything about Lee Harvey Oswald's claim that, "It's the fashion to hate people in the United States." (Although originally said in 1959 when he was living in Moscow, the sentence was repeated endlessly after Oswald's death at the hands of Jack Ruby on November 24.) The Beatles, lacking the guilt complex that overshadowed the nation and hung there for months after the event, were allowed to perform with a palpable sense of joy that seemed crass for American singers at the time. America was beating itself up about having created Oswald, about the death of Kennedy and the assumed end to the great dreams he had expressed in the future of the country.

It wasn't only that the Fab Four happened to come along just as the newspapers, T.V., and public were desperate to experience something other than the after-effects of a presidential assassination, of course. There was also the fact that American rock 'n' roll had stagnated and there were no new, original talents emerging. Just as the British kids had turned to an older form of music to fill the gap left by Elvis' entry into uniform, so did America, who embraced more folk and traditional sounds.

As they had in Britain, the Beatles brought an end to the dominance of the charts by old-fashioned music. It's worth noting that the Kingston Trio, one of the most successful and prominent of the folk-boom artists who had helped fill the charts between 1959 and 1963, didn't have a single hit following the arrival of the British Invasion bands. Rick Nelson's career stalled in 1964 after 26 top 40 hits, and he did not enter the charts again until 1970, after the Beatles had gone.

Left: The press was so taken with Beatles' humor that they made up quotes of their own.

Right: Rock 'n' roll may have been on a temporary hiatus but the folk revival of the early sixties had in its midst a number of closet rockers.

THE FREEWHEELIN' BOB DYLAN

th Country

onna Fall

Don't Think Tw

B

Talkin' Wo

Honey, Just Allow Me

If I Had a Hammer

Folk singers of the thirties and forties such as Pete Seeger and Woody Guthrie had enjoyed some success across the country with their protest songs and revivals of old folk and country tunes. The McCarthy anti-Communist witch-hunts of the early fifties brought a temporary halt to a folk-music revival that had begun with Seeger's trio the Weavers, who enjoyed a 13-week run at number 1 with their version of Leadbelly's Goodnight Irene in 1950. However, ten years after that, a new generation of folk singers, which included Bob Dylan, the Kingston Trio, Joan Baez, Judy Collins, Josh White, and Peter, Paul & Mary, among others, began to fill the charts with protest songs and old American folk songs sung in three-part harmonies, accompanied by acoustic instruments only.

Greenwich Village in New York was the recognized center of the folk-music scene of the late fifties, and it attracted thousands of would-be troubadours to flock there. Some went in search of a great performer at one of the many coffee houses that punctuated Bleecker Street and the surrounding area. Others went

Dylan's manager, Albert Grossman, created a folk "supergroup" by bringing together "a tall blonde [Mary Travers], a funny guy [Noel "Paul" Stookey], and a good-looking guy [Peter Yarrow]."

52

to become folk singers and be "discovered" at coffee houses, or perhaps when singing at one of the regular, open-air, impromptu sing-alongs that occurred at Washington Square Park, by MacDougal Street, on Sunday afternoons. In 1961, though, the City of New York put an end to the Sunday afternoon concerts and sent police in to break up a meeting on April 9, with the result that heads were broken by police batons in what the *New York Mirror* called the "Beatnik Riot."

However, the coffee shops remained open and the wave of protest singers who graduated from them began to take a positive role in the developing civil-rights movement. Joan Baez traveled to Grenada, Mississippi, with Martin Luther King to help with the integration of African-American kids into previously segregated schools. She also sang We Shall Overcome at Dr. King's Washington march in August 1963—her recording of the song was her first single to hit the American charts.

Even latin balladeer Trini Lopez jumped on the folk music bandwagon. Folk was in danger of being watered down and destroyed by the same commercial forces that had emasculated rock 'n' roll a few years before.

While the civil rights—and burgeoning anti-Vietnam War movement—attracted folk singers to write songs and perform at political rallies, the softer, lighter style of folk song made for big pop hits. Peter, Paul & Mary made number 10 in America with their version of Pete Seeger's If I Had a Hammer (The Hammer Song) in 1962 (and Trini Lopez got it to number 3 a year later), and their version of Puff, The Magic Dragon scored the trio their second-biggest hit when it reached number 2 early in 1963 (it was number 1 for two weeks on the Easy Listening chart that year, too). In the 12 months preceding the arrival of the Beatles, Peter, Paul & Mary had two more top 10 hits with their saccharine versions of Dylan's Blowin' in the Wind and Don't Think Twice, It's Alright. Their next top 10 hit did not arrive until 1967 (I Dig Rock and Roll Music reached number 9) and their only number 1 came in 1969, courtesy of John Denver's Leaving on a Jet Plane. They split the following year.

Despite the success of Peter, Paul & Mary, it was Dylan and Baez who were the recognized king and queen of the folk revival in 1963. Other singers such as Phil Ochs and Tom Paxton followed their lead and wrote solely protest and politically themed songs. Teenagers in the Midwest with money to spend, a hot-rod car, and energy to burn could not dance to songs about dying soldiers and changing seasons, though. And many couldn't easily hear the R&B and soul music that was beginning to emerge from Detroit, Memphis, and Chicago because of the segregation of the airwaves (and dance halls below the Mason-Dixon Line).

In 1964 America's teens were waiting for someone to come along who could play hard, fast, tuneful, and melodic rock 'n' roll. Which is why so many of them turned up at JFK airport on February 7, 1964.

They had heard on the radio that just this sort of act was coming. The honor of being the first D.J. in the U.S.A. to play the Beatles goes to Dick Biondi at WLS-AM, a 24-hour music station in Chicago. He was a friend of Vee-Jay Records president Ewart Abner who sent him a copy of the Beatles' first record Please Please Me early in February, 1963. Biondi gave it a spin and liked it enough to include it on his Friday night show on February 8, 1963, which ran from 9:00 to midnight. This means that he aired the Beatles exactly one year before Murray the K played them on his Swingin' Soiree program on WINS-AM.

As It Happened

Exactly how a 42-year-old former Borscht Belt compere got to be the "fifth Beatle" is a tale of sheer persistence and endeavor. Not that Murray Kaufman was ever actually a Beatle, of course; it was just that—according to the man himself—either Ringo Starr or George Harrison called him that after he had managed to latch on to the traveling circus that accompanied the Fab Four on their first visit to the United States. Ringo later said, "Murray became the so-called 'fifth Beatle' because he was really big on playing our record; he helped to make it a hit." It was a mutual admiration society. The Beatles were desperate to make it big in America and anyone prepared to help them do that was welcomed on board. Paul McCartney: "Murray the K was the man most on to the Beatle case; he had seen it coming and grabbed hold of it. Actually he was just a cheeky journalist who asked a few cheeky questions at the front of the press conference instead of standing back and being aloof." Murray the K knew his star would rise with theirs.

In 1958 Kaufman became a disc jockey very much in the mold of Alan Freed on New York's WINS-AM station. In fact his first show, which he called "The Swingin' Soiree," followed on from Freed's slot and played the same kind of

with God on our side

joan baez

fontana

doo-wop and rock 'n' roll. Shortly after a Freed rock 'n' roll stage show ended in violence in Boston in 1958, WINS-AM declined to renew his contract and tried "Cousin Brucie" Morrow—unsuccessfully—in Freed's seat. They then put Murray the K into the prime night-time (7–11 p.m.) slot instead. It worked, and Murray developed a frenetic, loud, and shamelessly self-promoting show which prompted Tom Wolfe to call him "the original hysterical D.J." He was the hottest rock 'n' roll D.J. on the East Coast at the tender age of 36.

Unsurprisingly perhaps, Murray the K found his way to the bottom of the stairs of the B.O.A.C. jet that deposited the Fab Four on the tarmac at JFK Airport on February 7, 1964. From that moment, wherever the Beatles went in America, so did Murray. He traveled on the train from Grand Central Station in New York to Washington with them for their first gig, sharing a compartment with George Harrison along the way. He stood backstage at *The Ed Sullivan Show* as they made their first, ground-breaking national television appearance. He recorded and broadcast interviews with them as often as he could. George Harrison recalled, "I've often wondered how Murray could barge into the room and hang out with us for the entire trip. It's funny, really, I never quite understood how he did that."

There's little doubt that the exposure that Murray the K gave the Beatles on his radio show in the weeks prior to their landing in the U.S.A. helped enormously to swell the numbers of fans who gathered at the airport to meet them as they landed, and the constant playing of their singles helped to put them in the top five of the New York and then the national charts. Many other local D.J.s— among them Long John Wade of Connecticut, Hy Lit in Philadelphia, Art Schreiber in Cleveland, Jim Stagg in Chicago, Rick Shaw in Florida, and Dave "The Hullabalooer" Hull in Los Angeles—were very happy to play Beatles music.

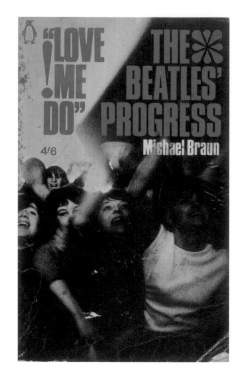

Above: One of the first books on the Beatles, and still regarded as one of the finest, Michael Braun described the madness of Beatlemania after accompanying them on tour.

Left: The Beatles, understandably, attracted some of the world's greatest photographers. This iconic and much imitated image is by Robert Freeman.

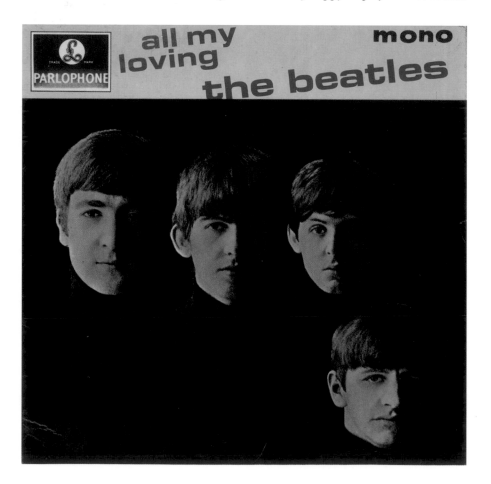

IMPORTANT EDITOR'S NOTE: A lot of material has been written on the Beatles during the past couple of years. Some of it is fact, the rest is fiction. Some of it is done with integrity and honesty, the rest is not. I am in touch with several people in the Beatles' Nems Ltd. organization and my promise to them is the publication of good, accurate and perceptive stories. The following article by top deejay Murray Kaufman is an excellent job of reporting facts, not artificial nonsense. It has humor, candidness, insight and we are happy to present it to you. But, above all, it is true and written by a man who knows the Beatles intimately, not a hack reporter with a grudge against them. Journalistic integrity is the philosophy of the entire staff of this magazine. We hope you like this approach enough to make us successful so that we can keep on bringing you the very best teen articles and stories available anywhere! Let us hear from you.

BEHIND THE SCENES
WITH THE BEATLES

BY MURRAY KAUFMAN

It was about nine o'clock at night in the Deauville Cottage at the Balmoral Club, Nassau, Bahamas. Paul and John were sitting on a sofa with Susan DeWilde, mate of actor Brandon DeWilde, who was resting nearby on the floor. George was on a big, rather awkward collapsible chair, and Ringo and I shared one in an opposite corner, the two of us making idle conversation.

We were talking about the film, "8 Arms to Hold You," and were having a good laugh in recounting what took place on the set that same day, when John stabbed me in a scene which depicted me as a Thug. Instead of falling dead when it happened, I *looked* at him and in full view of the camera, glanced inside my shirt where the stab "wound" was. Suddenly, John blared out, "You're supposed to be dead, ya nut!" "Oh!" I said, and obligingly fell back in the sand, realistically deaded (I hope!).

Just then, a deejay at a radio station in the States announced that Dorothy Kilgallen's column that day had mentioned that Paul had been married for a year, to Jane Asher and that he (the deejay) had spoken to the boys but they were too busy that evening to come to the phone and speak to the listening audience.

Paul and I exchanged glances, as though to say, "Who's he kidding? He never spoke to anyone."

George, in his Liverpudlian matter-of-fact way, asked me: "Who's Dorothy Kilgallen?"

I said: "She's a columnist."

He replied: "A Communist."

"No . . . a *columnist* for a New York newspaper."

Paul turned to me and said: "I don't know, Murray, what I have to do to convince people that I am not married. All this nonsense is just a bunch of lies and rubbish. I hate to sound corny but Jane is my girlfriend, and that's all. It's boyfriend and girlfriend, and that's it! You know what's going to happen, don't you, Murray. If ever I *do* get married, I'll probably make the announcement and they won't believe it!"

George, who believes in candid honesty, said consolingly: "What do you care what some little old lady writes? She's just trying to make a living, I guess, and doesn't care how she does it."

I felt, at this point, that I must make the boys aware of Kilgallen's feelings, so I said: "I'm really surprised at Dorothy writing that without checking, because she really *is* a Beatle fan. In fact, on a couple of TV shows with her, I have found that she always came to the defense of you fellas, and referred to *me* as 'the fifth Beatle.' "

George replied: "Then she probably is listening to the wrong people when she gets her column information."

Meanwhile, Paul — who had walked out of the room and come back smiling — turned to me and said: "Murray, you've got to promise us that you won't repeat the titles of these songs if I play them for you. These are the new ones for the picture."

He proceeded to play nine songs, seven written by John and himself, and two written by George. Without prejudice, I can say that they were the best recorded, best arranged, best vocal treatment of any of their songs to date. And, although I am sorely tempted to mention some of the titles, I can't now, or ever, break a promise that I made to them nor misuse a trust.

The phone rang, and John said to Neil Aspinell, their road manager: "I thought you took that phone off the hook."

Neil answered, his face breaking out into a big grin: "There's someone on the phone who says that Murray the K. wants to speak to the boys."

The boys started kidding me. "Hey, Murray, I thought you were *here*. How come you're *there*?"

Neil hung up and then took the phone off the hook. We started talking about games that we'd played when we were travelling together the first time the boys had come to the states. We started to play a game called Word Association, which they had taught me. The game goes like this. Everybody keeps a beat by hitting his hands against his thigh, and

59

HELLO ARTHUR

Question: "What do you call your haircut?"
George Harrison: "I call it Arthur."

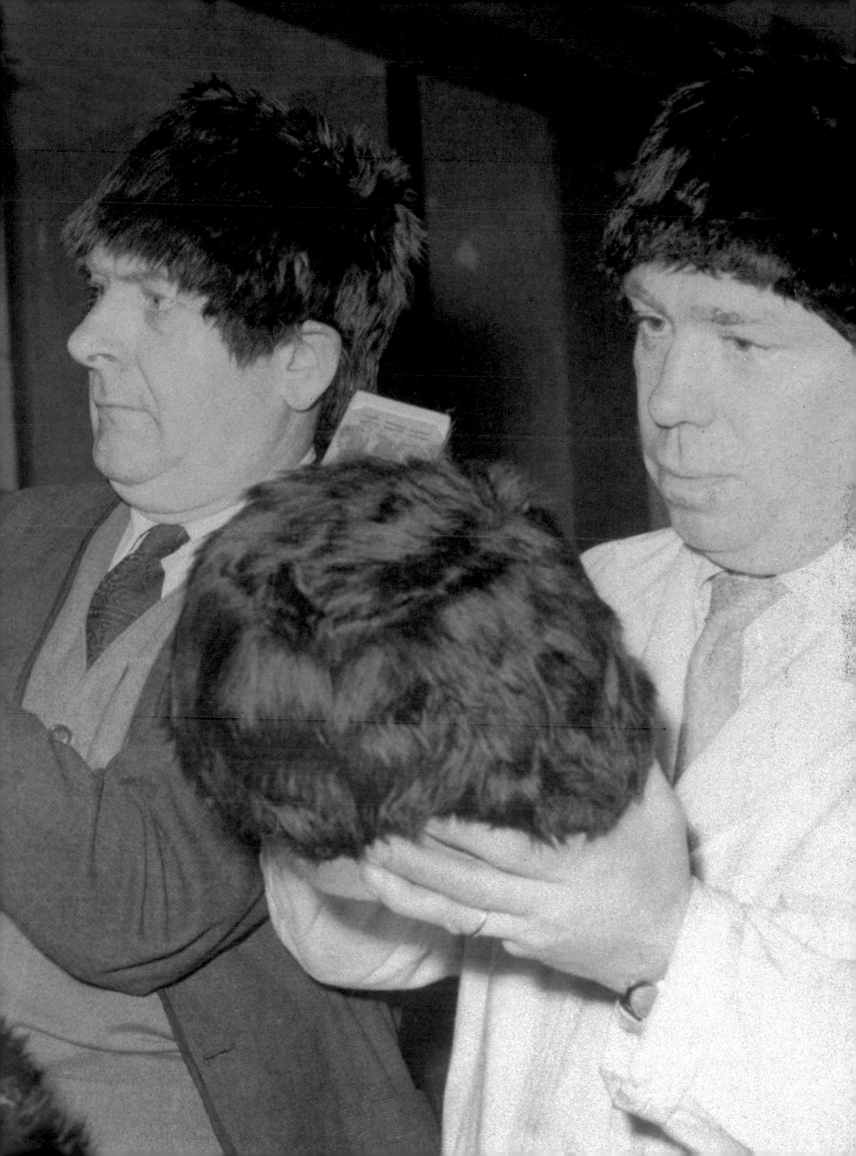

How Do You Do It?

Years of playing in Hamburg in tough late-night clubs in the red-light district meant that the Beatles knew how to please an audience. Their hundreds of performances in Liverpool, most of them at the Cavern, had given them a fan base and a distinct identity. There were hundreds, if not thousands, of groups in Liverpool and in order to stand out and shine you had to have original material. The Beatles were unique in that even in the early days they wrote some of their own material. However, most of their act came from obscure American R&B and show songs, often B-sides of records that no other groups in Liverpool had ever heard and therefore that no other group could copy. Add to this their musical ability, their obvious charm, and an almost perfect mix of personalities and you have the essential ingredients for an entertainment success of almost Disney-esque proportions.

The obvious personality types of the Fab Four were so well established that it was not long before there was a hit U.S.A.-based Beatles cartoon series. George was the sensitive one (despite John's Aunt Mimi trying to stop her nephew from seeing "that right little Teddy Boy"); Paul was the romantic ladies' man (though Cynthia Lennon described him as being "a bull in a china shop"); Ringo was the funny one (and it's true that many of the famous one-liners credited to Lennon came originally from Ringo); while John was the smart edgy one (even though much of the rapier-like wit he was credited with was really old-fashioned rudeness). There was someone for everyone and they appealed in a way that no previous musical act had—perhaps the best comparison would be with the impact the Bowery Boys of the movies had in the previous two decades. (Two of whom, Leo Gorcey and Huntz Hall, featured on the sleeve of *Sgt. Pepper's Lonely Hearts Club Band*, though Gorcey's photo was removed after his agent demanded a $400 payment.)

After the first wave of teen adulation for the Beatles had grown to the point where the press had to invent a new word for it—Beatlemania—the rest of the population had to join in. They could not resist.

As soon as his charges began to attract attention, Beatles manager Brian Epstein raced to sign up other Merseyside bands to his management company, N.E.M.S. He contracted most of them to Parlophone Records, the division of E.M.I. run by the Beatles' producer George Martin. Epstein took on Gerry and

No one could have anticipated the huge success of the Beatles, and their management was not equipped to control the merchandising that immediately sprang up to exploit them. The band never did gain control and even now their image is reproduced on thousands of unauthorized T-shirts and posters across the world.

The thing is, we're all really the same person. We're just four parts of the one.

PAUL MCCARTNEY

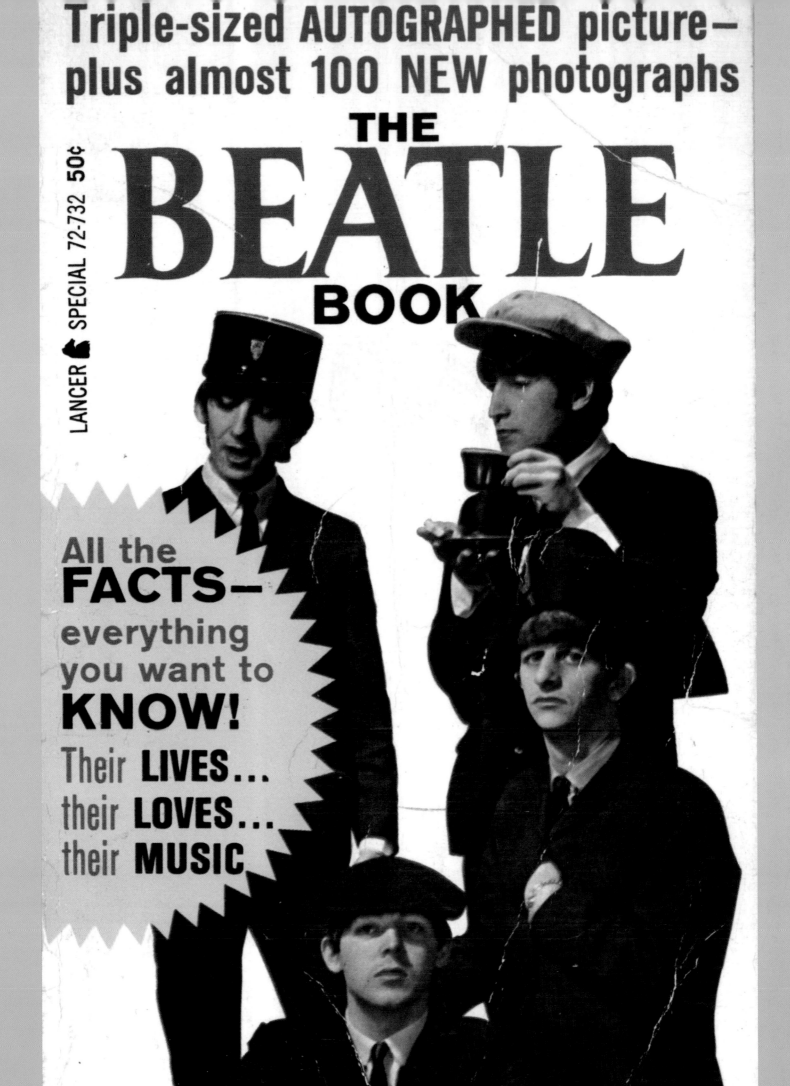

Triple-sized AUTOGRAPHED picture—
plus almost 100 NEW photographs

THE BEATLE BOOK

LANCER ♣ SPECIAL 72-732 50¢

All the FACTS— everything you want to **KNOW!** Their **LIVES...** their **LOVES...** their **MUSIC**

the Pacemakers and George Martin produced them singing How Do You Do It?, a song that the Beatles had refused to record. Martin's judgment that it was a commercial song proved to be sound as it went to number 1 in the British charts in April 1963. That outdid the Beatles, who so far had only reached number 2 with their second single, Please Please Me. But they needn't have worried. After three weeks Gerry was knocked from number 1 in Britain by the Beatles' From Me to You. It stayed at number 1 for seven weeks and sold half a million copies.

The Pacemakers didn't enjoy enormous success in America, though. In 1964 they made number 4 with Don't Let the Sun Catch You Crying, number 9 with How Do You Do It?, and number 17 with I Like It, but after a number 14 hit with I'll Be There and reaching number 6 with the title song from their movie *Ferry Cross the Mersey* in 1965, their popularity waned. There were no more top 20 hits for them again.

Brian Epstein (6th from right) flanked by his Merseyside signings. From left: The Beatles, Gerry and the Pacemakers and Billy J. Kramer and the Dakotas.

Brian Epstein also signed another Liverpudlian, Billy J. Kramer, whom he backed with a Manchester instrumental group called the Dakotas. George Martin created a nice arrangement of a Lennon and McCartney song, Do You Want To Know a Secret?, for him and he went to number 2 in Britain in June 1963. The same month Gerry and the Pacemakers replaced the Beatles at number 1 with I Like It, to be followed by Billy J. Kramer with yet another Lennon and McCartney song, Bad to Me. Lennon and McCartney knocked their own song from number one, with She Loves You, which went on to sell over 1.5 million copies before the end of the year. It seemed that anything from Liverpool would sell and Epstein went on a signing spree. N.E.M.S. signed up the Fourmost, the Big Three, Tommy Quickly, and even the cloakroom attendant from the Cavern, a girl called Priscilla White. He changed her name to Cilla Black and she had a number 1 with Anyone Who Had a Heart in February 1964.

Ken Ferguson investigates the cult which has swept the country

Beatlemania. A new word for the dictionary. What does it mean? What is the definition? What is it?

Beatlemania, is a form of hysterical worship instigated by four young men who call themselves The Beatles.

John, Paul, George and Ringo have written themselves into musical history with their savage, pulsating, hypnotic sound.

The other evening I felt the full blast and fury of Beatlemania as I sat in a theatre along with almost 2,000 screaming, hysterical worshippers of The Beatles. It was fantastic. On stage, the four boys moved their lips and went through the motions of a performance but nothing could be heard above the roars of mass appreciation.

HOW did it begin? *WHY* did it begin? *WHERE* will it end?

It began simply in Liverpool as we all know, in a small club which has now become a shrine—The Cavern.

Why did it begin? Simply because the older idols of the pop business, the Cliffs and the Elvises were growing up fast and so were their fans. The screams had weakened.

Those who were just entering their teens needed someone new to scream about—not just scream but *SCREAM!* They demanded a new idol and they almost cried out for a new cult. Not since the birth of the rock era with Bill Haley, did they have something new to idolise, apart from the eras of Presley, Richard and Faith which were, and still are, but (Continued on page 24)

ARE THE BEATLES A RELIGION

THE MERSEYBEATS
FASHIONABLE BRITISHERS

Described as the group with one of the most distinctive sounds ever to emerge on the beat scene, "The Merseybeats" are four young fellows who originate from the hometown of British beat music — Liverpool, England. While other groups were constantly turning out carbon copy discs, each one fighting the other for the same identical sound, The Merseybeats decided to be different and daring. In August, 1963 they cut their first record record, "It's Love That Really Counts." It was an overnight sensation, zooming straight into the English music charts where it stayed on top for sixteen consecutive weeks. The outcome was the first ballad-styled record by a group ever to hit the charts since the first beat was beat.

The Merseybeats are not only leaders of the "Mersey Sound" but they have revolutionized the groups image by their endless source of creative ideas and have long been recognized in England as the trend setters in the world of male fashion.

Their mode of dress, both on stage and off, is both original and unique. The Merseybeats wear lace, ruffled shirts (designed for them by one of England's top female designers) together with black mohair slacks, tapered to 16 inches with large six inch vents from the ham, revealing the buttoned sides of their spat-styled boots. The boys take as much pride in their appearance as in the music they produce.

Yeah, Yeah, Yeah

After the success of the Beatles, Gerry and the Pacemakers, and Billy J. Kramer, Liverpool was teeming with A&R men (the "Artists and Repertoire" talent scouts) from the London record companies. Pye Records signed the Searchers and their very first single, Sweets for My Sweet, went to number 1 in August 1963. Some record men from Parlophone got off the train at nearby Manchester instead and signed up the Hollies, who reached the top 20 with an old Coasters number, Searchin', while Columbia's A&R man who also alighted in Manchester signed Freddie and the Dreamers, a jolly, good-natured group who had three top 10 hits in 1963 with If You Gotta Make a Fool of Somebody (number 3), I'm Telling You Now (number 2), and You Were Made For Me (number 3).

After the long trip north, Columbia Records decided to stay closer to home and create a competitor to the Merseybeat with the Tottenham Sound, named after the London suburb where the Dave Clark Five (a.k.a. DC5) lived. Their fifth single, though only their second for Columbia, was Glad All Over, which gave them a number 1 in November 1963. The DC5 had first surfaced in summer 1962 as a less harmonic R&B act, but after being repositioned as a Beatles-competitor after the Liverpudlians' success, they really took off.

The year preceding their American trip had been a remarkable time for the Beatles in Britain. They had topped the charts for 16 weeks including over Christmas with the enormous hit, I Want to Hold Your Hand. With almost complete control of the British charts, Epstein now turned his sights on America.

To begin with, E.M.I.'s wholly owned subsidiary in America, Capitol Records, had turned down the chance to release the Beatles in the States so their early singles were out on a variety of small labels. Both Please Please Me/Ask Me Why and From Me To You/Thank You Girl had come out on the Vee-Jay label (with little chart success) in February and April 1963 respectively. Previously, Vee-Jay had released R&B luminaries such as Jimmy Reed, Memphis Slim, and John Lee Hooker but scored their biggest hit, Sherry, with their first white act, the Four Seasons, in 1962.

The Beatles' third U.S.A. single release had been on the Swan label, which was notable for giving gameshow host Chuck Barris his only songwriting hit, Palisades Park, as performed by Freddy Cannon in 1962. She Loves You/I'll Get You was released in September 1963 and sank without trace—at first. When Capitol finally

got round to releasing I Want to Hold Your Hand/I Saw Her Standing There in America, it was picked up by radio stations all over the country. After the band's appearance on *The Ed Sullivan Show* it hit number 1 in the *Billboard* Hot 100. The single was flipped and I Saw Her Standing There was played across the country with the result that it made number 14. Swan subsequently re-released She Loves You in late January 1964 and saw it reach the top slot in March.

At the end of January 1964 Vee-Jay—who had been dropped by Epstein for its failure to pay royalties—then re-released Please Please Me and that reached number 3. On the B-side, From Me to You also earned a place on the charts this time around, though only at number 41. Vee-Jay went on to release Twist and Shout (number 2) with B-side There's a Place (number 74) on its subsidiary label Tollie in March 1964; Do You Want to Know a Secret (number 2) with B-side Thank You Girl (number 35) the same month; and, again on Tollie, Love Me Do (number 1) with P.S. I Love You (number 10) in April.

The success of the re-releases demonstrated exactly what the effect of a television appearance could have on a young pop act. The excitement surrounding the arrival of the Beatles was considerably amplified on January 12, 1964, by the release of the Beatles' film, *A Hard Day's Night*, which opened simultaneously in 500 American cinemas to very favorable reviews.

New York Times: "This is going to surprise you—it may knock you right out off your chair—but the film with those incredible chaps, The Beatles, is a whale of a comedy."

New York World-Telegram & Sun: "A Hard Day's Night turns out to be funnier than you would expect and every bit as loud as the wildest Beatle optimist could hope."

New York Herald Tribune: "It is really an egghead picture, lightly scrambled, a triumph of The Beatles and the bald."

New York Daily News: "The picture adds up to a lot of fun, not only for the teenagers but for grownups as well. It's clean, wholesome entertainment."

New York Journal-American: "The picture turned out to be a completely wacky, off-beat entertainment that's frequently remindful of the Marx Brothers' comedies of the '30's."

New York Post: "A Hard Day's Night suggests a Beatle career in the movies as big as they've already been in stage and dancehall. They have the songs, the patter, and the histrionic flare. No more is needed."

Washington Post: "The main thing about it is that you can't hear it because the audience sort of over-participates."

It was not just fans who saw it multiple times: budding musicians across the States were astonished and impressed. *A Hard Day's Night* appears to have influenced half the next generation of musicians to pick up a guitar and form a band. It was hard to resist the lure of girls screaming as you make music, appear on television, flirt with models and joke with the older generation.

Above: It took some time before Capitol Records recognized the commercial potential of the Beatles, by which time they had been released on several smaller U.S. labels; something which caused confusion in the charts when they finally hit.

Right: The view from behind Ringo. A scene from A Hard Day's Night.

Following pages: The Beatles' fame spread as far as the world of comics, and the March 1965 edition of Strange Tales included a story of Human Torch and The Thing meeting The Beatles.

Till There Was You

The Ed Sullivan Show was the longest running television variety show of all time, transmitted by C.B.S. from 1948 until 1971. It always went out at the same time slot, eight on a Sunday night, and always with the same host, Ed Sullivan. The reason for its longevity was the wide variety of acts that it presented, from opera singers to rock 'n' rollers, comedians and circus performers, to ballet dancers. Sullivan was always on the lookout for the latest thing to keep his show ahead in the ratings. He happened to arrive at London's Heathrow Airport on October 31, 1963, just as the Beatles flew in from a successful tour of Sweden. Fifteen thousand screaming girls were there to greet the band, all gathered on the roof of the Queen's Building. The scenes were broadcast on the national television news in England, heightening the media frenzy about Beatlemania. Sullivan had no idea who they were, but he was impressed by the enthusiasm and excitement of the fans. His instinct told him to get his people to contact their people and book them for his show.

Beatlemania in the UK was a runaway train. The press loved it because it sold newspapers; the record companies loved it because it sold records; the promoters loved it because it filled their venues. And the fans loved it because they loved the Beatles. Sullivan booked them for three consecutive appearances at $4,000 apiece, on the strength of which Epstein was able to convince Capitol Records to finally release Beatles records and to allocate a large publicity budget to breaking the band in America.

A secret internal memo circulated to Capitol Records marketing executives on December 23, 1963.

On Monday December 30, a two page spread will appear in Billboard . . . We have also ordered easel-backed reprints of this ad in large quantity . . . Put it where consumers will see it, where they'll be impelled to buy both the Beatle single and LP.

Shortly after the first of the year, you'll have bulk quantities of a unique see-through plastic pin-on button. Inserted in each button is a shot of the Beatles, with each boy identified. What to do with the buttons? First, have all your sales staff wear one. Second, offer them to clerks and jocks. Third, arrange for radio station give-aways of the buttons.

Again shortly after the First, you'll have bulk quantities of a Beatle hair-do wig. As soon as they arrive - and until further notice - you and each of your sales and promotion staff are to wear the wig during the business day! Next, see how many of the retail clerks in your area have a sense of humor . . . Then offer some to jocks and stores for promotions and you'll find you're helping to start the Beatle Hair-Do craze that should be sweeping the country soon.

As soon as possible after the First, you'll have fantastic quantities of "THE BEATLES ARE COMING" teaser stickers . . . Put them up anywhere and everywhere . . . It may sound funny but we literally want your salesmen to be plastering these stickers on any friendly surface as they walk down the street . . . Make arrangements with local high school students to spread the stickers around town. Involve your friends and relatives . . . it's going to be "BEATLES ARE COMING" stickers everywhere you look.

Above: Freelance newsreel reporters made a fortune from unauthorized film of the Beatles.

Opposite: The Beatles on The Ed Sullivan Show: *"I've heard that while the show was on there were no reported crimes, or very few. When The Beatles were on* Ed Sullivan, *even the criminals had a rest for ten minutes."* George Harrison

America should put up statues to the Beatles. They helped give this country's pride back to it.

BOB DYLAN

After the booking, the full record-business hype machine swung into action: D.J.s received wigs and badges; "Beatles are coming" stickers covered lampposts across the country from New York to California; and anyone calling Capitol Records was greeted by a receptionist saying, "Capitol Records, the Beatles are coming!" Suffice to say, no British band had received so much attention before. It is unlikely that Capitol put more than $50,000 into the publicity campaign which, though a lot of money in those days, does not account for the eager anticipation of their arrival, nor the genuine enthusiasm with which thousands of (mostly) girls welcomed them at J.F.K. airport and screamed and waved as their motorcade entered New York.

Their first appearance on *The Ed Sullivan Show* on February 9, 1964, drew a record audience estimated at 73 million viewers, keen to see what all the fuss was about. Many of the next generation of American musicians, from Bruce Springsteen to members of the Grateful Dead, were introduced to the idea of forming a band by watching that show. The Beatles performed All My Loving and Till There Was You, while their names were projected on screen. When they reached John his name was captioned "Sorry girls, he's married." They continued with She Loves You and then, to close the show, returned with I Saw Her Standing There and their hit, I Want to Hold Your Hand. They had also recorded a show earlier that day on tape. This was shown two weeks later and consisted of Twist and Shout and Please Please Me, closing once again with I Want to Hold Your Hand. It was screened on February 23, by which time they were already back in Britain.

The Beatles' second *Ed Sullivan Show* performance was broadcast live from the Deauville Beach Resort Hotel in Miami, where the group was staying. The show went out on February 16 and the set consisted of She Loves You, This Boy, All My Loving, I Saw Her Standing There, From Me to You, and I Want to Hold Your Hand.

The press coverage was enormous. *The New York Times* ran the headline "The Beatles Invade, Complete With Long Hair and Screaming Fans" and four days later reported "Wild-eyed Mob Pursues Beatles."

"Imagine the thrill for us going on The Ed Sullivan Show. *I still remember one of the producer guys coming into our dressing room just before we went on and saying 'It's being watched by seventy million people you know.'"*
Paul McCartney

Teen Life magazine

DEC.
25c

BEATLES' SECRET DIARY

50 SCOOP PIX • 5 EXCLUSIVE STORIES

- I LIVED WITH THE BEATLES • PAUL McCARTNEY'S KISSES MADE ME CRY
- WHAT TRINI LOPEZ DID TO THE BEATLES • WIN 6 BEATLE RECORD PLAYERS
- THE SCARED-MAD WORLD OF THE BEATLES

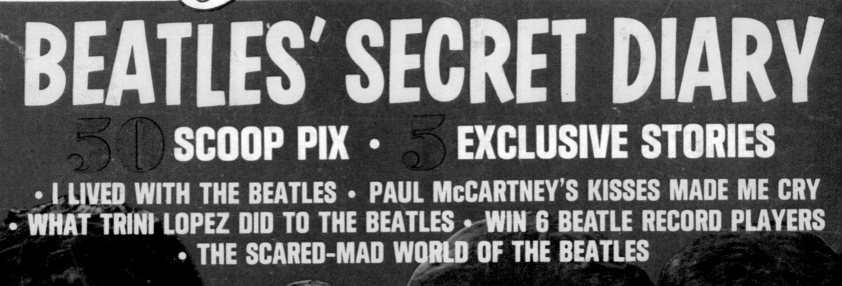

PATTY DUKE DISCOVERS LOVE

PAUL'S STRANGE NEW KICKS!

4 GREAT GROUPS
- THE ANIMALS
- BILLY J. KRAMER
- GERRY & PACEMAKE
- THE BEACH BOYS

Roll Over Beethoven

The effect of the Beatles' singles release schedule was unprecedented and has never been equaled. In the week of April 4, 1964, the Beatles held all top 5 positions in the *Billboard* Hot 100 singles chart and seven other places lower on the list. The top 5 were: Can't Buy Me Love, Twist and Shout, She Loves You, I Want to Hold Your Hand, and Please Please Me. Their first U.S.A. album release, *Meet the Beatles*, topped the album charts and on March 13 was reported as having sold a mighty 3.6 million copies; far more than any other album ever released. That same month, four Beatles tribute songs made it to the charts: We Love You Beatles (by the Carefrees), My Boyfriend Got a Beatle Haircut (Donna Lynn), The Boy With the Beatle Hair (the Swans), and A Letter to the Beatles (the Four Preps).

In February 1964, after a visit by the Beatles to New York's Peppermint Lounge, the club's nightclub act The Younger Brothers donned Beatle wigs and false noses to form one of the first Beatles tribute acts.

Every conceivable variety of product is now available in almost every country of the world with the Beatle name on it. These products range in price from just a few pennies to about $30 dollars. But where the Beatle fans are concerned money is no object!

BEATLE PRODUCTS

Beatle products are flooding the market throughout the world. No country seems to be able to escape from the deluge of various items that are on sale. Fans all over the world are spending their shillings, dollars, lira, cruzeros, and dinero for such items as Beatle wall-paper, Beatles cups and saucers, Beatle hats, Beatle shirts, Beatle pens, Beatles guitars and so many other Beatle products.

Today it is possible to do everything in the Beatle way. You can drink out of a Beatle cup while eating out of a Beatle plate. You can wear a Beatle hat, jacket, stockings and pin when you listen to Beatle records on the radio or phonograph. And when you go to sleep you can take a Beatle doll with you as you cover yourself up with a Beatle blanket.

The biggest selling Beatle items, apart from the many records, are Beatle shirts (180,000 Beatles shirts a week in America) and Beatle dolls (100,000 dolls sold every week also).

English sales promoter John Fenton says, "The first shipment of Beatle clothes are on their way to the Continent: shirts, pullovers, leather jackets, stockings and even jewelry is already on the way from New York. A Copenhagen firm has even got a license to produce silver Beatle lockets."

In England and the United States, children are now collecting Beatle Ringo cards as they once collected bubble-gum baseball cards.

The prices range from just a few pennies for chewing gum to many dollars for an 18 carat gold piece of Beatle jewelry.

The latest item to hit the market is a sliced loaf of bread called The Ringo Roll.

Where are the most sales made? Why the Lone Star State of Texas, of course!

Where the phenomenal Beatles are concerned nothing is sacred—and nothing about can be kept secret for long. When the fans discovered John Lennon's address (13 Empress Gate, S.W. 7) they descended and maintained a constant vigil.

While waiting outside the white pillared house they read Beatle magazines, look at Beatle pictures and some even read aloud from John's book, "In His Own Write".

The sentiments of the Beatlemaniacs in England can be seen scribbled on the stone pillars outside the front door. Sentiments which express in no uncertain terms their feelings towards girls whose names have been linked with various members of the group. Still others peer through the letter box in the hopes of perhaps *seeing* John.

The phenomena of Beatlemania continues and spreads even wider than before. Also, Beatlemania has become diversified. On the next few pages we have collected the newest and *gear-est* groups to come out of Liverpool in the past few months.

Their increasing popularity has caused many fans to wonder—and four Beatles to worry!

By the end of the year the Beatles had sold more than 25 million records in the U.S.A. including 15 that sold a million each: nine singles and six albums. Can't Buy Me Love sold 940,225 copies on the first day, a record in both senses, and sold more than 3 million by year's end. These mind-boggling statistics naturally paved the way for other British groups as American record companies scrambled for air tickets to sign up every British band that had appeared in the British charts in the last year—and some that didn't. Before the Beatles had even left for Britain a banner front-page headline in *Variety* on February 19, 1964, warned: "Rocking Redcoats Are Coming—Beatles Lead Massive Drive."

America's love affair with the band was in full flow and it was seemingly reciprocated. From the beginning of their career the Beatles had always insisted that their music be taken seriously and that their fans be given good value for money. With the exception of their first album they never included singles on their British albums, thinking correctly that the fans had already bought the singles and it would be a rip-off to sell them a second time. Unfortunately, though, they did not have control over the American record companies. To the executives at Capitol it was all just product. American companies regularly gave the public fewer tracks on albums, and in the Beatles' case they broke albums down and added all the A- and B-sides from the singles to make two albums. In this way the integrity of the Beatles early releases was destroyed when they often appeared in the U.S.A. with different titles like *Meet the Beatles!* or *The Beatles' Second Album* and with different tracks. It was not until *Sgt. Pepper's Lonely Hearts Club Band* in 1967 that they were able to insist that the tracks not be broken up and spread over more albums: it had to appear in the U.S.A. as it did in Britain.

Everything from Beatles mugs, hats, socks, and posters was available to avid Beatles fans. Rolls of—preferably unused—Beatles wallpaper sell for large sums at rock 'n' roll auctions.

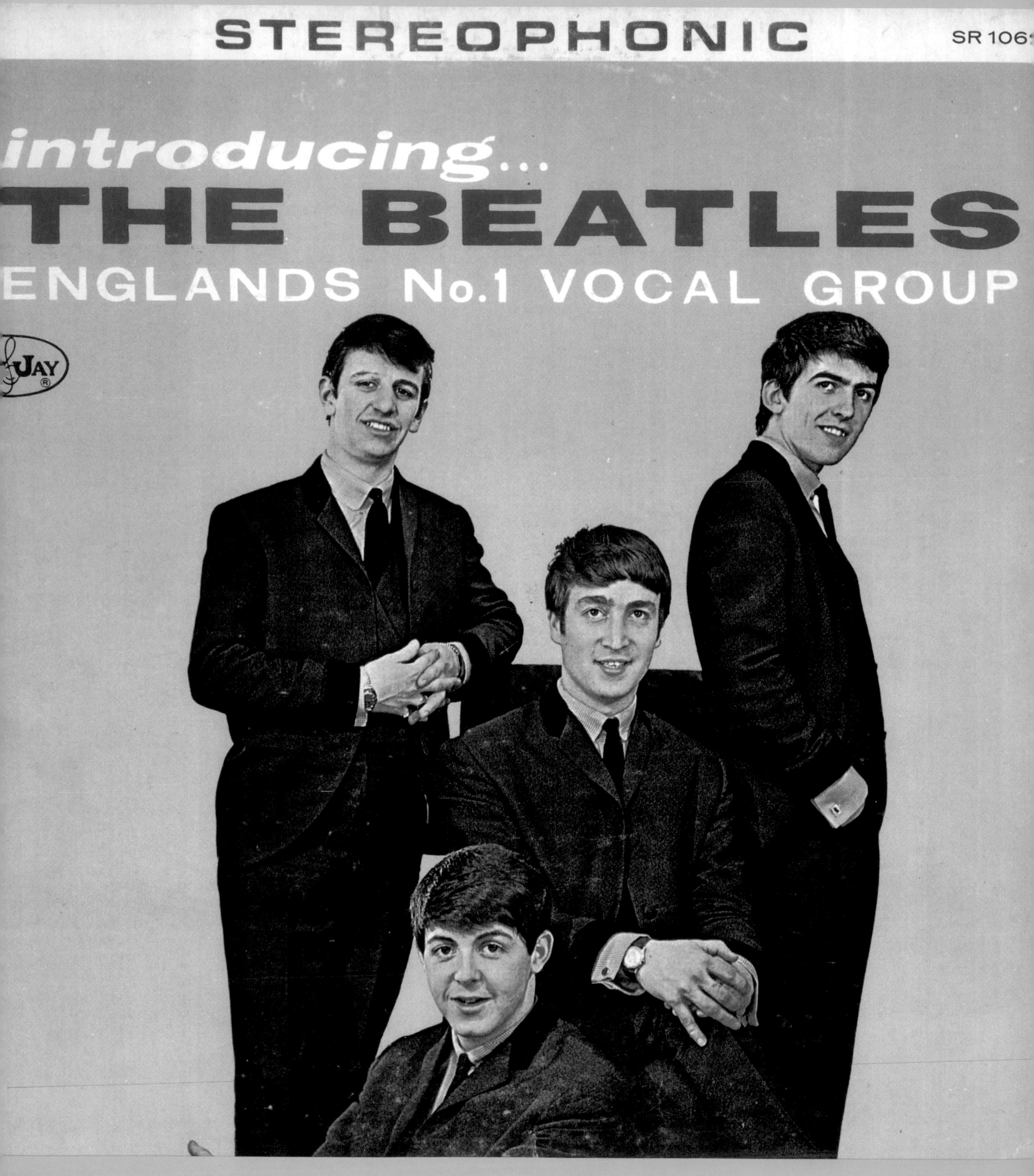

STEREOPHONIC SR 106

introducing...
THE BEATLES
ENGLANDS No.1 VOCAL GROUP

VEE JAY ®

Introducing . . .

The first company to get a Beatles album out in America was Vee-Jay, whose *Introducing . . . The Beatles* was released in January, 1964, before the band had even arrived. It consisted mostly of cover versions including Arthur Alexander's Anna (Go to Him), which was originally a minor hit for the composer in 1962 and was one of John Lennon's favorite songs (Alexander's first hit, You Better Move On, was recorded by the Rolling Stones). Chains was a Gerry Goffin and Carole King composition, originally recorded by the Cookies, the backing group for Goffin and King's babysitter-turned-singer, Little Eva. The Beatles and many other Merseyside bands played it in their live set. Boys was originally recorded by the Shirelles and was Ringo's token vocal. It later became a crowd pleaser in gay clubs because although the Beatles changed the lyrics to "My girl says when I kiss her lips" the song is still about boys. Paul McCartney said, "Ringo would do 'Boys', which was a fan favorite with the crowd. And it was great—though if you think about it, here's us doing a song and it was really a girls' song. 'I talk about boys now!' Or it was a gay song. But we never even listened. It's just a great song." There was also a second Shirelles song on the album, Baby It's You—again part of their live act—as well as A Taste of Honey, which was originally a hit for Herb Alpert and the Tijuana Brass, although the first vocal version was by Lenny Welch in September 1962. The Beatles had immediately made it part of their act and it was one of McCartney's favorite songs, perhaps because it gave him a chance to stretch his vocal range a bit after so many shouting R&B numbers.

Another all-time live favorite was Twist and Shout. Though originally recorded by the Top Notes, it was the Isley Brothers' version that the Beatles knew and copied. Lennon's raucous vocals on the recording offer perhaps one of the best examples of how the Beatles original live shows must have sounded.

All these cover versions had been included on the Beatles' first British album, Please Please Me, and show the wide range of influences they brought to their music. Paul McCartney recalls, "We started off being influenced by Carl Perkins and Chuck Berry and Bo Diddley and people. But after a bit I think we just got bored with 12 bars all the time so we tried to get into something else." There was only one cover on the Beatles' second American album, *Meet the Beatles!*, which was released by Capitol in January 1964, again before the group arrived in the U.S.A. This was Till There Was You, a song Paul McCartney knew from the Peggy Lee version released in the Britain in March 1961, which was introduced to him by his cousin Bett Robbins. The Beatles used it in their Star Club act in Hamburg as a way of appealing to the females in the audience and of slowing the pace to give themselves a breather. It was years later that McCartney found out it was from the 1957 Broadway musical *The Music Man*; it was the only Broadway number the Beatles ever recorded.

Beatles fans in the U.S.A. have very different memories of the music from fans in the UK, because the track selections on the albums were so different.

The Beatles saved the world from boredom.

GEORGE HARRISON

DAVE CLARK FIVE

The DC5 made their first tour of America in style, using their own rented plane. Not that it always meant they got away from places smoothly. Just as they were about to leave Miami after a gig they were stopped by police on their way to the plane. They told Clark to come with them, and drove across the tarmac with a motorcycle escort to Air Force One, parked on the other side of the airport. There Clark was presented to Lyndon Johnson who wanted his autograph for his daughter.

The DC5 made a record 18 appearances on The Ed Sullivan Show and had 15 top 20 hits in three years, making them one of the most successful of the British Invasion bands after the Beatles. Clark: "The American press pitted us against the Beatles, but there was no rivalry between us . . . the magazines made it up. The magazines in America made a war out of it."

GLAD ALL OVER
(Featuring "Bits and Pieces")
THE DAVE CLARK FIVE
All of the Time / Chaquita / Do You Love Me / I Know You
No Time to Lose / Doo Dah / Time / She's All Mine / Stay

Photo: Bruce

VE CLARK FIVE

Glad All Over

The same week that the Beatles occupied the top 5 positions in the *Billboard* Hot 100, seven other British groups were already in the charts including the Dave Clark Five, the Searchers, and the Swinging Blue Jeans. Though many of the new bands had reached number 1 in the British charts before the British Invasion began, it was the Dave Clark Five's luck that they replaced the Beatles' I Want to Hold Your Hand at number 1 in the British singles charts. It was seized upon by publicists and exploited for all it was worth, with the DC5 depicted as "giant killers" for having toppled the Beatles. Naturally, the Tottenham Sound was heralded as the next big thing. Which was just as well, since when Glad All Over reached the top of the British charts all of the band except for Clark had yet to give up their day jobs.

Though only 20 years old, Dave Clark was tremendously savvy. He was not only the drummer—with his kit placed at the front of the stage—and the

The Dave Clark Five in Central Park, New York, imitating Dezo Hoffmann's famous jumping shot of The Beatles, though with slightly less exuberance.

songwriter, but he managed the group, produced the records, and kept all the rights. He paid for the sessions and paid the band a weekly wage. As he succinctly put it: "We're all in it to try and make money." He marketed the group as more family-friendly than even the Beatles: the group all had short hair with partings and the sleeve notes to their first U.S.A. album (*Glad All Over*, of course) commented on the "floppy-haired" Beatles.

DC5 were the first group to reach the States in the wake of the Beatles and got off to a prestigious start by playing New York's Carnegie Hall on May 30, 1964. The band always wore smart jackets with white hankies tucked in the top pocket, and smiled and smiled at the camera. Dave, whose previous job had been as a film-stunt extra, clearly thought the best approach was to make as much money as fast as possible and inundated the market with records. In 1964 they released eight singles, four of which made the top 10. Because got to number 3, *Bits and Pieces* and *Can't You See That She's Mine* both reached number 4, Glad

BEATLES: TRUTH ABOUT THEIR GIRLS

OCT / 25c

16
MAGAZINE

McCALLUM
OPENS HIS HEART TO YOU
BIGGEST COLOR PIN-UP EVER
FAB GIFT FROM "ILLYA"
FOR EACH OF YOU

DINO
DESI
BILLY
"I Confess

"Miss
16"
contes

HERMAN
"MY HATES & LUVS" PLUS SUPER NEVER-SEEN-BEFORE PIX

PAUL · GEORGE · JOHN · RINGO
HUGE KISSABLE COLOR PORTRAITS

SEAN "007" CONNERY
HIS WHOLE LIFE IN 50 PIX

STONES: 101 Sizzling Secrets

CHAD & JEREMY
answer 80
very SNOOPY ?'s

BEATLES
NEED
HELP
SEE INSI

PLUS — PETER & GORDON · ROBT. VAUGHN
BYRDS
KINKS

Every city was beginning to look the same. The fun was going out of it. It was becoming a job of work and that's when I decided to stop (touring).

DAVE CLARK

All Over made it to number 6, while Do You Love Me?, Anyway You Want It, Everybody Knows (I Still Love You), and Come Home all reached the top 20. The coveted number 1 position was denied to them though, until Over and Over was a hit in late 1965.

Dave Clark learned a lot from the American girl groups (the DC5 were the only British Invasion group to use a saxophone, for instance) and, as the drummer, he made sure his productions had "The Big Beat," a loud stomping drum sound that characterized all their records. The perfectly crafted pop songs of the Dave Clark Five had no pretensions and didn't attempt to be anything other than pure entertainment. Clark had never heard of Ed Sullivan when they were asked to appear on his show. Dave Clark: "They offered us five thousand dollars to fly us over for the week and do the show on the Sunday. They guys were still doing their daytime jobs . . . what had we got to lose?"

Their appearance was so well received that they were asked to appear again the following week. But the group were exhausted from all the hysteria attendant on their success in Britain so Clark turned him down, saying the group needed a break. "Where would you like to go?" Sullivan asked. Clark remembered a billboard he'd seen on the way in from the airport. "Montego Bay," he said. Sullivan sent them there for a week. "So off we went, came back on the Friday and there were 30,000 people at Kennedy Airport. They had to stop the planes from coming in and they got us out by helicopter! We had five records in the charts at once. It all exploded."

British Invasion groups dominate the cover of 16 Magazine. 1964 was the greatest year of them all for British groups—and actors—in the U.S.

A World Without Love

Peter Asher and Gordon Waller were school friends at Westminster, one of Britain's top private schools. They began as a folk duo playing Soho Clubs, but got their big break through Paul McCartney. Peter lived with his parents in their large townhouse in Central London along with his sister Jane, who happened to be going out with Paul McCartney—and Paul had moved into their home, residing on the top floor in a small attic room next to Peter. When Peter and Gordon got a record contract, Paul gave them a song, World Without Love, which went straight to number 1 in Britain and also reached number 1 on the *Billboard* chart on June 27, 1964, making them the first British act to follow the Beatles to the top in the U.S.A.

Polite, intelligent, and personable, Peter and Gordon had many fans and, although they had long Beatles-style haircuts, were seen as being less threatening than the fast-talking, witty Beatles. They were enviable recipients of unused Beatles numbers, including their two follow-ups, Nobody I Know, which reached number 12, and I Don't Want to See You Again, which reached 16. After a string of further chart hits—not written by Lennon and McCartney—they had a top 20 hit in 1966 with Woman, written by Bernard Webb—who was Paul McCartney using a pseudonym to find out if it was his name or the music that made his songs sell. Peter Asher: "When we first came to the States in June of '64 and landed at the airport, there were crowds of screaming girls with signs, jumping all over us . . . It was a terrific time to be an English rock 'n' roller, and have girls tearing your clothes off. It was wonderful." Peter and Gordon enjoyed 14 chart singles and seven chart albums in the U.S.A. They broke up in 1968 when Gordon went solo, and Peter became head of A&R at the Beatles' Apple Records. He later became manager and producer of James Taylor and Linda Ronstadt.

PHOTO CREDIT: Courtesy of London Records

THE ZOMBIES
THEIR SECRET LIFELINES REVEALED!

The inside story on the hot group that rocketed to fame with "SHE'S NOT THERE" and "TELL HER NO."

She's Not There

Like Peter and Gordon, the Zombies were the product of an expensive, fee-paying school, theirs being St. Albans School, founded in A.D. 948 and one of the oldest schools in Britain. Rod Argent (co-leader and pianist), Paul Atkinson (guitar), and Hugh Grundy (drums) all attended there, whereas vocalist Colin Blunstone and Chris White (bass) went to nearby St. Albans Boys' Modern school (founded in 1938). Much was made of this upper-class background when the group signed to Decca in 1964 and recorded their first single, She's Not There. The song's catchy hook line, its minor key, and Blunstone's breathy, almost whispered vocals attracted attention and soon the band were on their way to the States to promote it. All through the fall it climbed the charts to peak at number 2. One of the most memorable gigs they played on their American trip was at Murray the K's Christmas Show at the Brooklyn Fox Theater. They not only played seven sets a day but drummer Hugh Grundy had the additional job of revving the motorcycle when the Shangri-Las played Leader of the Pack.

The Zombies' follow-up, 1965's Tell Her No, made number 6 on the *Billboard* Hot 100 and after a few subsequently low charting singles they reached number 3 in 1969 with Time of the Season. However, by then the group had disbanded with Rod Argent forming his own group (just called Argent) and Colin Blunstone embarking on a solo music career (after a few years working as an insurance clerk). The Zombies were perhaps ahead of their time: their music was more experimental and challenging than people were expecting from a British Invasion group. Had they arrived a couple of years later, maybe they would have been better appreciated.

In a bizarre coda to their story, an unscrupulous Midwest promoter assembled a band in 1988, called them the Zombies, and put them out on the road. Even *Rolling Stone* magazine was fooled when the band told them that Blunstone (who is still alive) had been killed in a car crash and they were continuing to play his music out of respect. It was not until they played the Whisky a Go Go in Los Angeles that they were exposed as phonies. Local D.J. Rodney Bingenheimer, who ran the English Disco club on Sunset Strip in the early 1970s, knew his British groups.

The Zombies display their intellectual image (note the two pairs of horn-rimmed glasses) and show off their matching velvet vests.

HOUSE OF THE RISING SUN

As if any further proof was needed that the British Invasion was a force to be reckoned with, in the summer of 1964 a previously unheard of group from Newcastle called the Animals suddenly appeared in the American charts. They reached number 1 on September 5, staying there for three weeks and becoming the second British group to follow the Beatles to the top. It was a remarkable achievement in that the song was a traditional ballad, The House of the Rising Sun, collected by Alan Lomax in the thirties and already recorded by many artists including Roy Acuff, Woody Guthrie, Leadbelly, Frankie Laine, Joan Baez, Josh White, Nina Simone, and Bob Dylan (who claimed a writer's credit).

The House of the Rising Sun clocked in at 4 minutes 30 seconds, which was regarded as being far too long for a pop single if it expected to get airplay. So a hasty edit was made for the American market, reducing it to 2 minutes 58 seconds, just under the fatal 3-minute mark. (The full version appeared on the Animals' 1966 Greatest Hits album.) In many ways it was a fluke that it became a hit as Eric Burdon's vocals were uncompromisingly raw and bluesy, and his only real interest was R&B. It proved difficult to find suitably commercial material for a follow-up single. I'm Crying got to number 19 but the next two singles did not reach the top 40. The Animals' British producer, Mickie Most, decided that the answer was to give them commercial Tin Pan Alley-created material and let Burdon's heavy blues voice add an edge to the classic Brill Building riffs. It worked and Don't Let Me Be Misunderstood made number 15, with It's My Life reaching number 23, but even as it was climbing in the charts Burdon (third from left on the cover, right) was giving interviews saying how much he disliked the song.

Soon the other original members of the Animals were lost, and Burdon was left with a set of unknown sidemen under the name Eric Burdon and the Animals. He progressed through all the vicissitudes of sixties' pop stardom, including total immersion into hippiedom: his 1967 San Franciscan Nights went top 10 and the follow-up, Monterey, reached number 15.

Long before then though, the original Animals' keyboard player Alan Price (far right) left to form the Alan Price Set and his first single, a 1966 cover of the Screamin' Jay Hawkins number I Put a Spell on You, reached the British top 10 but only got to number 80 in the States. The bass player with the Animals, Chas Chandler (second left), noted that managers seemed to always make much more money than their acts so he looked around for a group to manage. At the Café Wha? in New York's Greenwich Village he came across a brilliant guitarist named Jimi Hendrix. He took him to London, fixed him up with a bass player and a drummer, and created the Jimi Hendrix Experience.

E niMALS

heir hit single "House Of The Rising Sun"

MGM
HIGH FIDELITY

® © Metro-Goldwyn-Mayer, Inc./Printed in U.S.A.

I'm into Something Good

It was something of a surprise to people back in Britain that certain groups were taken up in America who were regarded as minor in Britain. Herman's Hermits was one such group who had two American number 1 hits with songs that were not even released back in Britain. It is hard to imagine that Herman's Hermits could be regarded as up there with the Beatles and Rolling Stones in the U.S.A., but for a period in 1965 and 1966 they were at the very top. Years later Joey Ramone from the Ramones cited them as a major influence on his band.

Herman's Hermits came from Manchester and lead singer, Peter Noone, was already familiar to British audiences for his work as a television child actor in programs such as the popular soap *Coronation Street*. When producer Mickie Most seized upon the band, Noone was 17 years old but had already been the band's spokesman and lead singer for two years. Most aimed the group at the prepubescent girl audience, knowing that the screams would drown out the fact that the group could not play their instruments. In the studio he used session musicians such as Jimmy Page and John Paul Jones, both from the future Led Zeppelin. The songs were carefully chosen, among them innocuous American standards such as Silhouettes and Wonderful World, as well as British music-hall classics such as I'm Henry VIII, I Am.

They first reached the charts with a cover of Gerry Goffin and Carole King's I'm into Something Good, which had been originally recorded by Earl-Jean McCrea, the former lead singer with the Cookies. The song was to give the Hermits their only number 1 in Britain, but only reached 13 in the U.S.A. They did better with next single though, and Can't You Hear My Heartbeat? climbed to number 2 in the States. Mickie Most concentrated his efforts on the American market from then on and it paid off with the next single, the March 1965 release, Mrs. Brown, You've Got a Lovely Daughter, which was not released in Britain. It made number 1. The same happened with I'm Henry VIII, I Am in June 1965.

Noone was a good frontman; wide-eyed and innocent looking, he appealed to young girls and seemed safe enough to the mothers though in point of fact his mentor was John Lennon. Peter Noone: "John Lennon drank Bacardi and Coke and smoked Lark cigarettes. For five years after I found that out, I only drank Bacardi and Coke and smoked Lark cigarettes." Nor were they as innocent as they might seem: "We came to the States and it was unbelievable. I was very interested in meeting girls–the more the merrier." The Hermits went on to have U.S.A. top 10 hits with Wonderful World, Just a Little Bit Better, A Must to Avoid, Listen People, which got to number 3, and Dandy, an American number 5, again not released in Britain. After February 1967's There's a Kind of Hush, which reached number 4 in the U.S.A., their records fell away and the last eight singles did not reach the Hot 100. Oddly enough, they all did quite well in Britain, though, with three of them entering the top 10. Peter Noone: "Herman's Hermits was a singles act, and in the future it was all to be album acts. We were not prepared to be an album act." Their time had been a good one, though.

Above: Herman stars with equine companion on the back cover of Blaze.

Opposite: Herman and the Hermits in a characteristic sixties pose, combining bowler-hatted, furled-umbrella Britishness with a joke use of the "Gentlemen" sign, which is the British term for a men's restroom.

We didn't write songs.

PETER NOONE

WHY THE

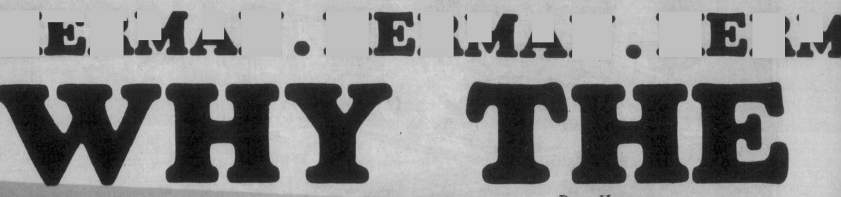

ON CAMERA, Herman gives out with the impression of a young, lively schoolboy. His innocent charm is the special element that sets him apart from other performers. Movie producers in Hollywood already have their eye on Herman for roles in films. Starting out as an actor, Herman made the change to singer easily.

Dear Herman,

The first time I heard you sing, I knew everything had stopped for me . . . that is until I saw you in person in Syracuse, New York. If ever there was a boy to meet any girl's dreams, it's you. Those dreamy eyes and that smile of yours. It's the absolute most! I just wish there were four of you to go around so my girlfriends and I could share you.

But one question: Why the Hermits? Why not just plain Herman? You're the greatest.

Love,
Angie

Dear Herman,

Of all the groups from England, I like yours the very best and that even includes The Beatles. But all I want to know is, don't you think it would be better if you were a solo singer? Maybe you could be like Sinatra someday. There's nothing wrong with your group, but I just think you'd be better alone. What do you think?

Your devoted fan,
Jane S.

These letters are just two samples of the mail that Herman's been getting since the Hermits hit the big time . . . and to Herman, himself, these questions are alarming! Here he is for the first time really being successful at something he loves, and suddenly the question is creeping back into his mind about whether he's doing the right thing.

Having begun his career as a child actor, Herman (real name Peter Noone) got much of his initial experience without benefit of any group. He liked acting, but somehow there always seemed to be something missing in his life.

He had sung a little at school and although at first just having drama lessons, he combined these with singing lessons when a part he had in one of the TV series "Knight Errant" required him to sing.

Singing wasn't easy at first for Herman so he was enrolled in the Manchester School of Music for both drama and singing lessons. These started when he was 14 and lasted for two years.

Herman always thought the Pops Clubs were gear and attended whenever he could. He loved going to hear a group called The Heartbeats at a

Continued

ARE HERMAN'S HERMAN'S HERMITS?

HIS FANS ARE BEGINNING TO ASK HIM TO STAND ALONE. HOW THIS WILL CHANGE HIM, NO ONE KNOWS!

Yesterday's Gone

At the end of 1963, Britain's first folk duo, Chad & Jeremy, released their first single, Yesterday's Gone, which reached number 40 in the British charts. It was to prove their only UK hit and, ironically, when they reached the U.S.A. in 1964 on the coattails of the Beatles they achieved the kind of successes that American folk acts had suddenly found wanting. They reached number 7 on the *Billboard* Hot 100 with A Summer Song in August, and in November enjoyed another hit with Willow Weep for Me. They went on to enjoy five more *Billboard* Hot 100 hits, and stopped releasing records in the UK in early 1965.

Yet another British group prepare to take off for America. Chad and Jeremy at London Airport, 1964.

There were other one-hit British Invasion bands, of course, such as the Nashville Teens, who got to number 13 with Tobacco Road in 1964, and the Swinging Blue Jeans from Liverpool who made number 21 with Hippy Hippy Shake early the same year. In October 1964, an unusual British duo had a number 5 hit with Have I the Right? The Honeycombs were a hairdresser, Dennis D'Ell, on vocals and his assistant, Honey Lantree, on drums; their name combined his profession and her name. The record was the last time that independent British producer Joe Meek had an American hit. Many of the groups simply didn't make it. The Hullaballoos, for instance, had a gimmick: they all had long blond Beatle-style hair. Strangely, they did not name themselves after the popular American television music program, but all came from Hull, in England: thus the Hullaballoos. Their records did not take off, however. Liverpudlian Jackie Lomax, who later recorded for the Beatles' Apple label, attempted to storm America in 1965 with the Undertakers: they dressed in long frock coats and arrived at gigs in a hearse and opened their set with The Funeral March. Again, no luck. In the main, though, the bands from Britain who landed in New York in the wake of the Beatles found at least some sustained success with American teens.

The Searchers got to number 3 with Love Potion No. 9 in 1965, which was their best U.S.A. chart showing, and Sugar and Spice (a British number 2) got to number 44 on the *Billboard* Hot 100 at the end of 1963. Strangely, their catchy British number 1 hit Sweets for My Sweet didn't chart at all in the States but their

The Beatles were perfect for opening doors . . . When they went to America they made it wide open for us. We could never have gone there without them.

KEITH RICHARDS

other UK number 1s, Needles and Pins and Don't Throw Your Love Away, made number 13 and 16 respectively in 1964.

In May of 1964 a new band from England—south-west London in fact—landed in the States and began what would prove to be a long and complicated love affair with America. The Rolling Stones began their first U.S.A. tour on June 2 and by August had three singles in the top 100, although none made the top 20: Not Fade Away, Tell Me, and It's All Over Now.

Wishin' and Hopin'

The American charts had not been totally devoid of British acts before The Beatles; the Springfields, for instance, had a number 20 hit with Silver Threads and Golden Needles in September 1962. The Springfields were a folk trio consisting of Tim Field and Tom Springfield along with Tom's sister Dusty. In 1963 Dusty went solo and had eleven Top 40 hits in the U.S. beginning with I Only Want to Be With You in February 1964—still pre-Beatles—and including Wishin' and Hopin in '64 and You Don't Have to Say You Love Me in '66. Dusty, with her gravity defying beehive and huge kohled eyes, was an iconic figure on the British pop scene. Her soulful voice was more subtle than most British invasion shouters, in fact she belonged much more in the soul tradition. One of her greatest achievements was the album *Dusty in Memphis*. Backed by the Memphis Cats, the top notch Atlantic Records session musicians who had previously backed everyone from Wilson Pickett to Elvis Presley, she felt somewhat intimidated. This, combined with an obsessive search for perfection, led to her rejecting every single track recorded in Memphis and recording new vocals tracks for the album in New York. It is regarded as her finest work and Son of a Preacher Man from the album was a Christmas hit in 1968 reaching number 10 in the Billboard charts. Dusty did Atlantic Records a huge favor by recommending that they sign the newly formed Led Zeppelin.

Another British act to have considerable American chart success in the sixties was Petula Clark. "Pet," as she was known in England, made her first film at age 11 in 1944, a war weepy called *Medal for the General*, her first record in 1949, and had been a British TV child star with her own show, *Pet's Parlour*, at the age of 11. She first hit the American Top 40 in 1964 with Downtown which went to number 1 and earned her a gold record. This was followed by I Know a Place, which reached number 3. In 1966 My Love went to number 1, and in 1967 This Is My Song, from the film *A Countess from Hong Kong*, starring Marlon Brando, made number 3. More hits followed including Don't Sleep on the Subway which reached number 5 in 1967. Though older than other British Invasion acts, she rode in with the first wave and had 15 Top 40 hits in all from 1965 until 1968. With her help, by January 2, 1965, more than a quarter of the songs in the *Billboard* Hot 100 were by British acts.

The rest of 1964 belonged to the Beatles, though. On August 19, they began their first American tour at the Cow Palace in San Francisco after being welcomed with a ticker-tape parade. Their *A Hard Day's Night* album reached number 1 on July 25. The big holiday season hit in the U.S.A. was the Beatles' I Feel Fine, which reached number 1 on December 26, 1964.

America had been well and truly invaded.

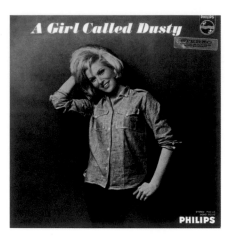

Above: Dusty Springfield's overlooked A Girl Called Dusty album went on to become regarded as a classic.

Right: Petula Clark made her first record in 1949 but the 1964 British Invasion enabled her to break into the American charts with Downtown.

3

BEATLES LIVE!
COAST TO COAST!

IN THE MID-SIXTIES *most bands were still on relatively small royalties from their record sales and the best way for them to capitalize on chart success was to tour. The Beatles were not only the first Brit band to conquer America, but also the first to use large venues such as the Hollywood Bowl and Shea Stadium. Their Shea Stadium concert on Sunday, August 15, 1965, set an audience record of 55,600 which would not be broken until 1973, when another British band, Led Zeppelin, topped it with a concert at Tampa Stadium in Florida. It was the Beatles who first earned enormous amounts of money from playing huge stadiums, something that promoters and other bands quickly copied. They also showed that this type of touring has to be organized with military precision to make sure that nobody gets hurt. It was an extraordinary experience for the Beatles and their crew, and not an altogether pleasant one. The sheer scale of Beatlemania in the U.S.A. is something people tend to overlook, but nothing like it had ever happened before.*

The Beatles began their first tour in San Francisco, landing at the International Airport on August 18, 1964, to scenes of mass hysteria as 9,000 fans screamed and ran riot. The original plan was for the Beatles to go first to "Beatlesville," a small stage located about a mile north-west of the main airport buildings, surrounded by a cyclone fence and guarded on all sides by 180 San Mateo County Sheriffs, where they would wave to the fans before being driven by limousine to the Hilton Hotel. But the scene at Beatlesville was chaotic. The Beatles waited in their limousine, debating what to do. Eventually, they risked a brief appearance, led by Ringo, but as soon as he appeared, thousands of girls

Below left: More product for Beatles fans. John Lennon: "Beatles fans don't copy us. We don't wear Beatles wigs."

Right: The Beatles rehearsing for their second appearance on The Ed Sullivan Show *in the Napoleon Room of the Deauville Hotel in Miami, February 15, 1964.*

BEATLEMANIA

Today's modern Beatle fan can wear Beatlemania, speak Beatlemania, play Beatlemania—and even eat Beatlemania!

Left: Safety for the group and for their fans was paramount, and Epstein always insisted on a high stage to prevent stage invasions.

Right: In reality the Beatles were rarely as animated as in this sculpture, except in the early days in Hamburg.

Presently being exhibited at the Chenil Galleries, King's Road, Chelsea, London are these "Beatles." They were modeled by Anthony Gray, A.R.B.S., who has sculpted the forms of many equally as famous people.

pushed forward, trying to scale the fence. After a brief appearance by Paul, George, and John, the deputies ushered them all quickly back to their limousine and drove them away from the hysterical scene just as the link fences were pushed over by the sheer weight of fans.

The Beatles had been big in Britain, but in America a new approach was needed to ensure their safety and that of their fans. At the Cow Palace 50 fans were hurt in the crush, 50 more were physically ejected from the stage, and back at the hotel 35 girls, some dressed as hotel maids, were caught trying to sneak past the guards.

The Beatles were supported on that tour by the Bill Black Combo, the Exciters, the Righteous Brothers, and Jackie DeShannon. At their first venue, the Cow Palace in San Francisco, they played to 17,130 screaming fans and earned a gross take of $91,670 (the net was $49,800). The screams were so unbelievably loud that the Beatles were unable to hear themselves play. Not only that but the stage lighting was rendered unnecessary by the constant bath of flashes from the girls' cameras which hit the stage like sheet lightning. *The San Francisco Examiner* reported:

Although it was publicized as music, all that was heard and seen of the Mersey Sound was something like a jet engine shrieking through a summer lightning storm because of the yelling fans. It had no mercy, and afterwards everyone still capable of speech took note of a ringing in the ears which lasted for as long as the Beatles had played.

When the Beatles appeared the girls screamed for a solid 4 minutes 45 seconds. It was an indication of things to come.

Please don't throw jellybabies, they get in my mouth.

GEORGE HARRISON

The Beatles played a short, 29-minute set on their 1964 American tour, consisting of Twist and Shout, You Can't Do That, All My Loving, She Loves You, Things We Said Today, Roll Over Beethoven, Can't Buy Me Love, If I Fell, I Want to Hold Your Hand, Boys, A Hard Day's Night, and Long Tall Sally. Sometimes they would open with I Saw Her Standing There and close with Twist and Shout.

Hit the Road, Whack!

That first 25-date tour was a steep learning curve for the band and their management. They were used to being screamed at and chased by fans, but the British police did not assail their fans in the way American police did. The Beatles did not want to see a repeat of their gig in Las Vegas where fans were attacked by the police wielding billy clubs.

At their concert at the Seattle Center Coliseum on August 21 the police rehearsed different tactics. The *Seattle Post-Intelligencer* reported:

> The original plan was for 16 Seattle police officers to escort the British quartet down a corridor, across 18 feet of open space and onto the stage. As the Beatles and their cortege whipped from the corridor, a phalanx of youngsters swept down a ramp from the balcony. The officers nearest the ramp pivoted like grid-iron tackles. Youngsters bounced off blue clad soldiers. Ringo, John, Paul and George were gone like gazelles, down a short tunnel toward the stage. Out of the chute like Brahma bulls, they bounced to their places as the Coliseum rose in one vast adolescent moan. Then the screams split the vaulted ceiling.

Seeing that they were in danger of being overwhelmed, the police recruited navy volunteers from the audience and formed them into a two-deep line to protect the Beatles for the short distance from the stage to the dressing-room corridor. So the Beatles played their final note, did the Beatle bow, dropped their instruments, and were gone. Hundreds of teenagers charged down the ramps, straight into a cordon of navy officers standing with locked arms. Unfortunately, the car that was to have driven the Beatles back to their hotel was so badly damaged by fans that it had to be abandoned. It was another hour before the crowds had dispersed enough for them to be spirited out of the building in an ambulance.

At the Empire Stadium in Vancouver, Canada, speed was of the essence. As they bowed to the audience the Beatles were already unstrapping their guitars.

Touring was not all hotel rooms and airports: The Beatles relax in a private villa in Brown Canyon, Bel-Air.

They ran from the stage and were in their waiting limousines in less than 30 seconds and, accompanied by motorcycle outriders, drove straight to the airport for a plane to Los Angeles. Unfortunately, thousands of teenagers rushed the stage, which was protected by a metal restraining fence. Hundreds of girls were crushed against it; dozens were treated for broken ribs, and hundreds for hysteria and shock.

The August 23 concert at the Hollywood Bowl had sold out four months earlier but hundreds of people without tickets turned up anyway, leading to several arrests. This being Los Angeles, there was a huge traffic jam afterwards as thousands of parents converged on the Bowl to collect their children. Police and firemen had set up roadblocks to control the traffic and local residents were given passes in advance to get to their homes. A good example of the levels of teen hysteria and fanaticism is the fact that even at 3:02 a.m. some 3,000 fans were waiting for the group at JFK airport when they flew in from Cincinnati and hundreds more were waiting outside the Delmonico Hotel at Park Avenue and 59th Street, New York. Fans used all manner of ingenious ways to gain access to the band: two girls arrived dressed as nurses, claiming to be their medical staff, while others delivered fake packages and made tempting offers to the security guards. The police asked the Beatles to stay away from their windows because every time they were seen from the street the fans surged into the roadway, blocking the traffic.

Help!

All 15,983 of the seats in the Forest Hills Tennis Stadium in Queens, New York, had sold out and extra field seats were added at $6.50 each (which was expensive in those days). An 8-foot high barbed-wire topped fence protected the stage and the group arrived by helicopter from the Wall Street heliport. On September 5 they played the International Amphitheatre in Chicago. Promoters the Andy Frain Organization had sent 10 of its ushers to attend the Beatles' concert in Milwaukee the previous night in order to study the tactics and behavior of Beatles fans and plan their security accordingly. At the Chicago concert, the 170 ushers and 35 usherettes were specially selected as being non-Beatles fans so that they would not join in the mass hysteria and 320 tough Chicago cops were stationed around the auditorium. One of them, patrolman Anthony Dizonne, remembered the Frank Sinatra days, saying: "This is kind of like Sinatra multiplied by 50 or 100." Fans were frisked on the way in and all large signs confiscated because they would block the view for others. Anything brought along to throw at the group, such as jelly beans and candy kisses, was also confiscated. Despite this, Paul was hit in the face by a used flashbulb. As usual, they drove straight to the airport after the show while police mounted a guard over their hotel rooms to stop fans from tearing them apart for souvenirs.

Canadian security was not so good: in Toronto the Beatles only just made it into the King Edward Hotel. They got separated by the crowds of fans and Paul's shirt was ripped and torn: "I thought I was [done] for it, but an immense copper lifted me up and shoved me into the elevator." John said, "The best view of the country is over the blue shoulder of a policeman." A police van was used to get them to the gig, leaving from the hotel's service entrance. Five blocks around Maple Leaf Gardens were roped off and patrolled for 12 hours before the group were due to arrive, and 4,000 male and female police and Canadian Mounties were on duty at the Gardens. The Beatles flew out with a check for $93,000.

At the time a reporter asked John, "How long do you think you'll last?" He replied: "Longer than you."

At the Gator Bowl in Florida, the Beatles encountered a new problem when newsreel and television cameramen refused to leave the arena; they could make considerable amounts of money selling Beatles footage, particularly of them playing. Beatles Press Officer Derek Taylor had to go onstage and explain to the audience: "The Beatles are 100 feet away. They came thousands of miles to be here. The only thing preventing their appearance is cinecameramen." He said that the film made as newsreels was ultimately sold and shown in movie theaters with no royalties paid to the Beatles. The police captains gave the order for filming to stop and police physically restrained eight of the cameramen, covering their lenses with their hands as they escorted them from the arena.

Virtually all Beatles concerts ended with half a dozen or so girls being taken to hospital in various states of emotional and physical exhaustion.

We're going to remain normal if it kills us.

JOHN LENNON

In Pittsburgh, the security force was larger than that used for presidential visits to the city. There were 120 police at the airport, including 15 on horseback, and more lined the route of their motorcade to the city. Five thousand fans surrounded the Civic Arena for hours before the concert. In Cleveland, a boy hid in a packing case and had himself delivered to their hotel, and at Public Hall the concert had to be stopped for 10 minutes after the audience had pushed the police line too close to the stage. Afterwards, John told a KYW reporter: "This has never happened to us before. We have never had a show stopped. These policemen are a bunch of amateurs." Things were worse in New Orleans where 700 teenagers rushed the barriers, keeping the group from the stage, and it took 225 police more than 20 minutes to restore order. Mounted police had to patrol the area around the stage. More than 200 fans collapsed and one girl had her arm broken. It was the same in virtually every city: the Beatles could not leave their hotel rooms and remained cooped up while the screams and cheers of fans drifted in through the hotel windows that they could not even go near.

Bigger Than Jesus

The Beatles' 1965 tour of America saw similar events. When the group played Shea Stadium for the second time on August 15 the police were concerned that their motorcade would block the East River tunnels. Consequently, they insisted that the Beatles travel by helicopter to the World Fair site, where they transferred to a Wells Fargo armored van. They flew from gig to gig in their own Lockheed Electra hired from Lockheed Flyers. Years later, George was on a flight from New York to Los Angeles and met the pilot, who told him, "You'd never believe that plane! It was just full of bullet holes, the tail, the wings, everything—just full of bullet holes. Jealous fellows who would be waiting, knowing that the Beatles were arriving at such-and-such a time. They'd all be trying to shoot the plane!"

Sometimes the local police were poorly organized. When the Beatles arrived in Houston, Texas, at 2 a.m. the police had made no arrangements and fans swarmed all over the plane before it had even come to halt at the terminal. Because of this, Chicago's O'Hare airport would not let them land, so they had to fly into the little-used Midway airport instead.

The band's inability to see any of the cities they were playing in, the fact that they could not hear what they were playing because of the screams, and their fears for their own safety meant that by their third major American tour, in 1966, the Beatles had become very disenchanted with the idea of life on stage. The problems were exacerbated on this tour by the fact that on July 29, 1966, *Datebook* magazine had published Maureen Cleave's interview with John Lennon in which he had commented, "We're bigger than Jesus now." When it had been published originally in the London *Evening Standard* on March 4, no one had commented, but in America it caused outrage. Television film showed zealots in Birmingham, Alabama, burning Beatles records just as the Nazis had burned books. There were fears that the entire 1966 tour would have to be canceled because of death threats. Thirty American radio stations banned Beatles records and one, Radio KLUE in Longview, Texas, who got on the bandwagon a bit late, organized a public burning of Beatles' records. The station manager said, "We are inviting local teenagers to bring in their records and other symbols of the group's popularity to be burned at a public bonfire on Friday night, August thirteenth." On August 14, Radio KLUE was taken off the air when a lightning bolt hit their transmission tower, knocking their news director unconscious and destroying much of their electronic equipment.

Richard Freeman's famous black and white image, used here on the second Beatles LP released in Britain, was shot using natural light at the Palace Hotel, Bournemouth, on August 22, 1963, during the band's summer tour.

The Grand Dragon of the South Carolina Ku Klux Klan attached a Beatles record to a large wooden cross which he then set on fire as part of their ritual. At the Mid-South Coliseum in Memphis, Tennessee, Klansmen picketed the stadium in their costumes and firecrackers and rubbish were thrown on the stage. Outside, the Beatles' bus was surrounded by hoards of Christian demonstrators screaming abuse. Paul recalled, "They were zealots. It was horrible to see the hatred on their faces," while John said, "When they started burning our records . . . that was a real shock, the physical burning. I couldn't go away knowing I'd created another little piece of hate in the world . . . so I apologized." George saw something humorously positive in the record-burning episode, though: "They've got to buy them before they can burn them."

At the Busch Stadium in St. Louis, Missouri, on August 21, the band played to 23,000 people in a heavy rainstorm. The Beatles were only protected by a flimsy tarpaulin which dripped water on to their amps. It was here that Paul McCartney finally gave in and agreed with the other three Beatles that it was time to stop live performances—something they had been trying to persuade him to agree to for some time. They only played four more stadiums and on August 29, 1966, at Candlestick Park outside San Francisco, 25,000 people saw the Beatles play their last live concert to a paying audience. The last number was their old Hamburg crowd-pleaser, Long Tall Sally. After it was all over John revealed:

On our last tour people kept bringing blind, crippled, and deformed children into our dressing room and this boy's mother would say, "Go on, kiss him, maybe you'll bring back his sight." We're not cruel. We've seen enough tragedy in Merseyside, but when a mother shrieks, "Just touch him and maybe he'll walk again," we want to run, cry, empty our pockets.

A lot of fans came to the concerts just to scream. Paul McCartney: "A lot of them don't even want to listen because they have got the records."

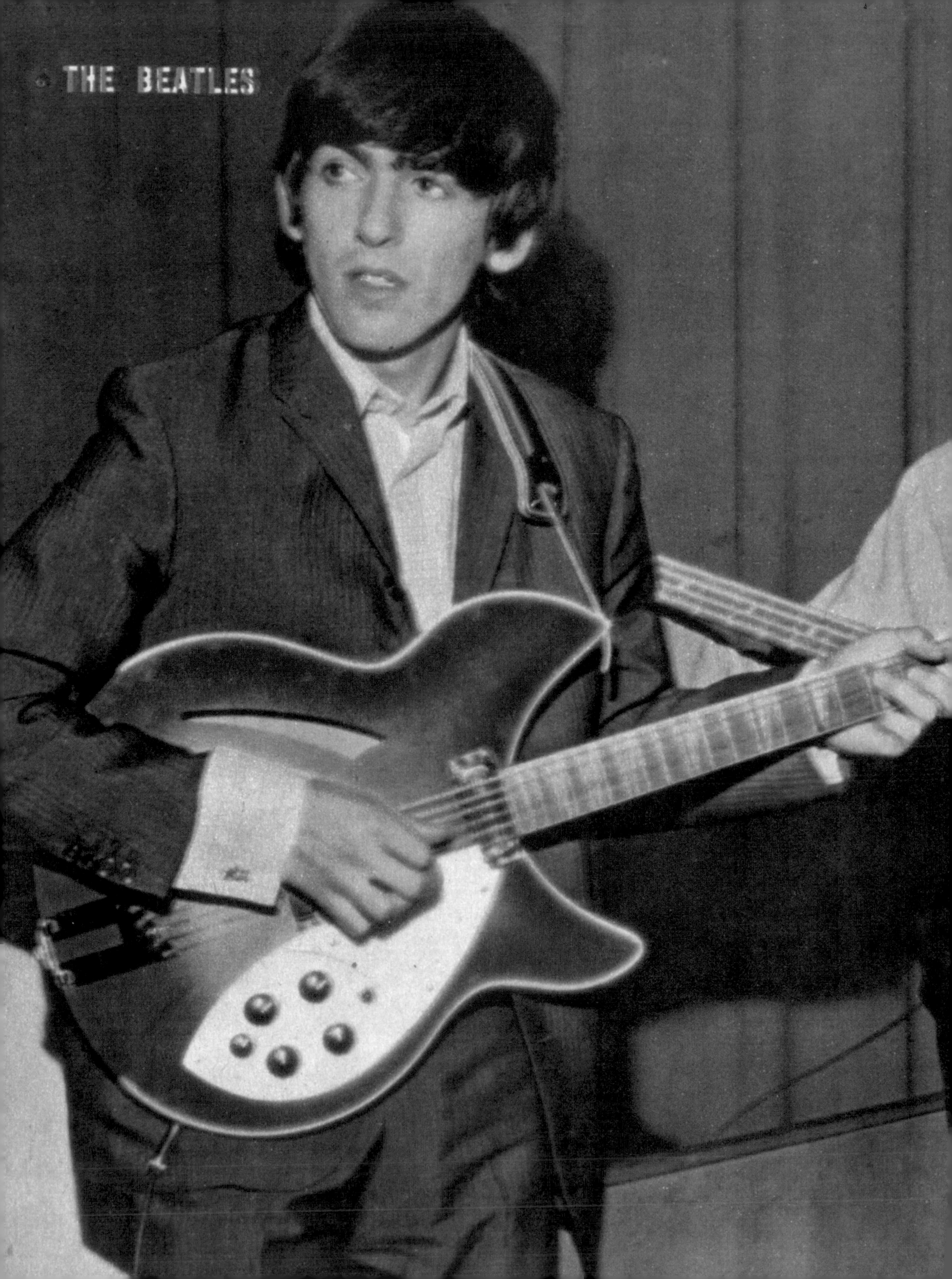
THE BEATLES

photoplay

Hoochie Coochie Men

It is a salutary fact that it required the British Invasion before America woke up to its own musical treasure, which lay buried in the South and in the black ghettos of the northern cities. As Muddy Waters said in *Time* on September 22, 1967, "Until the Beatles exposed the origins, the white kids didn't know anything about the music. Now they've learned it was in their backyard all the time.'

In the early 1960s, American bluesmen, who were mostly confined to playing the chitlin' circuit and segregated clubs in their homeland, had been amazed to find themselves playing at major, predominantly white clubs in European cities. European audiences became familiar with them thanks to the work done by German promoters Horst Lippmann and Fritz Rau, who instigated the influential American Folk Blues Festival that toured Europe every year from 1962 until 1972. After approaching Willie Dixon, the bass player and in-house producer at Chess Records, they gained access to a whole range of overlooked performers.

The first A.F.B.F. tour of Britain in October 1962 included Memphis Slim, T-Bone Walker, Sonny Terry & Brownie McGhee, Willie Dixon, John Lee Hooker, and Shakey Jake. Naturally, all the R&B-influenced musicians in London, who knew the lineup from their recordings only, went to the shows. They sat in awe, carefully noting guitar tunings—many of the bluesmen used their own unique tunings—makes, and models, scribbling down lyrics, and absorbing information like blotting paper: this was the real thing.

The October 1963 tour included Memphis Slim, Big Joe Williams, Willie Dixon, Victoria Spivey, Matt "Guitar" Murphy, Sonny Boy Williamson II, Lonnie Johnson, Otis Spann, and Muddy Waters. These people were treated like gods in Britain and, naturally, they sometimes reacted uneasily to the adulation coming their way. It was so unexpected.

Below left: Sonny Terry and Brownie McGhee became fixtures in the Soho blues scene and could often be found in Bungie's folk club.

Right: Memphis Slim was on the early American Folk Blues Festival tours and was astonished at the respect and even adulation afforded to the visiting bluesmen.

MEMPHIS SLIM

CLAP YOUR HANDS

fontana

ROBERT JOHNSON
KING OF THE DELTA BLUES SINGERS

62456
CBS ARCHIVE SERIES

Bright Lights, Big City

Some of the acts on the American Folk and Blues Festival lineup stayed in London after finishing their dates in order to play the clubs. When Jimmy Reed appeared at the Flamingo in Soho, he and his manager were so wary that Jimmy didn't take his overcoat off the whole time he performed. They simply couldn't understand the adulation and enthusiasm of the crowd, it had never happened to them before with a white audience. They were expecting a hostile crowd, so they were ready to grab the money and run.

Sonny Boy Williamson became the subject of numerous legendary—and possibly apocryphal—stories about his time in Britain. In one such tale he is said to have set his hotel room on fire during a tour by trying to cook a rabbit in a coffee percolator. Sonny Boy loved London and had a two-tone suit made for him which he wore with a bowler hat, furled umbrella, and a smart leather briefcase for his harmonica. In a 1964 recording made in London he played the song, I'm Trying to Make London My Home. Unfortunately, Sonny Boy had such a reputation for telling tall stories that when he returned to the Delta, few people believed his stories about recording in London and climbing the Eiffel Tower.

British bands brought a huge change of fortune for Willie Dixon. His songs were recorded by the Yardbirds, Cream, the Animals, the Rolling Stones, John Mayall, and later by American bands such as the Allman Brothers Band, Bob Dylan, the Doors, the Grateful Dead, and even the Monkees (You Can't Judge a Book By Looking at Its Cover'). When the Rolling Stones appeared on the American *Shindig!* television program, they insisted that Howlin' Wolf appear on the same bill; they had recorded his Little Red Rooster on their first album and he had been a huge influence upon them. Muddy Waters' career really took off after making several successful tours of Britain which took him back to his roots.

Opposite: As well as an interest in living bluesmen, there was an increased interest in the roots of R&B and blues, particularly in the legendary Robert Johnson, whose songs were in the repertoire of every self-respecting British blues player. This 1966 LP release gave many musicians their first chance to hear Johnson.

Left: The Blues Breakers "Beano" album lineup: John Mayall, Eric Clapton, John McVie, and Hughie Flint.

ELECTRIC BLUES

Howlin' Wolf in London on the 1964 American Folk Blues Festival tour with pianist Sunnyland Slim, guitarist Hubert Sunlin, and Willie Dixon on bass. The Wolf was probably the most powerful electric blues singer of all time.

Blues Inc.

Ever since the fifties there had been an R&B and blues scene in London that was quite distinct from Tin Pan Alley and the purely commercial pop-group scene. Many of the British Invasion bands had their beginnings in this milieu. In 1949, guitarist and vocalist Alexis Korner joined Chris Barber's Jazz Band where he met harmonica player Cyril Davies. After playing as a duo, they started the London Blues and Barrelhouse Club in 1955 and released their first record in 1957. Then in 1961 they formed Blues Incorporated, conceived of as an "informal band" with membership being intentionally fluid. An early stalwart was drummer Charlie Watts, taking time off from his real interest at the time, which was jazz. Jack Bruce was often on bass, Dick Heckstall-Smith was on saxophone, with Long John Baldry on vocals. However, the lineup for the album *R&B from the Marquee*, released in Britain in 1962, showed a Blues Incorporated lineup of Korner, Davies, Heckstall-Smith, Baldry, Teddy Wadmore on bass guitar, Big Jim Sullivan on vocals, Keith Scott on piano, and Spike Heatley on string bass. Interestingly, this album was produced by Jack Good who later moved to the U.S.A. and produced the *Shindig!* TV show. In 1962 Korner and Davies started a "Rhythm and Blues" night at the Ealing Jazz Club, usually known as the Ealing Club. It was here, on April 7, 1962, that Alexis Korner introduced Mick Jagger and Keith Richards to an Ealing Club regular called Brian Jones.

They all sat in with Blues Incorporated at one time or another, as did vocalist Rod Stewart, Zoot Money, Jimmy Page, John Mayall, and Paul Jones, who briefly sang with the Rolling Stones before being replaced by Jagger and going on to join Manfred Mann. Charlie Watts left the Blues Inc. to join the Stones and was replaced by Ginger Baker. When Korner decided to add a brass section to Blues Incorporated, Cyril Davies left with Long John Baldry to form his own group, the Cyril Davies All Stars. He was replaced by Graham Bond and Blues Incorporated began a residency at the Flamingo Club. Shortly afterwards Bond left to form the Graham Bond Organization, taking Jack Bruce and Ginger Baker with him. And so it went on, until the ever-changing lineups of the London R&B bands eventually settled into a series of fixed units including the Rolling Stones, the Cyril Davies All Stars, Manfred Mann, and, slightly later, John Mayall's Bluesbreakers.

Above: Sonny Terry and Brownie McGhee with Alexis Korner.

Opposite: John Lee Hooker with John Mayall.

THE ROLLING Has England Gone
Write and tell us what YOU think!

THE DADS are yelling and the Mums are pulling their hair out — but their sons and daughters just couldn't care less. The Rolling Stones may be sloppy, pallid, unkempt and weird-looking, but the teenagers of England have gone absolutely bananas over these five fantastic young men.

The Stones (that's the *only* hip thing to call them) are a thing unto themselves. No other group can touch them, either musically (a combination of hard-rock and down-home true rhythm 'n' blues) or for looks (let the pictures speak for themselves).

So here they are, one at a time, for you to meet and greet on their first trip to America!

MICK JAGGER

Mick plays the harmonica and is lead singer. He was born in Hampstead, London, England, on July 26, 1944. He is tall and dark, and when he starts to move in front of the mike, the girls go wild. His favorite dance is his own interpretation of. the Twist. He went to school at the London School of Economics and used to be considered an "egghead."

KEITH RICHARD

Keith, who vaguely resembles a brunet English sheep dog, plays the guitar with The Stones. He also was born in Hampstead, his birthday being December 18. He is 20 years old. Keith has a dry (oh, very dry, sense of humor), and insists that his previous occupation was a "la'yabout." His hobby is sleeping and his dislikes include "the fuzz." His likes include guitars, boats and gardening of a sort. He insists that the first film he ever starred in was *The Sheik* with Rudolph Valentino!

BRIAN JONES

Brian divides his first love equally between the guitar and the harmonica. Born in London on February 28, 1944, he lists his favorite composers as Lennon-McCartney — followed by Johannes Sebastian Bach! Because *gear* is one of his favorite words, he uses it to describe the kind of clothes he likes to wear. Brian, whose warm smile draws screams of delight from his avid fans (when he finally decides to turn it on), had various jobs before tying up with The Stones. His biggest concern in life right now is how to stop smoking.

Keith and Mick.

Bill Wyman.

STONES— Too Far?

BILL WYMAN

Bill, who looks like a young, handsome Abraham Lincoln, plays bass guitar with the group. He makes his home in Beckenham, Kent, England. He was born on October 24, 1941. Chuck Berry and Jimmy Reed have greatly influenced his musical thinking. He used to be an engineer, and likes cashew nuts and astronomy. Dislikes: arguments, marmalade and traveling.

CHARLIE WATTS

The last "nutty head" in this row of Stones is drummer Charlie Watts. Charlie makes his home in Wembley, Middlesex, where he was born on June 2, 1941. He digs the soul and "roots" music of Muddy Waters and Bo Diddley. For singing, he chooses Sammy Davis, Jr., and Mick Jagger. An art lover, he goes for Picasso. Charlie used to be a graphic designer (a hip one, of course), and he lists his hobbies as GIRLS!

Bill, Charlie, Brian and Mick in Ready Steady Go.

Rolling Stones—Mick Jagger, Keith Richard, Brian Jones, Bill Wyman and Charlie Watts.

WATCH OUT, WORLD—HERE COME THE ROLLING STONES!

Bill, Keith and Brian on Thank Your Lucky Stars.

Like Rolling Stones

Though it is hard to imagine now, there was quite some resistance in America to the Rolling Stones, caused in part by the way that manager Andrew Loog Oldham had chosen to market them—see the preceding spread from *16 Magazine*. Oldham was 19 years old and had worked as the Beatles press officer. He recalled the first time he saw the Beatles, then effectively eighth on the bill on the Helen Shapiro tour: "In one night you knew they were going to be very big. It was just an instinctive thing. From that night on it registered subconsciously that when they made it, another section of the public was gonna want an opposite." When he saw the Stones play the Crawdaddy Club at the Station Hotel in Richmond on the outskirts of London he knew that "The Stones were gonna be that opposite." He immediately offered to manage them: "I was about forty-eight hours ahead of the business in getting there. But that's the way God planned it . . . I wasn't coming on with a cigar and a silk suit going 'Listen kids.' I was the same age as them. We talked the same language."

The Stones arrived to tour America on June 1, 1964, to find more than 500 fans waiting for them at JFK airport. The next day their first gig was on the *Les*

The young Rolling Stones. In case you can no longer recognize them from this March 1964 Photoplay *spread, they are clockwise from top left: Bill Wyman, Brian Jones, Mick Jagger, Keith Richards, and Charlie Watts.*

LES CRANE:

This is your first appearance on American TV.

KEITH RICHARDS:

Yeah.

LES:

Isn't it exciting?

KEITH:

Yeah, knocks me out.

(MUCH LAUGHTER FROM CAMERA CREW.)

(Continued on page 62)

Crane Show, a network television talk show. Also on the tour were Bobby Vee, the Chiffons, Bobby Goldsboro, and Bobby Comstock. They opened on June 5 in San Bernardino, California, but it was already obvious that here was not just another Beatles-imitation act. They were far more threatening than that, and selling them was to prove more difficult. Their second promotional gig, on June 3, had been to tape an appearance on the *Hollywood Palace* television show, hosted by Dean Martin, where they shared the bill with a group of Hollywood celebrity wives singing for charity; a stand-up comedian called Joey Forman; the King Sisters; and Bertha and Her Daughter, a dancing elephant act. After the Stones performed I Just Wanna Make Love to You and Not Fade Away, Martin staggered back on-screen to insult them, saying "Rolling Stones . . . aren't they great?" while rolling his eyes upwards. "They're going to leave right after the show for London. They're challenging the Beatles to a hair pulling contest. I could swear Jackie Coogan and Skippy were in that group. Well I'm going to let you in on something . . . you know these singing groups today . . . you're under the impression they have long hair. Not true at all . . . it's an optical illusion . . . they just have low foreheads and high eyebrows."

After the ads, Martin continued his put-down. Following a comedy trampoline act by Larry Griswold, he commented, "Larry Griswold . . . isn't he wonderful? He's the father of the Rolling Stones. And ever since he heard them sing, he's been trying to kill himself." How the audience of Hollywood has-beens roared. Afterwards Brian Jones commented, "He was a symbol of the whole tour to us."

At the show in San Antonio, Texas, a trained monkey was brought back for an encore but not the Stones. Bill Wyman commented, "We all wanted to pack up and come home." Predictably, the New York Carnegie Hall audience was better, but it was still a hard sell.

As far as Stones manager Andrew Loog Oldham was concerned, bad press was good publicity. It all helped to build the Stones' "bad boys" image.

Not Fade Away

Not Fade Away was the first Stones single to reach the American charts, spending 14 weeks there and peaking at number 48, but they had to release eight more before they finally got a number 1 hit and captured the American public once and for all with (I Can't Get No) Satisfaction. This was partly due to the fact that what they were playing was closer to blues than to pop. In the end, Andrew Loog Oldham's strategy of marketing them as rebels paid off. They had longer hair than the Beatles (just) and they were ruder than the Beatles (but not as rude as Lennon in private). Mostly, they were cutting through show-biz conventions: they did not all dress alike, their hairstyles were different from each other, and they shunned stage makeup but sometimes wore makeup offstage. The fact sheet telling the waiting world about the band members' preferences was filled with information like "favorite color: black" and "blond Brian smokes sixty cigarettes a day." Amazingly, this slight departure from the norm was seen as deeply threatening—the stories of the band urinating on a gas pump (which had been a publicity stunt staged by Oldham) were well known in America, where they were considered dirty and surly. Not that they were really threatening. When asked to change the title of Let's Spend the Night Together for *The Ed Sullivan Show* on January 15, 1967, they complied because it was such an important show; even if Jagger did roll his eyes and look pained every time he had to sing the emasculated line "Let's spend some time together." After their initial *Ed Sullivan Show* appearance on October 24, 1964, the host had banned them from appearing again because he thought their act was lewd, and had apologized to the audience for having them on. Fans in the audience had rioted and a grim faced Sullivan told the press:

> I promise you they will never be back to our show . . . If things can't be handled, we'll stop the whole business. We won't book any more rock 'n' roll groups and we'll ban teenagers from the theater if we have to. Frankly, I didn't see the group until the day before the broadcast. They were recommended by my scouts in England. I was shocked when I saw them.

It was with some discomfort that he had to have them back, but by the time he did, they were second only to the Beatles in popularity in America and he had his ratings to think about. The Stones appeared on his show six times between 1964 and 1969.

While the Beatles were presented as four facets of the same "Beatle" person, the Stones were never anything but five individuals (there was a sixth member, piano player Ian Stewart, but he was kept behind a curtain because he did not have show-biz looks and Oldham was convinced that the public would never remember as many as six names.) Another difference between them was that the Beatles were never very animated on stage, they just stood and strummed, whereas Jagger danced, leapt, and bounced across the stage, Keith Richards shuffled forwards and then shuffled back, and Brian Jones, desperate not to be upstaged by Jagger, flitted about and posed and preened for the girls. The biggest difference between the Stones and all the other British Invasion groups of the time, though, was the music. As Brian Jones said in a 1964 interview: "The essential difference between ourselves and the British groups that are well known in the United States at the moment is that we're the first to have a really strong Negro rhythm and blues influence. We haven't adapted our music from a watered down music like white American rock 'n' roll. We've adapted our music from the

It took a lot of persuading to get the record company to release a record without the band's name on the front sleeve.

early blues forms." As far as the Stones were concerned, they played rhythm and blues, not pop, not even rock 'n' roll.

After Satisfaction, the Stones were away. Their follow up, Get Off of My Cloud, also went to number 1, as did Paint It, Black, released in May 1966, and January 1967's Ruby Tuesday. As Tears Go By, 19th Nervous Breakdown, Mother's Little Helper, and Have You Seen Your Mother, Baby, Standing in the Shadow? all reached the American top 10 in the same period.

Do Wah Diddy Diddy

On October 17, 1964, the number 1 position in the charts fell to yet another British group. This time it was Manfred Mann's Do Wah Diddy Diddy. The Manfreds, a group of R&B and jazz aficionados, used the same technique as the Animals: they blended sophisticated R&B delivery with the vacuous teenybopper lyrics of the Brill Building to create a commercial sound. They despised the songs, but singer Paul Jones had a great blues voice and phrasing, and he managed to make something of them. One look at the band's co-founder, Manfred Mann himself—real name Michael Lubowitz—would clock him as a jazz fan with his horn-rim spectacles and neatly trimmed beard with shaved upper lip.

In 1962 he and Mike Hugg had formed the Mann-Hugg Blues Brothers, who with the addition of Mike Vickers, Tom McGuinness, and vocalist Paul Jones (real name Paul Pond), became Manfred Mann and the Manfreds—and finally just Manfred Mann. Jones had a blues background, having sung with Alexis Korner's Blues Incorporated, and, at the invitation of Brian Jones, briefly with the Rolling Stones before Mick Jagger joined them. Despite the fact that the group looked like a jazz combo, Paul Jones' gyrations and tight trousers did the trick. The girls loved him, he had a twinkle in his eye and a big smile and, in the wake of the Beatles, Do Wah Diddy Diddy went to number 1. Sha La La reached number 12, but it was not until 1968 that they had another top 10 entry in the States with Bob Dylan's Quinn the Eskimo (The Mighty Quinn) and by then the lineup had changed. Mike d'Abo had replaced Jones, Jack Bruce had come and gone, and Mike Vickers had left.

Another band with roots in the London R&B scene was John Mayall's Bluesbreakers. Mayall had been persuaded by Alexis Korner to move to London from Manchester in 1963, and Korner helped him find gigs including regular employment at the Marquee. The first guitarist of Mayall's Bluesbreakers was Bernie Watson from the Cyril Davies All Stars. He was replaced by Roger Dean (not the album cover designer of the same name) and they went on to back John Lee Hooker on his first British tour in 1964. Then in April 1965, Dean was replaced by former Yardbirds guitarist Eric Clapton, and things began to look up. After some other changes, during which Clapton was replaced by Peter Green, Jack Bruce came in to play bass, Clapton returned again, and Green departed, an album called *Bluesbreakers with Eric Clapton* was recorded featuring the lineup of Mayall, Clapton, John McVie on bass, and Hughie Flint (later replaced by Aynsley Dunbar) on drums. It was released in July 1966 and is regarded as a seminal British blues album, making number 6 in the British album charts.

By this time, however, Clapton, Jack Bruce, and Ginger Baker had together formed Cream. Peter Green came and went to form Fleetwood Mac, taking with him John McVie and Mick Fleetwood, who had joined the Bluesbreakers to replace Aynsley Dunbar. Mayall replaced Peter Green with 19-year-old Mick Taylor, who two years later replaced Brian Jones in the Rolling Stones. Mayall's influence on the American musical scene via his sidemen was enormous.

No matter how they posed, the Manfred Mann group always looked like a university jazz combo. Manfred is the one in glasses AND the beard.

130

Heart Full of Soul

Also from the British R&B scene, the Yardbirds were a Kingston Art School group who first worked as a backup band for Cyril Davies. They got their break when they took over from the Rolling Stones at the Crawdaddy Club in Richmond, playing a set composed of American blues classics by Sonny Boy Williamson, Howlin' Wolf, Muddy Waters, Elmore James, and Bo Diddley. In August 1963 they reached a crucial lineup, replacing guitarist Anthony "Top" Topham with Eric Clapton. They were the first group to make their first release a live album, *Five Live Yardbirds*, which was recorded at London's Marquee early in 1964 (the album is the first recording to feature Clapton). Next, they toured Europe as the backing group for Sonny Boy Williamson, who cleverly adapted his style to a rock-oriented blues backing. He remarked: "Those English kids want to play the blues so bad—and they play the blues *so* bad!"

Released in the spring of 1965, the Yardbirds' third single, For Your Love, was a departure from the blues into pure pop, which so upset Eric Clapton that he left to join John Mayall's Bluesbreakers. Clapton was still a blues purist and thought that the 'birds had deviated from the one true path. Later, of course, he formed Cream and Blind Faith before going solo and leaving the blues far behind for much of his career. For Your Love reached number 3 in Britain and more importantly got to number 6 in the American charts. The Yardbirds were upset by Clapton's departure because his style was so distinct, but within two days of his leaving, they played their first gig with his replacement, Jeff Beck.

The Yardbirds undertook three American tours during Beck's 18-month tenure (the first in August 1965). His use of fuzz-tone, distortion, and feedback guitar effects helped usher in the era of psychedelic rock. Next, they became what must have been one of the first super-groups when bassist Paul Samwell-Smith left the group to become a producer. Jimmy Page joined, at first playing bass until original rhythm-guitarist Chris Dreja mastered four strings, when Page took over on lead guitar. John Paul Jones then became the band's bass player.

The Happenings Ten Years Time Ago single released in October 1966 featured Beck and Page on double lead guitar, Keith Relf on vocals, Jim McCarty on drums, Dreja on rhythm guitar, and Jones on bass. It is now regarded as one of the greatest psychedelic records of the era. Jones played bass on another Beck-Page collaboration, Beck's Bolero, which featured Keith Moon on drums and Nicky Hopkins on piano and was first released as the B-side of Beck's first solo single, Hi Ho Silver Lining, in March 1967.

The Yardbirds were much helped by the success of Antonioni's 1966 film *Blowup*, which featured the Beck-Page Yardbirds performing Train Kept a Rollin', and during which Beck smashed his guitar to pieces. He had been known to do this, but never on stage. Antonioni had wanted the Who for the movie.

The Yardbirds' most celebrated lineup. From top left: rhythm guitarist Chris Dreja, singer Keith Relf, lead guitarist Jimmy Page, drummer Jim McCarty, and guitarist Jeff Beck. They were a guitar band.

We were a white copy of a blues band.

CHRIS DREJA

My Generation

Part of the second wave of British bands to hit America, the Who were late comers to the U.S. charts and only reached the top 10 once, with I Can See for Miles in 1967.

In Britain, the Who had become renowned for their Mod roots. They were at the vanguard of the almost exclusively working-class movement that saw teenagers dress in Italian suits, which they protected by oversized parkas as they rode their Italian scooter motorbikes. With its roots in late-1950s London, the Mod scene was made up of the second generation of teenagers in post-war Britain who professed a love of all things "Modern"—in complete contrast to the Edwardian-dressed Teddy Boys, who took an instant dislike to the few Mods they ever came across. Mod clothes had clean, red, white, and blue graphics—the best example is Keith Moon's "target" T-shirt—and wore Italian loafers, button-down shirts, and skinny ties. They took cheap, pharmaceutical speed and liked their girlfriends to dress sharp, preferably in Mary Quant clothes (see chapter 5).

Another teenage cult on the increase were the Rockers, who wore their hair long and greased, and dressed in leather biker jackets over white T-shirts and jeans (in homage to James Dean and Marlon Brando). Mods and the Rockers hated each other and staged pitched battles on British seaside resort beaches over the holiday weekends of 1963 and 1964. In *A Hard Day's Night*, Ringo refers to himself as "a Mocker" in reference to the ongoing youth battles in Britain. The Mods

The Who in full Mod mode. From left: bass player John "The Ox" Entwistle, guitarist Pete Townshend, singer Roger Daltrey, and drummer Keith Moon.

and Rockers scene was brilliantly captured by the Who on their *Quadrophenia* album and the later movie. Mods loved American R&B soul from Memphis, Philadelphia, Detroit, and New York (the Who included a version of Martha & the Vandellas' *Heat Wave* on their second album, *A Quick One*, in 1967), while Rockers liked Elvis, Gene Vincent, Eddie Cochran, and old-time rock 'n' roll.

The Who had begun their life as the High Numbers, playing the Mod clubs of London before renaming and being taken on by a sharp young manager named Kit Lambert who signed them to the Brunswick label. Their records were loud, but were no preparation for the live act that the band put on. The Who were masters of the stage, with guitarist Pete Townshend's windmill arm blasting out power chords, singer Roger Daltrey whirling his microphone around his head on an increasingly long cord, and Keith Moon flaying away at a massive, double drum kit. Moon, who, among his other influences had spent months studying the Pretty Things' madcap drummer Viv Prince in 1964, adopted Prince's tricks of kicking the drum kit apart on stage, throwing his sticks away, and falling over while still always keeping up a merciless beat. Bass player John Entwistle, known as both the Ox and Thunderfingers, stood still at the side of the stage and just watched. No one had seen such energy before and the Who quickly entered rock 'n' roll legend.

The first Who record was played on U.S. radio on August 23, 1965, by D.J. Peter Cavanaugh on WTAC-AM. At the time, the Who were supporting Herman's Hermits on a tour in which the Who would demolish everything on the stage, causing half the audience to leave before the Hermits came on. During the tour, the band were celebrating Keith's 19th birthday (though he claimed it was his 21st so he could drink) at the Flint Holiday Inn. He celebrated by driving someone's Cadillac through a picket fence and into the swimming pool. A legend was born.

Below: The Who's early posters were often hand-drawn and reflected their interest in Pop Art.

SAT. 18 DEC 7·15-11: the, pop-art, guitar smashing epic (my generation) the WHO

now open sunday afternoon 3-5·30

dont miss our xmas and new year raves

coming in '66 soloman burke little stevie wonder the drifters and many more

All Day and All of the Night

Some people in America noted the similarity between I Can't Explain and a hit single called All Day and All of the Night by the Kinks, another British band, which reached number 7 on the *Billboard* Hot 100 in December 1964. The Who songwriter Pete Townshend agreed it was similar: "It can't be beat for straightforward Kink copying."

The similarities did not end there. If anything, the Kinks were even more badly behaved than the Who: they fought with other on stage, argued with promoters, and were famous for their drinking. Unfortunately, it had disastrous consequences for their American career. Riding on the coattails of the Beatles, like all the other British groups, they had their first big hit in August 1964 with You Really Got Me reaching number 7. January 1965's Tired of Waiting for You climbed a bit higher to number 6. They appeared to be following the Beatles and Stones to success, but after an altercation with the American musicians' union over an appearance on the television show *Hullabaloo* during their summer 1965 tour, the American Federation of Musicians refused to allow the group permits to appear in the United States for the next four years. This effectively destroyed their chances of ever making it really big in the States. Sunny Afternoon, which reached number 14 in 1966, was their last hit from that period. Artistically, this led to songwriter Ray Davies and the Kinks exploring their roots to produce a series of idiosyncratic and uniquely English singles like Waterloo Sunset and albums such as the classic 1968 album *The Kinks Are the Village Green Preservation Society* and *Arthur (Or the Decline and Fall of the British Empire)*, both of which were critically acclaimed in the U.S.A. but did poorly in the stores.

Not all the British R&B acts came from London's Soho scene. Them arrived from Belfast, Northern Ireland. Their leader, Van Morrison (George Ivan Morrison), discovered R&B early on: "I was doing what I was doing when the Rolling Stones were still in school."

By the time he was 17, he was already touring England and Germany with his band, the International Monarchs, who, after a few lineup changes, became Them. They moved to London in January 1965 but were soon disillusioned. They were a surly, difficult bunch and found it hard to relate to both Londoners and journalists. *Melody Maker* reported: "Them are switched off to such an extent that it is excessively difficult to cull enough words from them to form a sentence." It was not all their fault: both their management and their record company, Decca, were inept. They threw away Van Morrison's classic Gloria by putting it on the B-side of Here Comes the Night and brought in session men like Jimmy Page when they were recording. However, the band persevered and in 1965 Here Comes the Night reached 24 in the American charts, while Mystic Eyes got to 33. When Gloria was released as a single in 1966 it only crept up to 71 because a Chicago band, the Shadows of Night, had already recognized how great the song was and had a gold record with it (though they had to censor a lyric to get it on American AM radio).

Van Morrison's soon-to-be legendary moodiness led to the lineup of Them constantly changing and only one original member of the band remained by the time they toured America in June 1966. They played the recently opened Fillmore in San Francisco and Van jammed with Jim Morrison at the Whisky a Go Go in Hollywood, where the Doors were their support act. After a dispute with his manager, Phil Solomon, over payment for their tour, Van almost quit the music business altogether—but was fortunately persuaded by Bert Berns, the writer of Here Comes the Night and Them's producer, to return as a solo act.

Obvious art students, The Kinks. From the left: Ray Davies, lead vocals and rhythm guitar, drummer Mick Avory, Dave Davies, lead guitar and vocals, and Pete Quaife on bass and backing vocals.

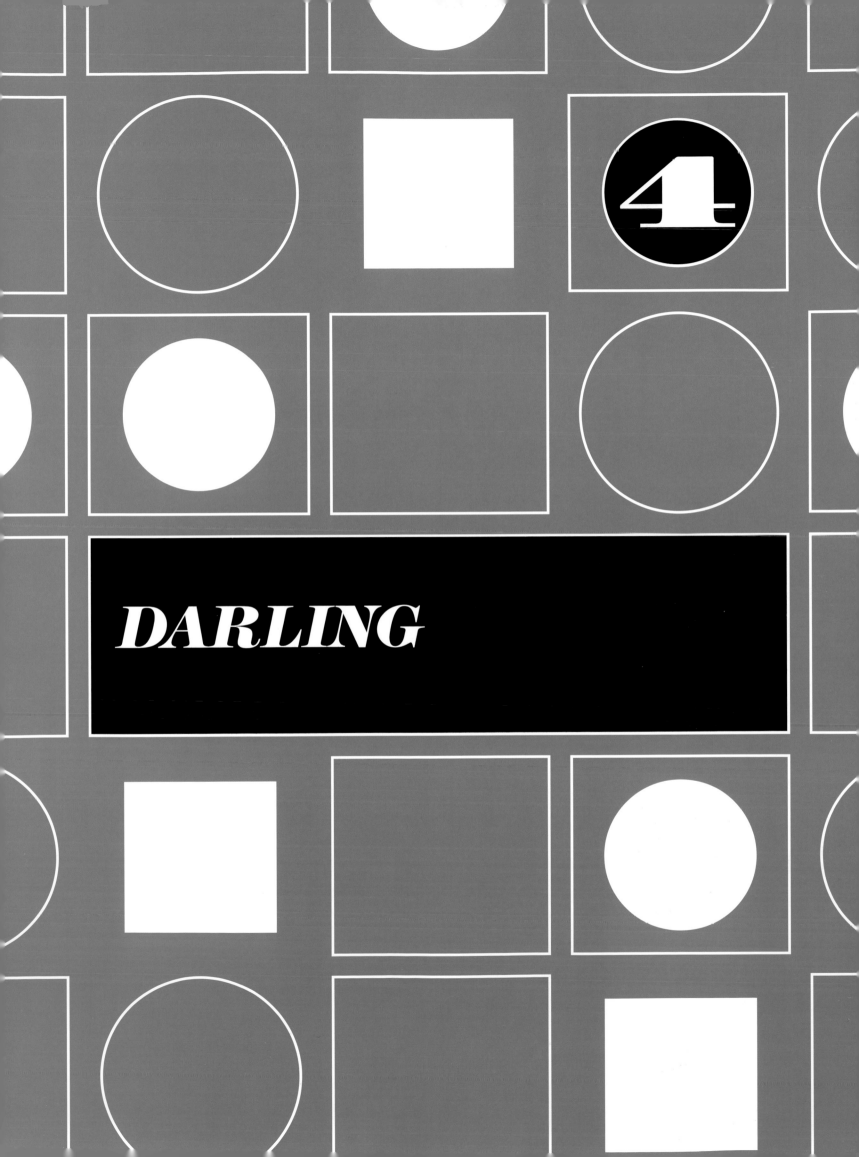

DARLING

4

THE BEATLES APPEARANCE ON *The Ed Sullivan Show of February 9, 1964, is usually considered the point at which the British Invasion came to the attention of the American public. Yet in truth, the American cinema-going public was already more than aware that the British had infiltrated some parts of their country—particularly Hollywood and the Broadway district of New York.*

It's more than just a coincidence that also appearing on that same *Ed Sullivan Show*, and watching the Fab Four's performance from the wings, was a 19-year-old Manchester-born star of one of Broadway's smash hit musicals that year, *Oliver!* by Lionel Bart. As Davy Jones, who was playing the part of the Artful Dodger and was soon to become a Monkee, tells it, "I saw the girls going crazy and thought to myself, 'I want a piece of that!'" (This was much the same as Brian Jones' reaction when he first experienced Beatlemania.)

Not that the Dickens-inspired musical was any kind of precursoR to the cultural impact that the beat bands and fashion models were to have on America's youth. The surprising success of the satirical revue show *Beyond the Fringe* on Broadway, which launched the careers of Alan Bennett, Peter Cook, Jonathan Miller, and Dudley Moore, was much more of a sign of things to come. With its irreverent humor, mocking satire, and surreal sketches, the 1962 show had helped prepare New Yorkers for the banter and shock of the Fab Four's arrival.

In Hollywood there had also been a major influx of new, young, British acting talent who exhibited a very different attitude and style to the more theatrical, classically inclined Brits who had given gravitas to historical epics. Nobody watching the movies of Alfred Hitchcock, Laurence Oliver, John Gielgud, Alec Guinness, or Trevor Howard made in the 1950s could have expected the shock of the new wave of British movies and their stars who were set to take the industry by storm.

Below: The Beatles made as big an impact on film as they did on record and 1964's A Hard Day's Night was credited with inspiring hundreds of sixties musicians to form bands.

Right: Peter Cook and Dudley Moore starred in Bedazzled. Here Dudley uses a cup of tea to protect himself from Raquel Welch.

BEDAZZLED

SPHERE

a novel by Michael J. Bird
from a screenplay by Peter Cook
based on an original story by
Peter Cook & Dudley Moore

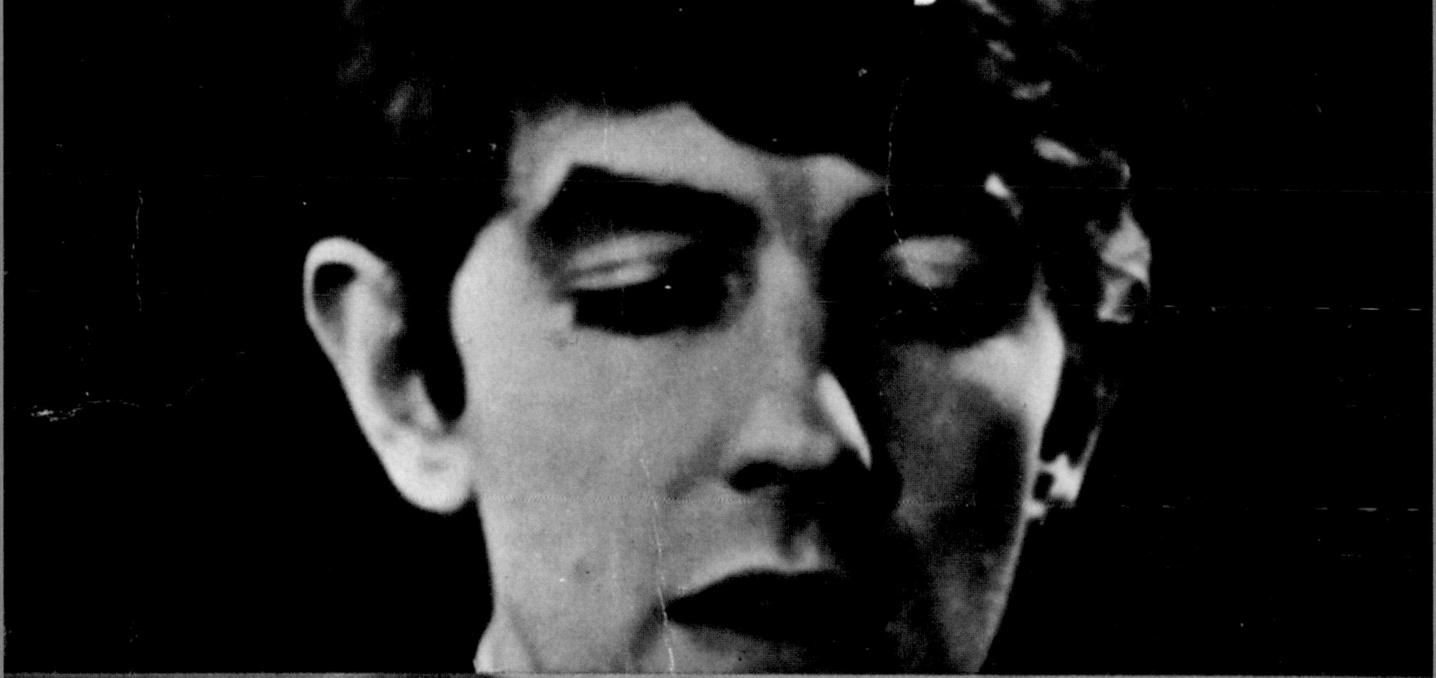

LAURENCE HARVEY: ROOM AT THE TOP

A new breed of actors was coming out of Britain in the early 1960s, led by the Lithuanian-born and South African-raised Laurence Harvey, who trained as an actor in Britain and made his name there before landing on the shores of America just ahead of the first British Invasion. In 1959 he won an Oscar nomination for his part as the lead in the movie of John Braine's novel Room at the Top. *It was directed by British director Jack Clayton, who went on to make* The Innocents *(1961) and* The Pumpkin Eater *(1964).* Room at the Top *was a surprising success in America. Surprising not only because it was a "small" British-made film, but because its subject matter—Harvey plays an ambitious working-class Englishman who marries up into the management class of an industrial town—included enough sexual content to earn it an X (18) rating in Britain. At the Oscars, Harvey lost out to Charlton Heston (for* Ben-Hur*), but his leading lady in* Room at the Top, *Simone Signoret, won the Best Actress award.*

The following year, 1960, Harvey's co-star, the very British Elizabeth Taylor, won the first of her two Best Actress Oscars for her part in the movie adaptation of John O'Hara's BUtterfield 8, *directed by Daniel Mann. Harvey made more than a dozen movies as leading man in the early 1960s, mostly in Hollywood. And in 1965's* Darling, *his image dominated the publicity—although once again his leading lady would win all the prizes.*

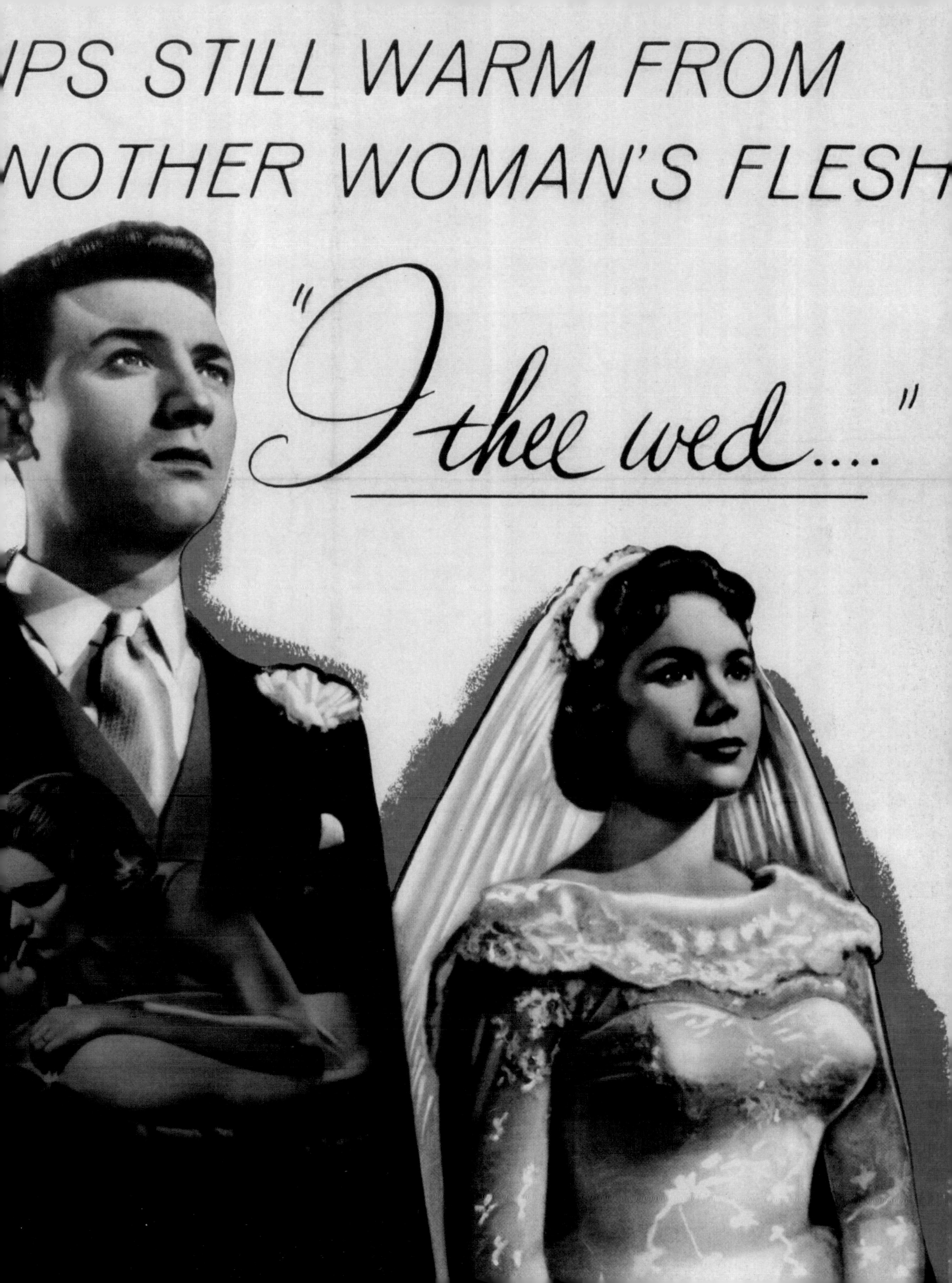
IPS STILL WARM FROM
NOTHER WOMAN'S FLESH
"I thee wed...."

The Running, Jumping, Standing Still Film

Barely six months after making their first appearance on national T.V. in America the Beatles' first movie, *A Hard Day's Night*, was released in American cinemas on August 11, 1964. It was a huge success and naturally prompted other bands from Britain to try their hand at comedic movies in which they play themselves.

The film was directed by Richard Lester, an American who had formed an immediate bond with the Beatles on meeting them. This was mainly because of their shared sense of humor, but also because he had directed one of John Lennon's favorite movies, *The Running, Jumping, Standing Still Film*. An 11-minute, mostly silent short, it starred two of Lennon's favorite comedians from the Goons—Peter Sellers and Spike Milligan—alongside Lester, who also wrote the film's music. There are sequences in both *A Hard Day's Night* and the second Lester-directed Beatles movie, *Help!*, which are similar in style and content to the sight gags acted out by the cast in *The Running, Jumping, Standing Still Film*, particularly in the editing.

Lester also had experience directing pop bands. After *The Running, Jumping, Standing Still Film* he took charge of a 1962 movie titled *It's Trad, Dad!*, featuring trad jazz (Dixieland) star Acker Bilk amongst a raft of British pop singers led by the 15-year old Helen Shapiro and various American artists, among them Gary "U.S." Bonds, Gene Vincent, Del Shannon, and Chubby Checker.

As the Merseybeat sound started to sell to teenagers, small British studios began to shoot cheap black-and-white films, helping to sell them by featuring as many of the new bands as possible. One of the first of these films to be successful was *The System* (a.k.a. *The Girl-Getters*), starring Oliver Reed, which came out in 1964 and featured songs by the Searchers, the Rockin' Berries, and the Marauders. The movie's director was Michael Winner, who would go on to make the very violent *Death Wish* series of films starring Charles Bronson.

Saturday Night Out (also made in 1964) featured the Searchers, but this time in person, playing in a pub. (The Beatles supposedly turned the part down because they could not afford the train fare from Liverpool to London for filming.) Starring nobody else of any importance, it was directed by Robert Hartford-Davis, who also directed *Gonks Go Beat* in 1965. That film featured the Graham Bond Organization (including Ginger Baker and Jack Bruce), Lulu, and the Nashville Teens.

Live It Up (a.k.a. *Sing and Swing*) was released in Britain slightly earlier, in 1963, and featured the very young David Hemmings and Steve Marriott as part of a struggling rock band. Marriott would go on to form the Small Faces (and then Humble Pie), but began life as an actor. Directed by British veteran Lance Comfort, the film featured performances from a number of British acts working with the film's music producer, the legendary pop songwriter and producer Joe Meek (who created "Telstar" in 1962). None of the groups made a big impression in the U.S.A., although among them are the Outlaws (with Ritchie Blackmore, later of Deep Purple, on lead guitar), Heinz and the Tornadoes, and Andy Cavell and the Saints. The film is mostly notable for the fact that the costumes are designed by Mary Quant.

Director Comfort made one more pop B-movie, hiring Hemmings and Marriott once again for *Be My Guest* in 1965. Set and filmed in Brighton, on the south coast of England, it is about the failing rooming house run by Marriott's parents. Marriott's band, Jerry Lee Lewis, and the Nashville Teens all play at the house and turn it into a popular destination. Luckily for Marriott's parents, rock 'n' roll saves their bacon.

One of the reasons that A Hard Day's Night *was such a success was not just because it featured the Fab Four but because they were natural comedians. They had the type of surrealistic British humor most associated with Peter Sellers and which led to the creation of the Monty Python Show.*

THE BEATLES
MAKE A MOVIE!

FIFTY CENTS • PDC

ALL NEW & Exclusive pics of the
BEATLES
in action!

YOU MAY TELEPHONE
FROM HERE

Plus

LATEST PHOTO REPORT
FROM ENGLAND AND
BEATLEMANIA!

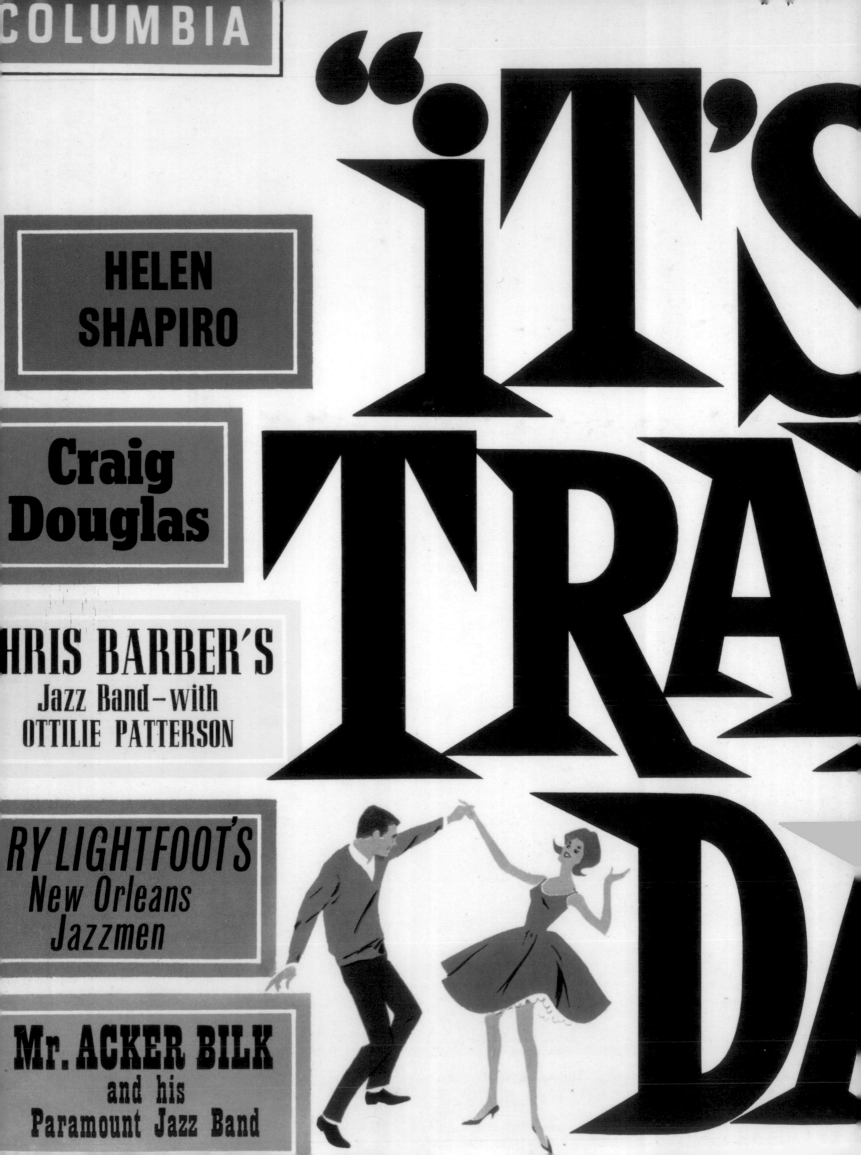

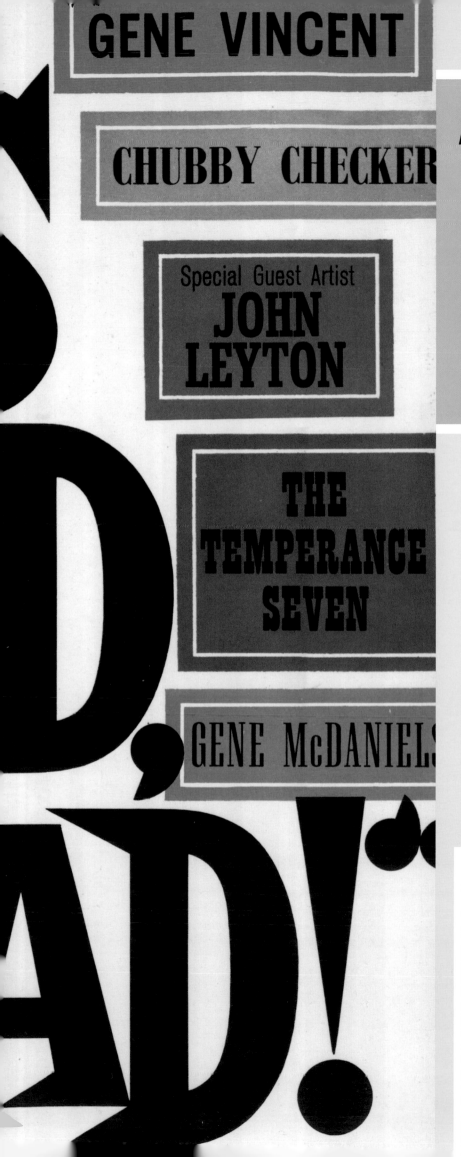

GENE VINCENT

CHUBBY CHECKER

Special Guest Artist
JOHN
LEYTON

THE
TEMPERANCE
SEVEN

GENE McDANIELS

IT'S FAB, DAD!

Originally intended to be a 15-minute short film, It's Trad, Dad! grew to 78 minutes as new acts, many of them part of the early 1960s trad jazz craze which swept Britain between 1960 and the coming of the Beatles in 1963, were added to the cast list. The movie was part of a tradition stretching back to the mid-1950s of rock 'n' roll movies made as B-flicks for the British and American cinema.

Such movies usually had a thin plot, which served to set up on-camera performances by the musical talent whose names sold the tickets to the kids. The Beatles redefined the teen movie market, though, with A Hard Day's Night and Help!

Party

MUSIC TO HAVE AROUND

TO JIVE TO:

THE EVERLY
BROTHERS
ELVIS PRESLEY

"Selection"
London LP
"King Creole" and
"Elvis' Golden
Records"

NAT 'KING' COLE: We
'velvety' Cole voice when
low. Listen to his new C
"Cole Espanole". Nat sing
You can dance to his "St.
album (Capitol)

TOMMY STEELE: Wide a
And who better to liven
spot in a party. Jive to his
"The Duke Wore Jeans"
earlier "Tommy Steele Stage S
albums on Decca

DORIS DAY: We must have
oice around. And when th
Doris's, then it's ideal for a

TO LAUGH TO:
STAN FREBERG

"The
Stan
—Ve

MORRIS AND
MITCH
JIM BACKUS

"Six
Spe
"De
a V
Lor

TO DREAM TO:
FRANK SINATRA

"S
Or
C

GEORGE
SHEARING
CARMEN MacRAE

You Were Made For Me

Disk-O-Tek Holiday (called *Just For You* in Britain) was released in America in 1966 and featured Peter and Gordon, Freddie and the Dreamers, the Bachelors, and the Merseybeats among others. However, the lead band was the Warriors, fronted by Jon Anderson–who would later form prog-rock giants Yes. The storyline was typical, concerning a hopeful band trying to make it big, which was the theme for most of the genre.

Pop Gear (a.k.a. *Pop Mania*) was different, though. Released in May 1965 it opened and ended with live performances by the Beatles, and in between gave screen time to the Animals, the Rockin' Berries, the Nashville Teens, the Fourmost, Peter and Gordon, the Four Pennies, Matt Monro, Billy J. Kramer and the Dakotas, Sounds Incorporated, Spencer Davis Group, Susan Maughan, Herman's Hermits, and Tommy Quickly & the Remo Four. The Spencer Davis

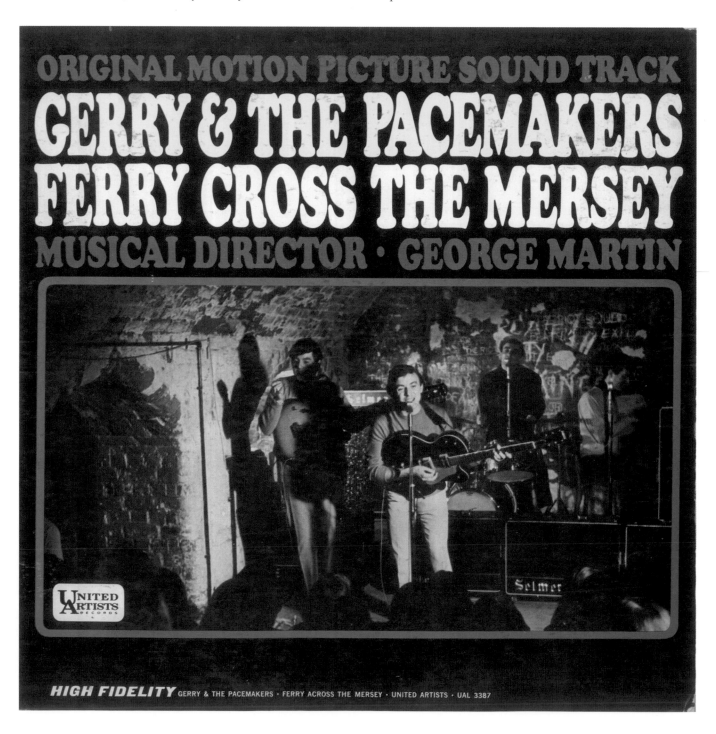

Gerry and the Pacemakers made an unabashed imitation of the Beatles. Drop the conformity kick, boys. The world isn't ready for more Beatles.

EUGENE ARCHER, *NY TIMES* REVIEW OF *FERRY CROSS THE MERSEY*

Group turned up in another unusual movie in 1966. Called *The Ghost Goes Gear*, it had the band playing at a haunted mansion in Britain, along with Dave Berry and the St. Louis Union.

After the enormous success of *A Hard Day's Night*, the other leading Liverpudlian bands to hit America wanted their own star vehicles. Many got them, but few with the same kind of success. Gerry and the Pacemakers filmed *Ferry Cross the Mersey* (1965) in their home city but it met with little Stateside success. Maybe the impenetrable accents put people off.

Freddie and the Dreamers appeared, bizarrely, as a band called the Chefs in a piece of pop fluff released in the States as *Seaside Swingers* (and as *Every Day's a Holiday* in Britain) in 1965. The director, James Hill, made *Born Free* the following year.

In 1965 Peter Noone as Herman, with his Hermits, had appeared in *Pop Gear* playing just one song, but they returned more fully as themselves in *When the Boys Meet the Girls*, starring Connie Francis and also featuring Sam the Sham and the Pharaohs, Louis Armstrong, and Liberace in an attempt to touch all musical bases. Herman's Hermits were so successful, though, that they made two more movies.

In 1966 they played themselves in *Hold On!* in which they arrive in Los Angeles to play a gig and are offered the opportunity to have a space rocket named after them. Director Arthur Rubin did not make another movie for five years after this. Cashing in on the recognition factor of their hit single of the same title, Herman's Hermits made *Mrs. Brown You've Got a Lovely Daughter* in 1968. Directed by American Saul Swimmer (a producer of the final Beatles movie, *Let It Be*) and shot in England, it has a convoluted plotline involving Mrs. Brown's daughter and Peter Noone. It was a box office flop and not even the songs could save it—the title song had been a hit three years earlier, and although the soundtrack also included There's A Kind of Hush (All Over The World) and Years May Come, Years May Go, the band failed to chart again in America.

Compare that with the Monkees' only big-screen picture, *Head*, made the same year, and you get an idea of why. The times had changed and the likes of the Hermits were by then outdated. *Head* was co-directed by Jack Nicholson (who was about to make *Easy Rider*) and full of psychedelic imagery and Technicolor dream sequences, and had no discernible plot. Even Frank Zappa, who had a walk-on part leading a bovine friend and interviewing Davy Jones about his responsibilities as a rock star, appeared to have no idea what was going on. Like many of the films listed here, *Head* did not get a nationwide big cinema opening but was seen in suburban or rural drive-in theaters.

Right: Having followed the Beatles across the Atlantic, Herman's Hermits attempted to use the same format as A Hard Day's Night and star in their own film. The director did not work again for five years.

Left: So many of the English groups looked alike that editors had to really stretch their imaginations to find new ways of presenting them to their teenage readers.

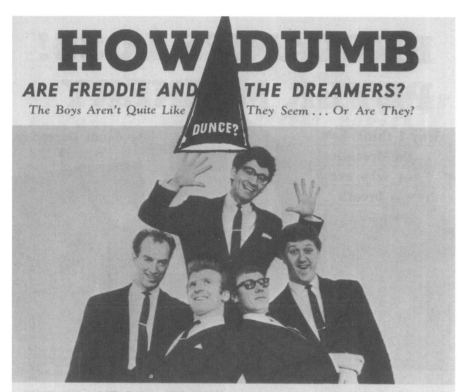

HOW DUMB
ARE FREDDIE AND THE DREAMERS?
The Boys Aren't Quite Like They Seem ... Or Are They?

DUNCE?

FIVE ZANY guys like The Dreamers can get into a whole pack of trouble. People react in strange ways towards Freddie and his boys and this is what's beginning to make Freddie wonder whether everyone gets his message.

"I resent Freddie and the Dreamers" claims one girl, "because they're making fun of today's great musical groups, and this is a crime!"

"They're the greatest," insists another, "because they're making our parents look at our music in a different way. They don't take themselves seriously and this is very appealing to adults because then the parents can take the rock sound much easier."

Freddie doesn't get too bugged by criticism, but he says, "I am surprised when people criticize us because they think we're dumb or stupid or something like that. We just try to get some laughs out of our numbers, that's all."

To watch the boys perform is to know what fun is. They're wild, zany and totally original. Though none of the boys is a typical group

singer or performer in the tradition of the Beatles, they can, when they wish, create a sound that is much like that of the great groups. "I'm Telling You Now" certainly will go down among the big hits of the past year, and it didn't need any comic gimmicks to sell.

Freddie and the Dreamers' fans react more unusually toward them than do fans of the Beatles or the Stones. They rarely scream or try to tear at their clothes and possessions.

"They're really sweet . . . all of them," says one 15-year-old Los Angeles girl. "When they came here to do 'Shindig' I got to meet them and it was so neat. They're so gentlemanly . . . not at all conceited. And they don't act goofy when they're not performing. Each of them, and especially Freddie, seems so interested in everyone who likes them. I think they're great guys and very talented."

A talent booker in Hollywood couldn't decide what he thought about Freddie and the Dreamers. "I don't think they're for real," he believes. "When they were staying

at a hotel here in town, they seemed to be as funny off stage as they are on. I don't think they're ever serious. But basically, they're good musicians as well as comedians. This is what makes me think they'll be around awhile."

One movie producer in Hollywood wanted to use Freddie in an upcoming film. "I wouldn't have him sing," the executive pointed out. "I would just let him be funny. Actually, he's one of the few people going that can get young people to laugh. Soupy Sales can and so can Freddie. I think we need more comics and I'd like Freddie to become big in this way. He's unique."

Freddie likes being thought of as a comic, but he's happy being part of a musical group for the time being.

Anyone who thinks Freddie and the Dreamers are anything but brilliant, had better take another look. No matter how silly they may seem, it takes terrific talent to create dances like The Freddie and put over sing hits like "I Understand." These boys will never have to worry about IQ's as long as hits continue to pile up!

55

MUSIC FROM THE ORIGINAL SOUND TRACK

Metro-Goldwyn-Mayer presents A Sam Katzman Production

HOLD ON!

STARRING HERMAN'S HERMITS

MGM RECORDS

RICHARD HARRIS
THIS SPORTING LIFE

Lindsay Anderson made his directorial debut with This Sporting Life *in 1963,
starring another new raw, talent, the Irish actor Richard Harris (far left, with Michael
Redgrave and Kirk Douglas in 1964). In* This Sporting Life *Harris plays a violent
Yorkshire miner who develops a talent for rugby and a lust for his older, widowed
landlady, played by Rachel Roberts. Like the other great kitchen-sink dramas of the
British New Wave there is no happy ending to the film, which is shot in black-and-
white and uncompromising in its vernacular. And yet it proved to be enormously
successful in America, gaining Oscar nominations for both Harris and Roberts.*

THE RANK ORGANISATION presents
A JULIAN WINTLE – LESLIE PARKY
PRODUCTION

'BEST ACTOR'
AWARD TO
RICHARD
HARRIS
XVI CANNES FILM FESTIVAL

CRITICS PRIZE
(F.I.P.R.E.S.C.I.)
XVI CANNES FILM FESTIVAL

THIS
SPORTING
LIFE

Saturday Night and Sunday Morning

In the same decade as these light pop movies were trying to ride on the back of the success of British bands in America, British film was undergoing a more serious renaissance that was gaining worldwide recognition. In 1960, *Saturday Night and Sunday Morning* launched what became known as the British New Wave of cinema, which, like the British Invasion in music, was led by working-class youth from the north of England. It made it acceptable for realistic dialogue, delivered in regional accents, to be used in movies rather than the B.B.C.-approved middle-class pronunciation favored by the old guard of classically trained British actors. Albert Finney, born in Salford near Manchester, gave a loutish, rough, and realistic portrayal of a sexual predator who tries to organize an abortion for the wife of a blue-collar co-worker with whom he's enjoyed an adulterous relationship. *Saturday Night and Sunday Morning* proved so successful that it enjoyed a long and profitable run in American cinemas. It also prompted Finney's elevation to leading-man status in Hollywood and helped British director Tony Richardson to pick and choose his films.

In 1961, Richardson directed *A Taste of Honey*, which Shelagh Delaney, also born in Salford, had adapted from her own play. It starred Liverpool's Rita Tushingham, winning her a Golden Globe for Most Promising Female Newcomer award, with Richardson picking up Best Director. Her doe-eyed, elfin looks and asymmetric bob haircut proved a big hit with teenage girls, and bangs were soon to be seen across Britain and America. In 1965 Tushingham starred in director Richard Lester's Swinging London opus, *The Knack . . . and How to Get It*, which was a hit in the U.S.A. despite not having a major male lead—Michael Crawford would make his American reputation later alongside Barbara Streisand in *Hello, Dolly!* in 1969. Among the cast of actresses that paraded through the house in Hammersmith, West London, where *The Knack* was filmed, are Pattie Boyd (of *A Hard Day's Night* fame) and Charlotte Rampling, Jane Birkin, and Jacqueline Bisset, all making their first movie appearances.

Also in 1965, John Schlesinger's *Darling* helped spread the Julie Christie look across the States, where many girls were already copying Pattie Boyd's long straight hair from *A Hard Day's Night*. The girls loved the Beatles, but it was Pattie Boyd they wanted to be, particularly after it became known she had become George Harrison's girlfriend. Julie Christie won an Oscar in the title role of *Darling* and the same year starred in a very different type of British movie, David Lean's *Dr. Zhivago*. The role of Lara made her a Hollywood leading lady and international star, but it was *Darling* which made Julie Christie a sixties icon.

Opposite: Liverpudlian Rita Tushingham promoting A Taste of Honey *at the 1961 Cannes Film Festival.*

Below: Despite starring Laurence Harvey and Dirk Bogarde, Darling *was seen by audiences as a Julie Christie vehicle and it established her as a sixties icon.*

Women never have young minds. They're born 3000 years old.

SHELAGH DELANEY/*A TASTE OF HONEY*

JULIE, DARLING

Julie Christie moves to London to start a new life as a model in Darling. Playing a shallow, manipulative woman, she moves from man to man (here played by Dirk Bogarde) until she is rich— but bored and unhappy.

ALBERT FINNEY
IS TOM JONES

In 1962, Tony Richardson directed playwright John Osborne's adaptation of Henry Fielding's 18th-century novel Tom Jones, starring Finney in the title role. The resultant movie was so successful that Richardson won Oscars for Best Director and Best Picture, Osborne won a statue for Best Screen Adaptation, and Finney was nominated for Best Actor.

RT FINNEY / SUSANNAH YORK / HUGH GRIFFITH / EDITH EVANS / JOAN GREENWOOD / "TOM JONES" / DIANE CILENTO

Lawrence of Arabia and the Oscars

Just as America's pop charts and teen magazine awards were being dominated by British bands from 1964 on, so too was Hollywood. It's an amazing fact that the same year the Beatles arrived there were no American-born actors nominated at that year's Oscar ceremony for the Best Actor award. Four were Brits and the other was Mexican (Anthony Quinn).

In fact, the Brits had landed in Hollywood long before the Fab Four. David Lean, who had long been a major star in Hollywood, won the Best Director and Best Picture Oscars for *Lawrence of Arabia* in 1962, and launched the young Peter O'Toole's film career. He was nominated for a Best Actor award in 1962, the only Brit nominated that year, and would go on to be nominated for another seven Oscars (four of them in the 1960s), but winning none, which makes him the most-nominated actor never to win an Academy Award.

French composer Maurice Jarre won the 1962 Academy Award for his haunting theme to the very British Lawrence of Arabia.

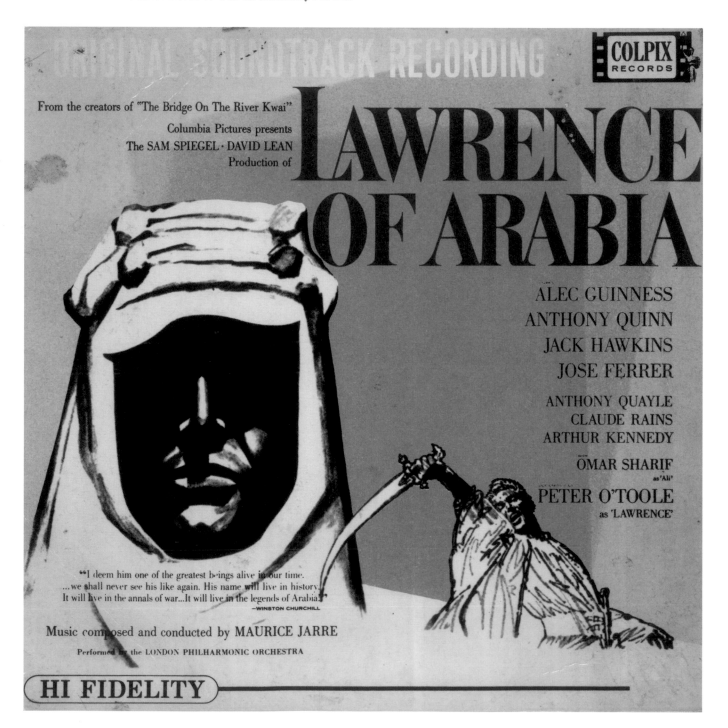

In 1963 Best Picture and Best Director went to Tony Richardson's *Tom Jones* and Best Supporting Actress went to Margaret Rutherford for her performance in *The VIPs*. Albert Finney was nominated Best Actor (for *Tom Jones*), along with fellow Briton Rex Harrison (*Cleopatra*) and Irishman Richard Harris (*This Sporting Life*); they lost to Sidney Poitier for *Lilies of the Field*. Harris' co-star Rachel Roberts was nominated for Best Actress along with Britons Edith Evans and Joyce Redman. Welshman Hugh Griffith was nominated for his supporting role in *Tom Jones*.

In 1964 Peter O'Toole was nominated for the Best Actor Oscar for his role in *Becket*, set in medieval England and made by British director Peter Glenville, but he lost out to his fellow countryman Rex Harrison for his masterful role in

Richard Burton (left) and Peter O'Toole star in Becket, *1964, for which O'Toole received an Oscar nomination.*

I am very proud to be British.

JULIE ANDREWS

My Fair Lady. Richard Burton was also nominated for *Becket*, as was Peter Sellers for Stanley Kubrick's *Dr. Strangelove*.

My Fair Lady, an adaptation of a British play by George Bernard Shaw, won the award for Best Picture, with another going to its British costume designer and art director, Cecil Beaton. Two of the British cast were nominated for supporting roles: Stanley Holloway and Gladys Cooper. Holloway lost to another British actor, Peter Ustinov (for *Topkapi*); also nominated was fellow Brit John Gielgud (for *Becket*), while Cooper lost to the French actress Lila Kedrova (for *Zorba*).

In the same year, Britain's Julie Andrews won the Oscar for Best Actress as *Mary Poppins*, beating two American actresses who were nominated for their parts in British movies: Anne Bancroft in *The Pumpkin Eaters* and Kim Stanley for the low-budget horror *Seance on a Wet Afternoon*, directed by Bryan Forbes and produced and co-starring Richard Attenborough. That year two of the five nominated Best Directors were British: Peter Glenville for *Becket* and Robert Stevenson for *Mary Poppins*.

The British kept up their strong showing at the Oscars of 1965. Richard Burton was nominated Best Actor for his role in *The Spy That Came in from the Cold* and Lawrence Olivier was nominated for *Othello* (they lost to Lee Marvin in *Cat Ballou*). David Lean was nominated Best Director for *Dr. Zhivago* and John Schlesinger for *Darling*, and both movies were nominated for Best Film, but lost out to Robert Wise's *The Sound of Music* on both counts. Julie Christie won the Best Actress award for *Darling*, with Julie Andrews (*The Sound of Music*) and fellow Brit Samantha Eggar (*The Collector*) also nominated.

In 1966 Fred Zinnemann's *A Man for All Seasons* did rather well for the British at the Oscars, winning Best Picture, Best Director, Best Actor (Paul Scofield), Best Screenplay, Best Costume Design, and Best Cinematography. It was shot on location in England and was based on British playwright Robert Bolt's adaptation of the life and death of 14th-century English Chancellor Thomas More. Robert Shaw was nominated for Best Supporting Actor and Wendy Hiller for Best Supporting Actress. An unlikely story to achieve such acclaim, *A Man for All Seasons* competed with another British film, Lewis Gilbert's *Alfie*, arguably the last successful British New Wave movie. *Alfie* also earned Oscar nominations for Michael Caine as Best Actor, Bill Naughton for his adaptation of his own book, Vivien Merchant for Supporting Actress, and for Burt Bacharach and Hal David's theme tune, sung by Cilla Black.

Also in 1966, Elizabeth Taylor won the Best Actress Oscar for *Who's Afraid of Virginia Woolf?*, directed by Mike Nichols, while her husband and co-star Richard Burton was nominated for Best Actor. Other Best Actress nominations went to the British Redgrave sisters—Lynn for her debut in the title role of *Georgy Girl* and Vanessa for *Morgan!*

Opposite: Julie Andrews is Mary Poppins.

Below: The original London cast recording of My Fair Lady, with Julie Andrews playing the part of Eliza Doolittle. She was replaced in the 1964 movie version by Audrey Hepburn, but Andrews won the Best Actress Academy Award that year.

Please Sir, Can We Have Some More?

There were no British actors nominated for Best Actor in 1967 and only Edith Evans was nominated for Best Actress. The big movie was Arthur Penn's *Bonnie and Clyde*, and its success, along with *The Graduate* (which won Best Director for Mike Nichols), signaled the start of a New Wave of American movies, which would even sweep up British directors—John Schlesinger won the Best Director Oscar in 1969 for the very American *Midnight Cowboy*.

There was only one British movie to make a major impact on the Oscars in the late 1960s, and that was the film adaptation of Lionel Bart's stage music of *Oliver!*, directed by Carol Reed in 1968. It won the Best Picture and Best Director awards, along with three other awards, and gained nominations for Best Actor for Ron Moody and Supporting Actor for Jack Wild, as well as introducing the director's nephew, Oliver Reed, as a brooding, big screen presence.

Also nominated for Best Actor awards that year were Peter O'Toole (for *The Lion in Winter*, by British director Anthony Harvey) and Alan Bates for John Frankenheimer's *The Fixer*, but that was the last time that three British actors won nominations in one year until 1983. British actresses did rather better as the sixties ended. Maggie Smith won the Oscar for her role as the lead in British director Ronald Neame's *The Prime of Miss Jean Brodie* in 1969 and the next year Glenda Jackson won for her part in British director Ken Russell's envelope-pushing *Women in Love*. She picked up her second in 1973 for *A Touch of Class*.

Despite the success of the British at the Oscars during the 1960s, there would be no British movie even nominated for Best Picture until *Chariots of Fire*, directed by Hugh Hudson, won in 1981. (In that year, Colin Welland, who won an Oscar for his screenplay for *Chariots of Fire*, rather prematurely proclaimed, "The British are coming!")

Below left: The soundtrack for the 1968 movie was an international hit.

Right: Oliver Reed was a truly frightening Bill Sykes, while Mark Lester was a saccharine Oliver in the 1968 movie.

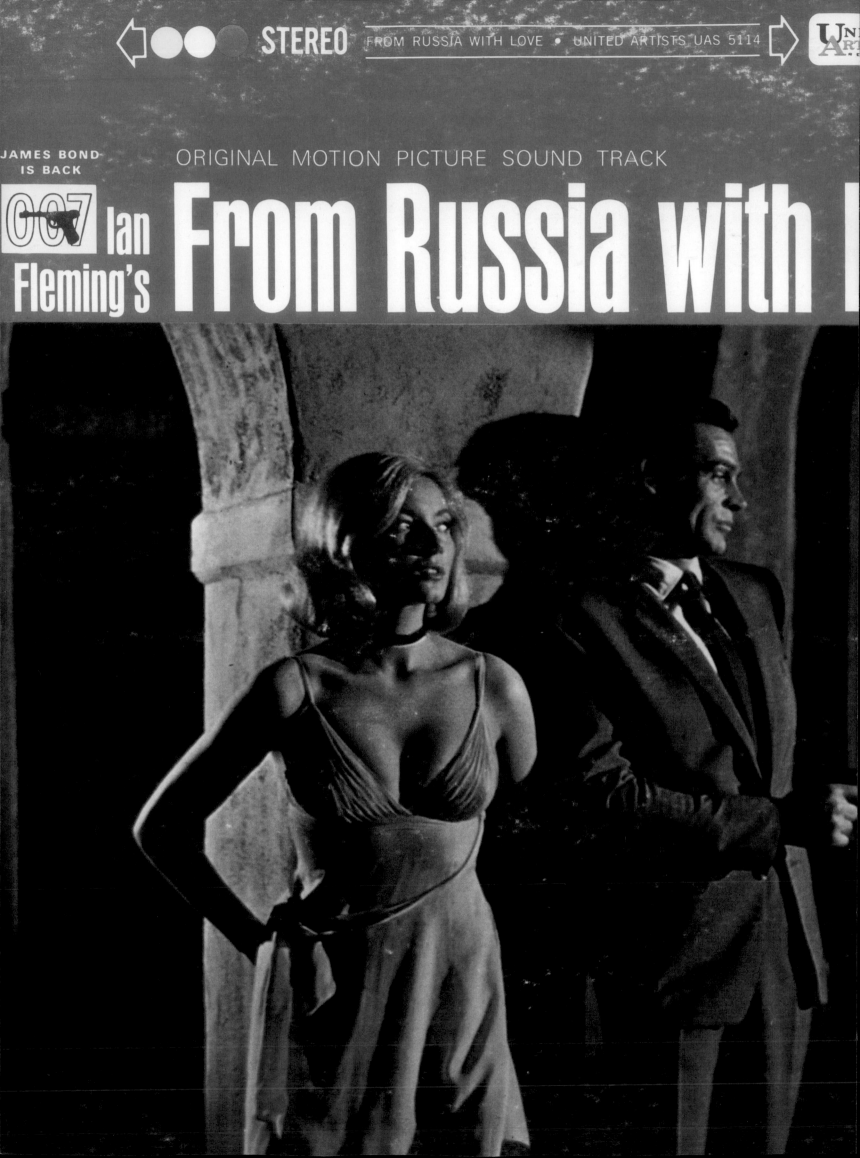

Russia with Lo

SHAKEN, NOT STIRRED

Just as it took a year or so for the new British groups to cross the Atlantic, the same went for a new British film hero. The same conviction and assuredness that permeated the Beatles and their music was to be found in the James Bond character and, though the first film, 1962's Dr. No, did not do that well when first released in the U.S.A. a year later, $16 million was not bad for film that only cost $1 million to make. However, the second Bond vehicle, From Russia With Love, was a huge box-office success, grossing $24 million in North America (and $78 million worldwide), and considered hip across the country. This was a time of great self-confidence in Britain, when there was a resurgence of belief and pride in Britain's cars, films, music, and clothes and that showed through in the films and music of the time.

Sean Connery, who played Bond in six of the first seven Bond films (plus 1983's Never Say Never Again, which was outside the main Bond franchise), is still regarded by many traditionalists as the ultimate Bond. Ian Fleming, the creator of the fictional Bond character, at first doubted Connery's ability to play the role. He had envisaged someone like David Niven for the part, but when he saw the Scottish Connery in Dr. No, he was so impressed that he created a half-Scottish background for his character. James Bond, British secret agent 007 with "a license to kill," was a suave, multi-lingual womanizer, invariably dressed in a dinner jacket with bow tie, but with an in-depth knowledge of firearms and the martial arts: it was a role perfectly suited to the tall, muscular Connery. In those non-politically correct days, the series had a winning formula of guns, cars, gadgets, and "Bond girls" (with double-entendre names), as well as exotic international settings and plenty of action sequences.

The Bond series has grossed over $4 billion—nearly $11 billion when adjusted for inflation—making it the highest grossing and most profitable film series ever. The films were a projection of a fantasy England of bowler hats, Aston Martin sports cars, and gentlemen's clubs, trading on the same clichés and images of tradition and modernity as the successful Avengers television series. Bond spawned a massive secondary industry of comics, books, cartoons, spoofs, parodies, imitations, and merchandising. After a slow start, companies vied with each other for product placement; after all, if James Bond wore a Rolex watch, then that was clearly the cool watch to have. However, the ultimate product that the films advertised was Britain itself, which made them one of the prime vehicles of the British Invasion.

Side One
ning Titles — James Bond is
FROM RUSSIA WITH LOVE (Ba
and JAMES BOND THEME (Nor
2. TANIA MEETS KLEBB (Barry)
3. MEETING IN ST. SOPHIA (Barry
4. THE GOLDEN HORN (Barry)

BOND MEETS HIS CREATOR

" Sean Connery makes a wonderful James Bond," says Ian Fleming, the man who created this larger than life character for a series of novels which have sold in their millions all over the world.

" Ian Fleming is a very likeable man," says Sean Connery, the man chosen to play his famous 007.

The two men met on the set at Pinewood during a break in shooting.

Fleming watched several scenes being filmed and looked pleased with what he saw.

" I think these boys have done a splendid job with the Bond films," said Fleming talking about producers Saltzman and Broccoli.

Fleming himself worked in Naval Intelligence. At the outbreak of the last war he went to Moscow as special correspondent for The Times before joining Naval Intelligence as Personal Assistant to the Director.

His first Bond novel, " Casino Royale " was published in 1954.

He writes a new Bond adventure every year. His books have been translated into German, French, Italian, Spanish, Japanese and the Scandinavian languages.

Sean Connery and Shirley Eaton meet author Ian Fleming

Honor Blackman (Pussy Galore) holds Sean (Bond), at gun point

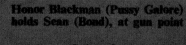

HONOR BLACKMAN AS PUSSY GALORE

" Pussy Galore is a woman who thinks like a man," Honor Blackman said as I sat down beside her on the set. " The kind of woman I would expect every woman dreams she could be in the same way as men may dream secretly of being James Bond. She is a woman who loves them and leaves them. Very much true to Bond type . . . who also loves them and leaves them.

" When Bond meets Pussy they are attracted to each other and desire each other and they both know this is all they want. Nothing permanent in a relationship. Neither one has a hold on the other."

Pussy is quite a girl—so, too, is Honor who could well become the most exciting feminine star in British pictures as a result of the contract she signed with Broccoli and Saltzman, who have big international plans for her.

Those two shrewd film-makers looked no further than Honor Blackman for the role of this seductively exciting Ian Fleming creation—Pussy Galore.

" What a wonderful name," Honor giggled.

Honor, now back in the big league, is needless to say glad to be back.

She says, " I loved doing the Avenger series because it got me away from understanding wife roles. But enough was enough. I didn't want to outstay my welcome. I had two years of being Cathy Gale. It was a terrible wrench leaving—but that was that."

Pussy Galore is Goldfinger's personal pilot.

" I've thoroughly enjoyed myself being Pussy," smiles Honor, " even if it has only been for a short while."

THE DAY SHIRLEY WAS PAINTED GOLD

Gold may be where you find it—but attractive 27-year-old British actress Shirley Eaton found it all over her body when she appeared in front of the cameras.

She plays Jill Masterson, a sexy English secretary, who is murdered by the millionaire criminal, Goldfinger, because she betrays him to Secret Agent 007 James Bond.

His method of murdering her is unique—but then, so is Goldfinger. As he has a maniacal obsession for gold he has her stripped nude and then painted all over with gold dust so that the pores of her skin cannot breathe . . . and she dies.

On the studio physician's recommendation a time limit of one hour had been set for filming the scene. Dizziness and nausea could have resulted from prolonged suffocation of the pores—even though Shirley's covering was only studio make-up.

" Although my reputation was launched in British comedies," comments Shirley, " I'm now more interested in finding unusual and dramatic roles. Being a James Bond girl is certainly that, even though I end up dead, looking like an Oscar statue."

A Bond picture means plenty of glamour. *Goldfinger* has a fine array of gorgeous lovelies. Apart from Honor Blackman and Shirley Eaton, there is the attractive Tania Mallett (middle picture), making her film debut as Tilly Masterson; Margaret Nolan (top picture), playing a Miami Beach beauty; and the sultry Nadja Regin (bottom picture), who stirs the blood with her seductive dancing in a night club scene.

Licensed to Kill

Conceived independently from the Bond movies, Len Deighton's first "Harry Palmer" novel, *The IPCRESS File*, was published just after the British release of *Dr. No*. Bond producers Harry Saltzman and Albert Broccoli approached him to write the second Bond film, *From Russia With Love,* but little of his screenplay was used. Saltzman decided that Deighton's books, which had a more realistic, gritty, downbeat street quality to them, would make a good parallel series of spy films. Michael Caine starred in all three: *The IPCRESS File* (1965, by Canadian director Sidney J. Furie), *Funeral in Berlin* (1966, by British director Guy Hamilton), and *Billion Dollar Brain* (1967 by British director Ken Russell). In the

Michael Caine as
Harry Palmer in
The IPCRESS File.
*Unlike most spies of
the sixties, Palmer
knew his way around
a kitchen.*

mid-1990s Michael Caine starred in two more Harry Palmer vehicles: *Bullet to Beijing* (1995) and *Midnight in Saint Petersburg* (1996), but Deighton had no involvement in them.

The immense impact made by the Bond movies could be seen by the number of spoofs and "tributes" made of the Bond genre. Australian Rod Taylor starred in *The Liquidator*, directed by Jack Cardiff in 1965, while Terence Stamp was a much cooler, oddly emotionless sidekick to Italian actress Monica Vitti as the eponymous heroine of *Modesty Blaise*, released in 1966 and directed by Joseph Losey. Richard Johnson, who had turned down the chance to play Bond in 1961, turned up as Bulldog Drummond, a proto-Bond character from a series of detective novels from the 1920s, in 1967's *Deadlier Than the Male* and 1969's *Some Girls Do*, both directed by Ralph Thomas. None of these were sold as being parodies of the Bond series, but dozens were—*Licensed to Kill* (1965, directed by Lindsay Shonteff and starring Tom Adams) is a good example. There were also two, equally spoofy, sequels: *Where the Bullets Fly* (1966, by British director John Gilling) and *Somebody's Stolen Our Russian Spy* (1967, by Jose Luis Madrid). Even the Beatles succumbed with a number of references to Bond films occurring in their second film, *Help!*, in 1965. The most blatant cash-in, though, was probably *OK Connery*, an Italian film starring Sean Connery's younger brother Neil, who plays James Bond's look-alike younger brother, hired by MI6 when 007 is unavailable. The best parodies came decades later, of course, with Canadian Mike Myers' three Austin Powers movies.

Bond also provided an endless source of material for television parody. The most successful was probably *Get Smart*, created by Mel Brooks and Buck Henry as a satire of the secret-agent genre. Henry said the show was created to capitalize on "the two biggest things in the entertainment world today: James Bond and Inspector Clouseau." Brooks modestly described it "an insane combination of James Bond and Mel Brooks comedy." The show began in September 1965 and ran for 138 episodes, ending in 1970 before being revived in 2008 for a feature film. *The Man Called Flintstone* was a 1966 cartoon parody of Bond featuring Fred Flintstone in his first full-length movie. This was the first of many Bond references in animated cartoons, including *The Simpsons*, *Family Guy*, and *American Dad!*

The show most indebted to Bond was *The Man from U.N.C.L.E.*, which began in September 1964 and ran for 105 episodes. Bond creator Ian Fleming helped in the show's genesis. At one point the show was to be called *Ian Fleming's Solo*, featuring the character Napoleon Solo (a "Mr. Solo" character was in *Goldfinger*). Fleming also named the lead character of the 1966 sister series, *The Girl from U.N.C.L.E*: April Dancer.

The Man from U.N.C.L.E. also gave American teen girls the biggest British TV heartthrob in the shape of Scottish actor David McCallum. The blond, Nordic-looking actor appeared young enough to be the nephew of co-star American Robert Vaughn, but in fact was only a year younger. McCallum's role as Illya Kuryakin—a Russian agent working for American bosses—managed to mix the Beatles (McCallum's haircut) and international espionage, guns, and girls as the dynamic, black-suited duo kicked the asses of enemy agents. McCallum was so popular that every teenage magazine carried pinups of him and in 1966–7 he released two albums of music which he conducted and arranged, but didn't sing on: *Music: A Bit More of Me* and *Music: It's Happening Now!* They featured arrangements for rock hits of the day—including the Beatles' Michelle, Louie, Louie, If I Were a Carpenter, and I Can't Control Myself.

DAVID MCCALLUM

Despite not being a musician or a singer, Scottish-born actor McCallum became a huge heartthrob and pin-up for teen magazines in America because of the success of the U.S.-made television spy series, The Man from U.N.C.L.E. He did release two LPs of instrumental music that he conducted, and which bore his fine chiselled features on their cover, but he was an actor, not a pop star. This spread is taken from 16 Magazine.

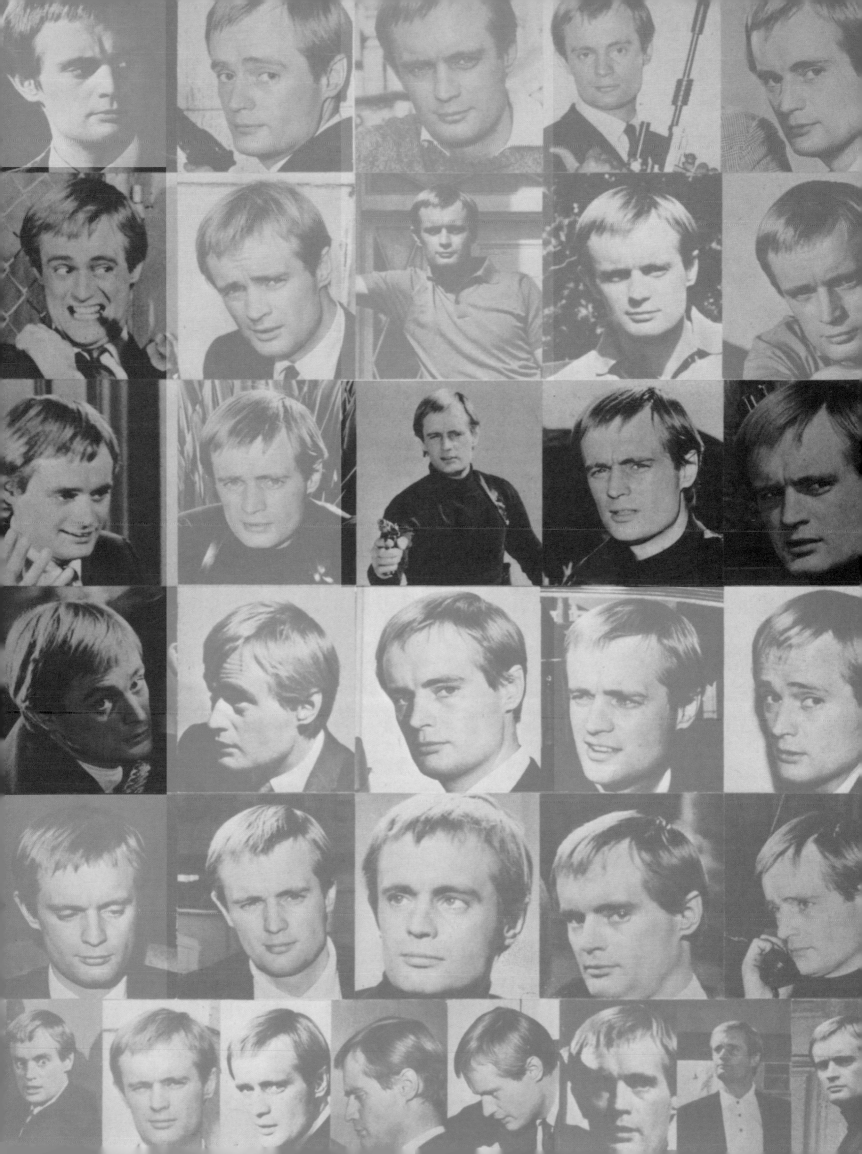

From Britain with Love

While the Oscars are a gauge of how the movie industry regards their peers, the box office is a better reflection of how the American people feel about movies, actors, and trends, and Bond was far from being the only British hit. Throughout the sixties there always seemed to be a British film, or a film filled with British actors, playing at the local cinema. Right at the start of the decade, in 1960, *BUtterfield 8*, with the double-British lead duo of Elizabeth Taylor and (adopted Briton) Laurence Harvey, was the sixth highest-grossing movie of the year, while the year's biggest hit, Disney's *Swiss Family Robinson*, was made by British director Ken Annakin. The following year Disney's *101 Dalmatians*, an animation that used British voices, was set in London, and was based on British writer Dodie Smith's novel, out-grossed the next highest-selling movie, *West Side Story*, by more than three to one.

In 1962 the two top-grossing American films were concerned with Britons at war—David Lean's *Lawrence of Arabia* and *The Longest Day* (this had five different directors), which offered the last chance to see a new Scottish actor Sean Connery in a non-leading role in the days before James Bond mania. That year Elizabeth Taylor once more provided the box-office gold when she starred as *Cleopatra* opposite real-life husband Richard Burton (as Anthony). However, it was the success of *Tom Jones* that surprised Hollywood. It made stars of Finney, Susannah York, and David Warner (who would later star in *Morgan!* and *Straw Dogs*) and was even featured on *Time* magazine's cover.

The year that the Beatles conquered America was also the year that the British really conquered the American box office, though. Seven of the top 10 grossing movies of 1964 were either British-made, or starred British talent. Listed according to box-office position, they were: 1. *Mary Poppins*; 2. *My Fair Lady*; 3. *Goldfinger*; 5. *From Russia With Love*; 6. *A Shot in the Dark*; 7. *A Hard Day's Night*; 9. *The Pink Panther*.

Both *A Shot in the Dark* and *The Pink Panther* starred Peter Sellers as the bumbling French Inspector Clouseau and were directed by Blake Edwards (later to become husband to Julie Andrews) in joint Anglo-American productions. Among the other British films released in 1964 were *Zulu*, starring Michael Caine; the Oscar-nominated *The Pumpkin Eater* and *Seance on a Wet Afternoon*; and the multi-award winning *Becket*.

In 1965 the Beatles released *Help!* (this time in color), a jolly film but without the depth of *A Hard Day's Night*. The obvious plot, their actual story, had already been done and it was virtually impossible to find another storyline that would incorporate equal roles for all four Beatles. Consequently, the Fab Four just romped mindlessly through Austria and the Bahamas. The American box office take that year was led by *The Sound of Music* with Julie Andrews, closely followed by *Dr. Zhivago* and the fourth Bond movie, *Thunderball*. The wholly British-made *Those Magnificent Men In Their Flying Machines*, starring Sarah Miles and directed by the McCarthy-blacklisted, ex-pat American Joseph Losey, was the fourth highest grossing movie of the year.

Peter Sellers and Peter O'Toole also made the top 10 during 1965 with *What's New Pussycat?*, directed by Briton Clive Donner and co-starring Woody Allen, Romy Schneider, Capucine, and Ursula Andress (who had first risen to fame from the surf in *Dr. No*). With *Darling*, *The Collector*, and *The Spy Who Came In from the Cold* offering different views of British society to the international jet-set lifestyle of the Beatles and Bond, the British film industry was in such good shape that American and Italian directors began to make movies there.

Peter Sellers as Inspector Clouseau, having blundered into a nudist colony with co-star Elke Sommer in A Shot in the Dark.

Swinging London!

By the mid-sixties it seemed that you could barely walk anywhere in London without bumping into a film crew making yet another movie in which the city played a starring role. The greatest of the Swinging London movies was—and still is—Michelangelo Antonioni's *Blowup* starring David Hemmings as a David Bailey-style fashion photographer who seems to capture a murder taking place in the corner of a photo he takes of a model in a park (actually Hampstead Heath). Vanessa Redgrave and Sarah Miles co-starred, but the film is as notable for the scenes in which Hemmings cruises though the city on foot or in his convertible Bentley as it is for the acting. In one night scene he attends a live performance by the Yardbirds, while in another there's a distinctly psychedelic party going on in a private house. It all contributes to paint London as being a decidedly "happening" place, full of mystery and glamour.

In Silvio Narizzano's *Georgy Girl* (1966), the other Redgrave sister, Lynn, skips her way through a different kind of London, one which is still both physically and morally recovering from WWII. Among Redgrave's co-stars are James Mason, Alan Bates, and Charlotte Rampling, but again the city of London is as much the star of the film as the actors. In *Bedazzled* (1967), a bikini-clad Raquel Welch is employed by director Stanley Donen to distract the viewer—and Peter Cook and Dudley Moore—from the charms of London as filmed from a bus. She only partly succeeds.

There were plenty of other, differing movies shot in London around the same time, among them Polish émigré director Roman Polanski's *Repulsion* (1965) and *Cul-de-Sac* (1966), the kitchen-sink dramas *Poor Cow* (1967, directed by Ken Loach) and *Up the Junction* (1968, directed by Peter Collinson), *To Sir, With Love (1967),* and the aforementioned *The Knack . . .*, *Alfie*, and *Morgan!*, but at the end of the decade two very different movies projected apparently very different sides to the same city.

In *Performance* (made in 1968 but not released until 1970), directors Donald Cammell and Nicolas Roeg tried to make sense of a convoluted, L.S.D.-laced plot involving immoral gangsters (James Fox) and an amoral rock star (Mick Jagger) living in a big house in Powis Square, Notting Hill. The area was at the heart of the burgeoning London underground scene, and the dark frames hint at the seamier side of the grimy underbelly of Swinging London. The subject of numerous books, *Performance* was called the greatest British gangster film of all time by film critic and academic Colin McCabe.

Made the following year, *The Italian Job* (1969, directed by Peter Collinson) features a different side to the gangsters of Notting Hill, and one much more in line with the perceived idea of what constituted Swinging London. In a memorable opening sequence, recently freed convict Charlie Croker visits his tailor, gets his convertible Aston Martin (which contains money from his last bank job), and awakes in his Portobello Road apartment with a gorgeous girl. Even in 1969, *The Italian Job* looked dated.

Opposite: Lynn Redgrave as Georgy Girl.

Above: The paperback cover of the novel that became a 1967 Clive Donner comedy, with title track by Traffic and shot in the new town of Stevenage, Hertfordshire.

Following pages: Handbill and still from Blowup.

Georgy Girl is BIG!

ORIGINAL POSTER TAGLINE

BLOWUP

UN FILM
DIRETTO DA

MICHELANGELO
ANTONIONI

VANESSA **REDGRAVE** DAVID **HEMMINGS** SARAH **MILES**

METROCOLOR

What Do You Want to Do?

The Beatles gave up touring in 1966 and the same year Paul McCartney contributed the soundtrack to *The Family Way* (directed by Roy Boulting), a British melodrama starring Hayley Mills and Hywel Bennett as a newly married couple with sexual problems. *Help!* it wasn't. Paul continued to contribute to movie soundtracks (most successfully the title song to *Live and Let Die*, the Bond movie in 1973), but kept away from acting until 1986's *Give My Regards to Broadway*.

George Harrison contributed songs and performance, though anonymously, to *Wonderwall* (1968, directed by Joe Massot) before taking to producing movies rather than starring in them—notable successes being *Time Bandits* (1981, directed by Terry Gilliam) and Neil Jordan's 1986 hit, *Mona Lisa*, plus all of the many Monty Python movies.

Between the release of *Sgt. Pepper* and *Abbey Road* the other Beatles took to acting with varying degrees of success. In 1967 John Lennon took a part in *How I Won the War* (directed by Richard Lester), an anti-war movie set during WWII. Lennon mumbled his lines and proved that as an actor he made a great Beatle. In 1968, he released the 19-minute *Two Virgins*, starring himself and new wife Yoko Ono as a sort of early promo video for their album of the same name. The couple made nine other short "art" films in a similar style but they were hard to find and only shown on the art circuit (thankfully).

Surprisingly, the most memorable cinematic performances by a Beatle came from Ringo Starr: in 1968 he starred alongside Marlon Brando, Richard Burton, Walter Matthau and Charles Aznavour in *Candy*. It was a psychedelic retelling of Voltaire's *Candide* with Ewa Aulin as a female extraterrestrial Candy, descended to Earth. Written by Terry Southern, the co-author of *Easy Rider*, it was made in Italy and directed by Brando's roommate at the time, Christian Marquand. It was a bigger hit in Europe than the U.S.A. Ringo also appeared in Joseph McGrath's 1969 *The Magic Christian* with Peter Sellers, again written by Southern but shot in Britain. Possibly his best acting is to be seen in 1973's *That'll Be the Day*, though, when he gave a convincing portrayal of a Teddy Boy working on a fun-fair. Ringo acted in several more movies but perhaps most famously voiced the children's cartoon series *Thomas the Tank Engine* in the mid-1980s.

The Beatles were involved in three more "movies" as a group. *Magical Mystery Tour*, a loose, would-be psychedelic road trip with British pensioners, was a TV film shown on British television at Christmas 1967. *Yellow Submarine* (1968, directed by George Dunning) is a feature-length cartoon to which the band contributed songs only, with the voices of the cartoon versions of them being spoken by actors. At least they sounded like the Liverpudlians, unlike the actors employed to voice the "tribute" paid them by Disney in *The Jungle Book* (1967, directed by Wolfgang Reitherman). Disney created four vultures seemingly wearing Beatle wigs and talking with Liverpudlian accents, who ask each other "What do you want to do?" before singing That's What Friends Are For. The accents were more Dick van Dyke than John, Paul, George, and Ringo, although the dialogue between the vultures proved to be sadly prophetic of their last cinematic outing, *Let It Be* (1970, directed Michael Lindsay-Hogg).

There's no acting in *Let It Be*, just real-life boredom, antagonism, quarreling, and thankfully some music making. It is a documentary shot over several months of 1969 as the band make what would be their last album together, while Yoko Ono sits almost silently throughout the film, perched at John's shoulder to the irritation of the other Beatles. By the time the movie was released the Beatles, like the British Invasion, was all over bar the lawsuits.

WALT DISNEY

PRESENTS

The Jungle Book

Vista RECORDS — BVE-201

ORIGINAL CAST SOUND TRACK

The Beatles

Yellow Submarine

From the song by JOHN LENNON & PAUL McCARTNEY

FULL STEAM AHEAD

Apple publicity for Yellow Submarine. Because the Beatles refused to
have anything to do with the film until the last minute, the producers were
reduced to sending out second-rate hippie publicity to teen mags (right).

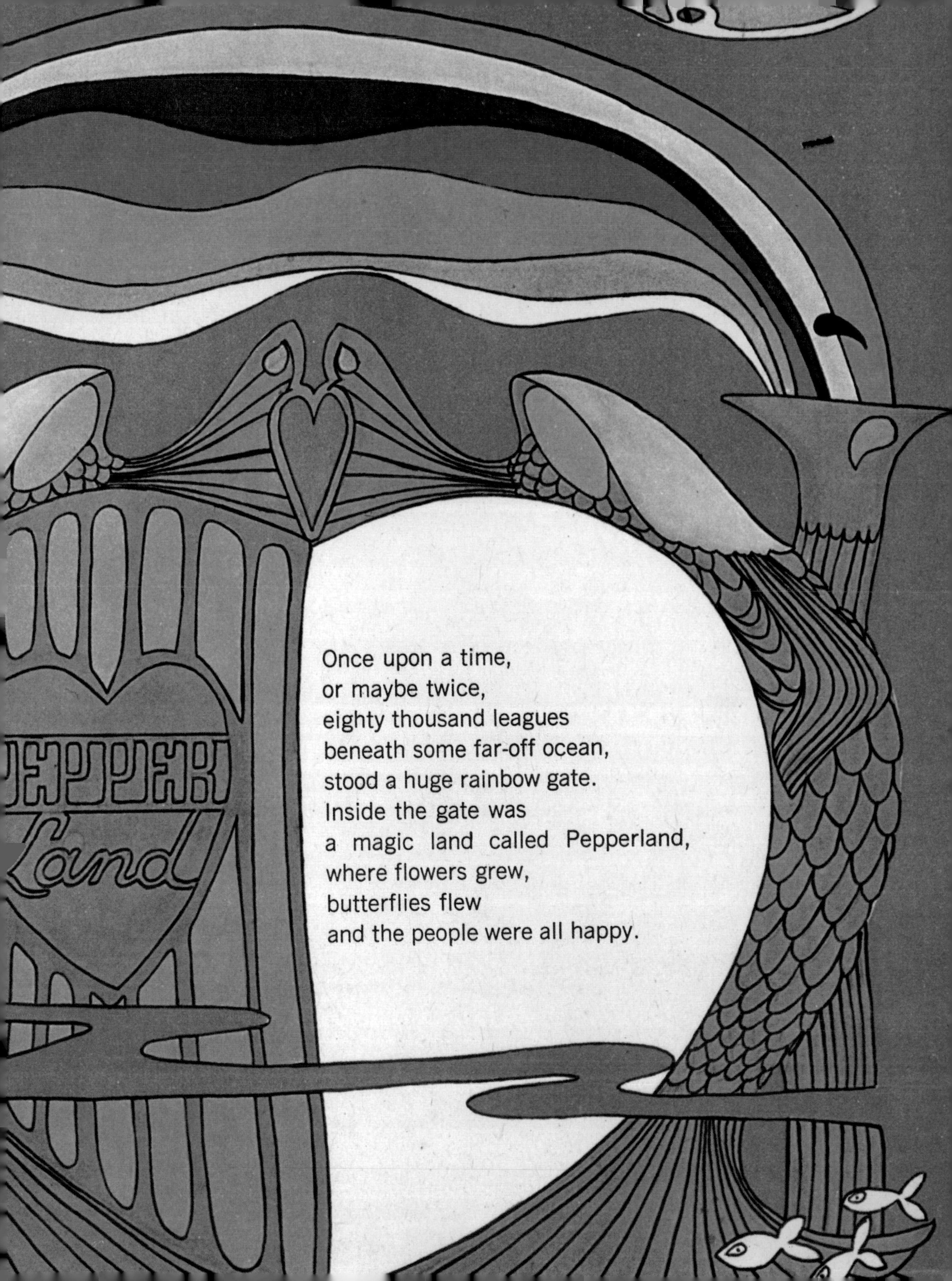

Once upon a time,
or maybe twice,
eighty thousand leagues
beneath some far-off ocean,
stood a huge rainbow gate.
Inside the gate was
a magic land called Pepperland,
where flowers grew,
butterflies flew
and the people were all happy.

5

THE LOOK . . . AND HOW TO GET IT

NOT ONLY DID THE BEATLES *sound fresh and new, and quite unlike almost anything else that American audiences had heard before, but they looked fresh and new, too.*

When they first stepped from the plane on to American soil in February 1964 they were decked out in stylish, smart but singularly unusual suits; black ties on white shirts; three-quarter-length dark, A-line raincoats; Cuban-heeled boots; and mop-top haircuts. They all had "The Look."

The Beatle's mohair suits were not like those worn by Elvis, the Four Seasons, or Fabian. They were not shiny or brightly colored, and there was no overstated Hollywood "flash" apparent in their daywear.

Pictures of The Beatles talking with Ed Sullivan before their first appearance on his program show them attired in casual London streetwear: Ringo in a dark chalk-stripe two-piece, black shirt, and black tie; George in a gray two-piece with four buttons and velvet collar over a turtleneck sweater; Paul in a black three-piece (with vest), white shirt, and black tie; John in a dark two-piece with all four buttons done up, short-drop thin lapels with black tie and white shirt. All showed the influence of the latest Italian menswear designers on London high fashion of the time. That influence had not even registered in America until the Beatles' appearance provoked such a reaction.

During the band's biggest British tour of the previous year they had worn matching stage outfits with a remarkable success. Each Beatle wore the same suit—but what a suit! They were not the regulation three-button suits, with thin lapels and flap pockets in a short, bum-hugging box shape, which were prevalent

The Beatles pose with their utterly unconvincing wax models at Madame Tussauds in London. At least the Dougie Millings suits were genuine.

among their peers (and had been worn only months previously by John, Paul, George, and Ringo). These Beatle suits had no lapels, nor even a collar: they buttoned up just under the knot of a thin necktie with pearl buttons. The tight-ankled, uncuffed trousers sat just on the top of the Beatle-boots, had flat fronts, and no hipster pockets. They were all silver-gray with black edging and were based on a suit seen on the catwalks of Paris only weeks previously, designed by Pierre Cardin.

The silver suits became something of a Beatle uniform—for instance, their waxwork dummies at Madame Tussauds in London wore them when they were unveiled in April 1964—and the man who made them, Dougie Millings, became famous as the Beatles' tailor.

The reason the Fab Four had found their way to a tailor was that in those days there was no alternative for young males wanting to look smart or different unless you went to Carnaby Street, then patronized only by the Mods and the gay

The Beatles backstage with Ed Sullivan, showing off their casual Carnaby Street outfits. For the show they changed into their traditional narrow leg, boxy jacket, black Beatle suits with skinny straight ties.

Keith Moon died in one of my suits . . . he hadn't paid for it.

DOUGIE MILLINGS

community. The British High Street menswear stores sold the kind of clothes worn by men, such as the fathers of young Mods, who wanted a "Sunday best" suit which was smart, conservative, and British. Casual clothes were also typically British in the main, and denim was non-existent in fashion stores: denim jackets and workwear could be found in hardware stores, but not in the big High Street chainstores that ruled men's fashion. Individuality came only at a cost; in the case of the first Beatle suits that cost was less than $100, but still a small fortune to most of Britain's youth.

However, once the band had conquered Britain, every small tailor in the country began advertising their own, handmade versions of the Beatle suit. Dougie Millings and the Beatles almost single-handedly caused a boom in menswear in 1963.

The Beatles liked his work so much that Dougie had a part in *A Hard Day's Night* (as a tailor, naturally) and went on to make the band's suits for the *Help!* movie, as well as those worn to collect their O.B.E.s at Buckingham Palace.

The lightweight gray and black suits with velvet collars that Dougie made for the Beatles' first tour of America had, like the Kinks' famous red suits of the same year, some stylistic reference to the classic English hunting jacket (with double vents and breast pocket). Across America the ubiquitous butt-freezer suit was gradually relegated to sale racks in favor of longer jackets as the young American male went for the British "look" as well as its sound.

Dougie Millings at Work

Dougie Millings had become known in the London music business after making suits for various stars of the early 1960s such as Billy Fury, Adam Faith, and Cliff Richard. In 1962 he was located in a small shop on Soho's Old Compton Street when Brian Epstein brought the Beatles in for a fitting. While Paul and John played the piano in Dougie's basement, he set about measuring them up and showing them some photos of Pierre Cardin's latest show. Paul and Epstein were taken enough with the idea to help finalize the design and the first Beatle suit was born. In the next few years Dougie would make all the band's stagewear—as well as that of numerous other British bands intent on looking as good as the Fab Four, including the Kinks, the Rolling Stones, and the Who. After the Beatles' success in America, Hollywood beat a path to Dougie's door and he made suits for, among others, Sammy Davis, Jr., Steve McQueen, and Warren Beatty. Bigger premises were required, prompting John Lennon to remark that, "He keeps moving with all the profit he makes."

Most people had no access to trendy clothes shops and the garment industry quickly developed a mail order trade catering to Beatles fans. At £5.10.0 ($14.00), this Beatles jacket was not cheap at a time when a shop assistant was earning about £9.0.0 a week ($25.29).

PATTIE BOYD

The interest in all things related to the Beatles led to a natural curiosity among their teen female fans about the band's girlfriends (and, as was soon discovered in John's case, his wife). Both George and Paul were dating gorgeous "dolly birds" at the time. Because of her fleeting appearance in the band's first movie A Hard Day's Night, *Pattie Boyd* attracted a great deal of interest, not only from fans but from the media, too. Aged 19 when she played the part of a schoolgirl in the movie, Pattie was already known in London for her modeling, most notably for the hip designer Mary Quant. George Harrison was only a year older than her and the attraction between them was immediate and mutual. With her blond, fringed hairstyle, big blue eyes with heavy eye-liner, and wardrobe of Mod dresses, Pattie was an obvious fashion role model for girls who also wanted to snag a Beatle. It was not long before the savvy editor of 16 Magazine, Gloria Stavers, offered Pattie a regular clothes and makeup column in the magazine. Advertised as Pattie's tips direct from London, it ensured that the Beatles could always be somewhere in the magazine and on the cover.

STEP 1

STEP 2

STEP 3

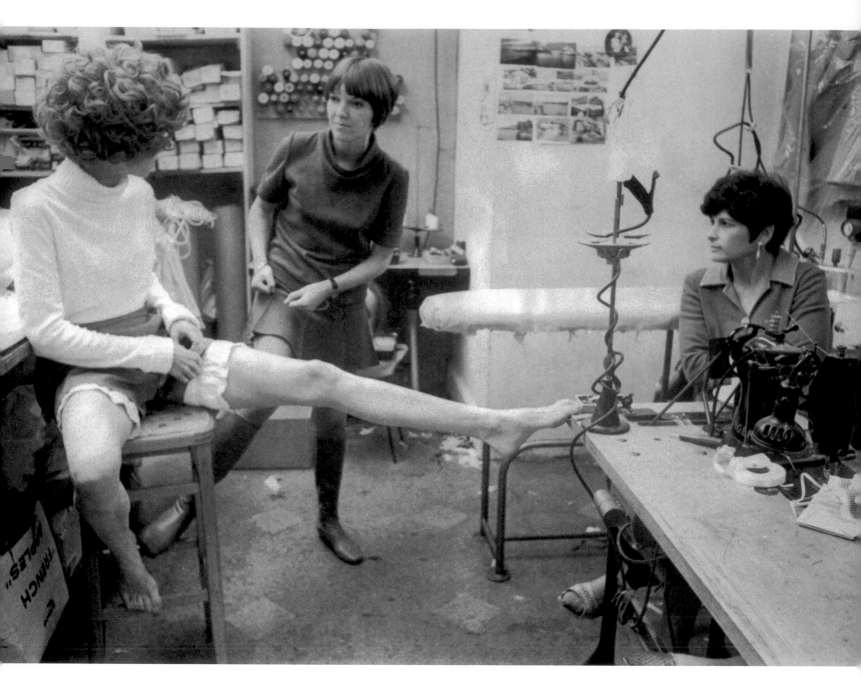

Mini Success

Mary Quant's arrival in America was almost accidental. Her success in turning
Britain's young women into "dolly birds" dressed in her trademark Mod designs
had been the result of tremendous hard work and by 1962 she was exhausted,
depressed, and on the verge of emotional collapse. After a short break in Paris to
recover, she returned to London where her partner (and husband) Alexander
Plunkett Greene, delighted that she had recovered, suggested that the time had
come for them to visit America. Seven years earlier she and Plunkett Greene,
along with their partner Archie McNair, had opened a boutique selling their own
designs in Chelsea (called Bazaar, it was on the King's Road, then just becoming
a highly affluent part of London). From the beginning Quant had wanted young
women to dress differently to their mothers, which was not the case in 1955. As
Plunkett Greene recalled: "When we started, we were really so bloody lonely. We
thought our parents' generation was mad, but thought we were the only ones to
feel like this. We seemed alone. Then we realized that a whole lot of young people
felt the same way."

*Mary Quant at work
with her assistants
developing self-hold
stockings in her
Chelsea workshop.*

Early in 1962, Quant and Plunkett Greene filled two suitcases with designs and, armed with a couple of telephone numbers given to them by journalist friends, set off to see America.

They had done no market research, they had no influential contacts, and had not intended to sell anything. They just thought they should see the American way of life, look at the shops, and note what kind of things the Americans liked. Mary recalled: "Nobody—not even us—thought my fashion thinking would ever have any influence outside London." For the first two days they were scared to even make a phone-call. When they did, their lives were changed. *Women's Wear Daily* raved over their designs: "English chic is fiercely NOW . . . by the young for the young." *Life* magazine, *Seventeen*, and the *New York Herald Tribune* picked up on the story and Mary had to model her own clothes ten times a day for the press and potential buyers.

They returned to London in shock, with orders worth thousands of dollars and a thick file of press clippings. They were still totally naive about the mechanics of mass production though, and did not even know who they were meeting when Paul Young, the buyer from J. C. Penney, called to arrange an appointment. It was J. C. Penney, with its 1,700 stores across the U.S.A., that made Mary Quant a household name among young American women, when she was selected by the chainstore to provide their outlets with a more up-to-date image, using her bright, geometric printed dresses. "It was the first time ever that the clothes of a named British designer had been promoted throughout a large chain of stores across the States," Quant recalled in her autobiography. "It was exciting but worrying too." Young asked them to design four annual collections for J. C. Penney. At first they did not think they would be able to do it. Quant:

> He just stood us on our heads. We didn't know how to produce these fantastic quantities. It's another lovely American characteristic not to accept "no." "Yes, of course you can do it" they told us. So we tried, with all sorts of consequences, but we did try! What we were doing here [in London] had anticipated something that was international. It was quite a shock—quite an exciting shock!

It was the first time that exciting, youthful clothes had been available outside the big cities in the U.S.A. and, shortly after the line was released, the fact that they were British made them even more desirable—these were after all the dresses and skirts worn by the Beatles' wives and girlfriends.

Quant's clothes—A-lines and pinafores—were designed for movement and for dancing along to the new Big Beat Sound. She could not make them fast enough and pretty quickly ran out of space for machinists to work up her designs. At one point, with Bazaar almost empty of stock, Quant was running down the street from the workshop toward it with a bunch of dresses over her arm, when a desperate shopper grabbed one and said, "I'll take that," without seeing it properly or trying it on. As Quant said, her clothes "happened to fit in exactly with the teenage trend, with pop records and espresso bars and jazz clubs."

Let Me Take You Higher
Mary Quant quickly capitalized on her position and, following on 1962's successful design partnership with J. C. Penney, she entered into design partnerships with two other big American companies in 1964: Butterick and Puritan Fashions. Meanwhile, there were racks of Quant designs in J.C. Penney's across the

In addition to her Mod clothes, Mary Quant's trademark Vidal Sassoon haircut quickly caught on among Britain's young women.

country, and they were constantly replenished as the nation's young women got the British Look to go with that sound. It came complete with a subtext: the clothes represented a new lifestyle, that of the new Swinging Sixties. British surrealist, singer, and writer George Melly wrote in *Revolt into Style*: "Quant chucked lady-like accessories into the dustbin, recognized the irrelevancy of looking like a virgin, took into account that pavements and restaurants were not muddy hunting fields nor parties and dances the antechambers of morgues. Innocent and tough, she attacked the whole rigid structure of the rag trade and won hands down and skirts up." These were clothes for active young woman.

Quant played up the British angle. When she was first promoting her clothes in America she had been surprised to find that rock 'n' roll music stations wanted to interview her about the whole British youth scene, the music, and attitudes, and not just about her clothes. She therefore quickly adopted the Swinging London iconography for her own use, and her presentations came complete with images of Big Ben, red double-decker London buses, red phone booths, Mini automobiles, black London cabs, and, of course, miniskirts. It took a while before American manufacturers dared to make their skirts as short as they were worn in Britain, but they could still be used to promote an image. The Beatles, miniskirts, Mini cars, and James Bond all combined to make Swinging London into a powerful brand. *Time* magazine's "London: The Swinging City" cover said it all: against a background of a Union Jack sky, a Mini Cooper, a Rolls Royce, and an E-type Jaguar jostle with a red double-decker bus amid crowds that include a photographer standing in the doorway of a discotheque, a pop singer wearing a Who T-shirt, and a dolly bird in an Op Art minidress. Meanwhile, a movie theater advertises the film *Alfie* in lights; there is a bingo hall and a roulette wheel, while Big Ben towers over the scene; and even the prime minister, Harold Wilson—name-checked by the Beatles in the song Taxman incidentally—appears puffing his trademark pipe and wearing his reversible Gannex raincoat (another big British export).

Although hemlines had been rising from the early fifties, and by the early sixties had reached the knee, Quant wanted them higher so they would be less restricting—they allowed women to run for a bus, she said—and much, much sexier. There is much debate about who exactly invented the miniskirt: was it Quant or André Courrèges, who was working independently in Paris? Or perhaps it was the model Jean Shrimpton who in 1965 had dressmaker Colin Rolf make up some of her designs, and, finding there wasn't enough material, told him, "Oh, it doesn't matter. Make them a bit shorter—no one's going to notice"? (Though they did notice: the results shocked Australian society when she arrived to present the Melbourne Cup in 1965 wearing a short skirt, no hat, no gloves, and no stockings.)

British Mod fashions finally made it into the mainstream in America by getting joked about in Betty and Veronica *comics. Astonishingly, this "pin-up" comes from the June 1967 edition, when for most people the mini skirt was no longer an issue.*

The London that has emerged is swinging.

TIME MAGAZINE, APRIL 15, 1966

Jane Asher

Born in 1946, the sister of Peter Asher (one half of Peter and Gordon) and like him a distinctive redhead, Jane Asher dated Paul McCartney for five years. She was an experienced actress, having begun as a child in the 1952 film *Mandy* at the age of six and played numerous other stage and screen roles as well as television and radio appearances. This meant that she was already something of a show-business veteran when she met the Beatles in 1963 to interview them for a B.B.C. radio program guide, and they were a little intimidated by her air of imperious coolness and composure. They were surprised to find she had red hair because on black and white television she had always looked like a blonde. Like Pattie Boyd, Jane Asher dressed in the latest London styles—including promoting paper dresses—wore her hair long, fringed, and straight, and made no attempt to look either older or younger than she was. Her liberal, middle-class parents saw no reason why Paul could not have a room in the family home (which he did for three years until he bought his own house), and from them Jane clearly learned the value of privacy and friendship: she remains the only close Beatle companion to never have told her story. In the mid-sixties her style inspired a million girls to be proud of their red hair and not dye it blonde.

For several years Paul McCartney and Jane Asher were the media's favorite couple, like Elizabeth Taylor and Richard Burton or Humphrey Bogart and Lauren Bacall before them. They did not disappoint and appeared together at first nights, premiers, and art openings on a regular basis.

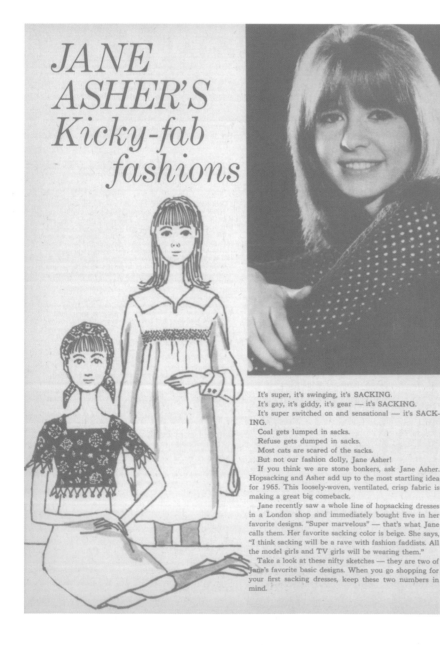

JANE ASHER'S *Kicky-fab fashions*

It's super, it's swinging, it's SACKING.
It's gay, it's giddy, it's gear — it's SACKING.
It's super switched on and sensational — it's SACKING.
Coal gets lumped in sacks.
Refuse gets dumped in sacks.
Most cats are scared of the sacks.
But not our fashion dolly, Jane Asher!
If you think we are stone bonkers, ask Jane Asher. Hopsacking and Asher add up to the most startling idea for 1965. This loosely-woven, ventilated, crisp fabric is making a great big comeback.
Jane recently saw a whole line of hopsacking dresses in a London shop and immediately bought five in her favorite designs. "Super marvelous" — that's what Jane calls them. Her favorite sacking color is beige. She says, "I think sacking will be a rave with fashion faddists. All the model girls and TV girls will be wearing them."
Take a look at these nifty sketches — they are two of Jane's favorite basic designs. When you go shopping for your first sacking dresses, keep these two numbers in mind.

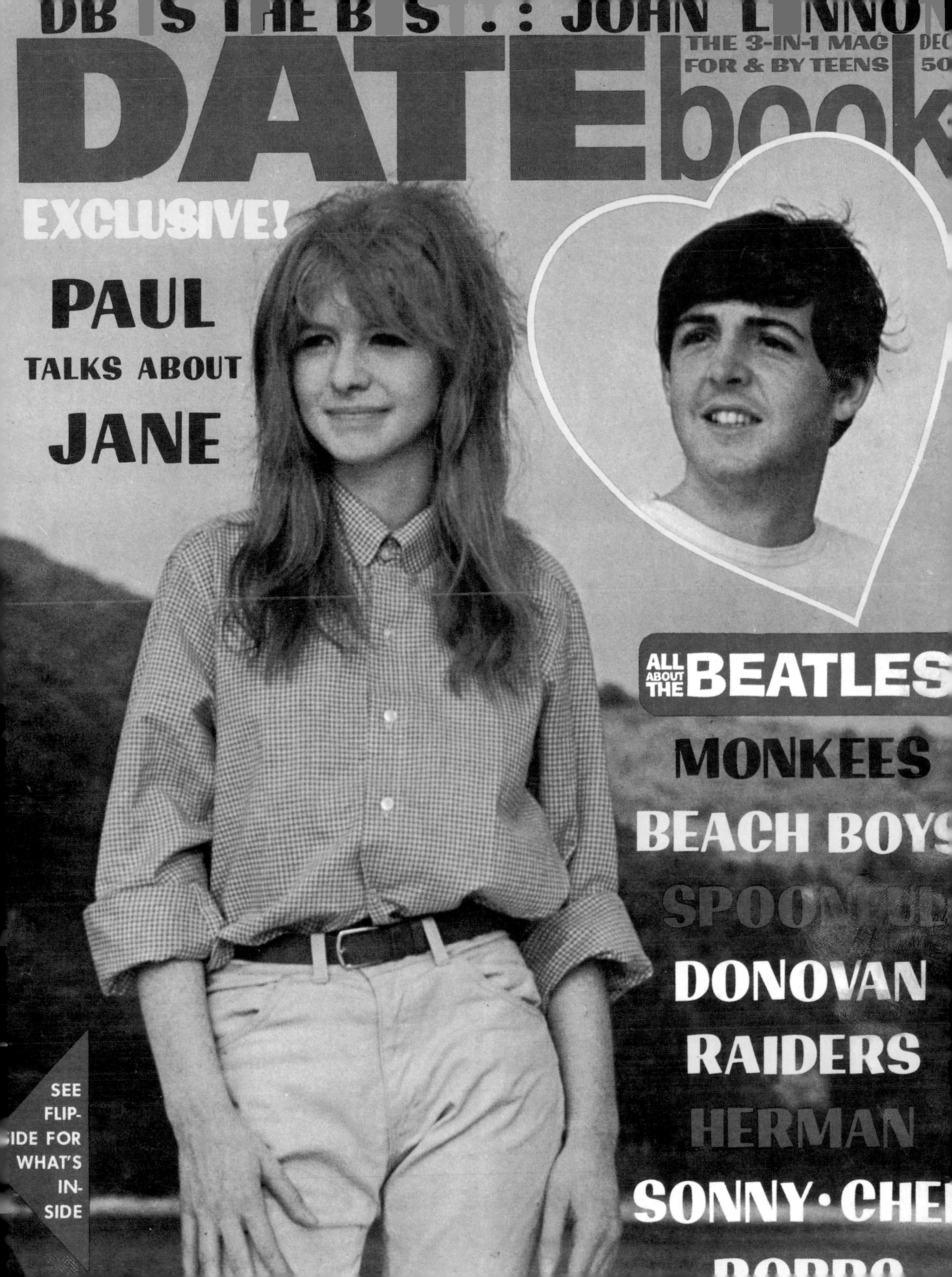

DATEbook

THE 3-IN-1 MAG | DEC
FOR & BY TEENS | 50

EXCLUSIVE!

PAUL
TALKS ABOUT
JANE

ALL
ABOUT
THE **BEATLES**

MONKEES

BEACH BOYS

SPOON

DONOVAN

RAIDERS

HERMAN

SONNY·CHE

SEE
FLIP-
SIDE FOR
WHAT'S
IN-
SIDE

This Is the Modern World

Just as British rock bands followed the Beatles to America, so British designers were quick to follow in Mary Quant's footsteps. One of the first was John Stephen, who was doing for men's fashions what Mary Quant had done for women. He opened his first shop, a one-roomed boutique called His Clothes, in Beak Street, moving to 5 Carnaby Street a year later in 1957. His stock was drawn from essentially Italian fashion: short boxy jackets and narrow pants. It was a look taken up by a group of fashion-conscious young people in London who styled themselves as "Modernists" or Mods. Fast forward to 1966 when *Time* magazine ran its Swinging London cover and nine of the clothes shops on Carnaby Street were his: Adam, Male West One, Paul's, The Man's Shop, His Clothes, and so on. He was known as "The King of Carnaby Street" and was frequently photographed with his Rolls Royce parked in the background. He bought it when he was 20 and the police were always asking, "Does your father know you're driving his car?"

Stephen followed Mary Quant to New York in the spring of 1966, taking his Rolls with him, as he always did, and got his clothes into J. C. Penney. The chain consolidated their lead in British designers by also signing John Michael, a new London designer, who was rather more conservative and expensive than Stephen. His clothes featured in the J. C. Penney catalog of fall 1966 in a section called "The Young London Look." Labeled "designed for Penney's by John Michael of Chelsea, London and tailored in England," they were shown alongside the range designed by Mary Quant.

By 1966, in a further echo of the groups in the wake of Beatlemania, the Fashion House Group, an organization set up to promote British fashion headed by Moss Murray, went beyond selling to British and European department stores

and took on America. Murray recalled: "We sailed on the *Queen Elizabeth* with a party of eighteen model girls, manufacturers and twelve top British journalists. We were a wow! It simply wasn't done for a big store not to have British fashions." One of their designers to do well in the States was Australian haute couture designer Bob Schultz, who had arrived in London in 1948. His ready-to-wear designs did extremely well at upmarket stores like Henri Bendel and Bloomingdales in New York and Neiman Marcus in Dallas. Also on the trip were John Bates, Maggi Shepherd, and designers from Burberry.

Jenny Boyd, Pattie's sister, worked in the Apple Boutique owned and run by the Beatles, in London, from December 1967. It closed in July 1968.

John Bates was yet another contender for title of the inventor of the miniskirt. Whether he did or not, his minis were certainly the shortest. "I think everything should show," he said in 1964. "Nothing should go underneath. All a girl needs is something to hold up her stockings . . . Newspapers loved stirring up a storm about indecency. But the mini was innocent. It was never tarty." He advocated that women should go braless and was the first to bare the midriff. He introduced trouser suits in 1962, string vests in 1963, and his white vinyl coats were very popular. Although he designed for Julie Christie (including her dress in *Shampoo* in 1975), he remained best known for Diana Rigg's black leather cat-suits in *The Avengers* television series. Throughout the sixties he designed under his Jean Varon label, only starting a label under his own name in 1970.

Mod for the Ladies

Sally Tuffin and Marion Foale started their own business shortly after graduating from London's Royal College of Art's fashion department, which was then unheard of; traditionally, you served a long apprenticeship in an established fashion house first. In August 1964 the influential American fashion newspaper *Women's Wear Daily* happened to be visiting Foale and Tuffin's tiny Carnaby Street showroom when Baby Jane Holzer, one of the Warhol Superstars, was also there, tearing the racks apart. "This stuff swings," she told them, "It's much better than New York." The newspaper described Holzer "jumping in and out of pantsuits, clean crepe dresses cut like cycler's shirts, or ferociously banded in rugby stripes—purple and jade—and the new Foale and Tuffin Pop Art prints." In 1965, Foale and Tuffin were among the designers featured in New York's new boutique Paraphernalia, and shoppers could not get enough of their pantsuits. The same year, they traveled to America to help promote Paraphernalia's wholesale arm, Youthquake, and appeared on television and radio talk shows. They were very amused to find that at runway shows all the buyers in the big suburban stores wore their clothes or similar, "But after the show, they changed back into their own clothes. They knew our work was commercially viable, but they didn't want to wear it. Fair enough. But at the time we were so dismayed."

Paraphernalia and Youthquake were created by Paul Young, the buyer at J. C. Penney, with Carl Rosen, the president of the Puritan Dress Company, who wished to imitate the success of the London dress boutiques. Together they brought in designers from Britain, such as Quant, Foale, and Tuffin, along with European designers and new American talent such as Betsey Johnson and future filmmaker Joel Schumacher. Paraphernalia was so successful that by 1968 they had 44 franchises across the States.

Leading the London boutique scene was Barbara Hulanicki, whose Biba label was enormously influential in London in the mid-sixties. *Women's Wear Daily* reported that when Biba opened in 1964, "she was *the* name in the lives of Britain's fashion hungry, fiercely individualistic Mods." (In Britain the use of the word Mod had only applied to young men, but the American paper identified a whole new women's fashion trend.) Hulanicki later said that, "The young market was so strong and it had suffered so much under their parents that it was all rebellion." Hulanicki's clothes were available in the boutique attached to the trendy New York discotheque Cheetah and were worn by the most fashion-conscious women in New York. They were quickly taken up by Bergdorf Goodman, Macy's, and Bloomingdales, but her clothes remained exclusive imports until February, 1971, when, trading on all the publicity she was getting in the States, Hulanicki opened a satellite branch of Biba in New York's Bergdorf Goodman.

This was clearly a good time to be English and living in the United States.

FIGURE

TWIGGY

- EYES..Blue
- BUST..31"
- WAIST..22"
- HIPS..32"
- THIGH..16½"

REAL NAME.. Lesley Hornby
NICKNAME..Twiggy
AGE..18 years old
PROFESSION..Model
HEIGHT..5' 6"
WEIGHT..6½ st.
DRESS SIZE..Smaller than 8
DRESS DESIGNER..Pam Procter who works with her on Twiggy Clothes
SHAMPOO USED..Leonard's own mixture
TIMES HAIR WASHED PER WEEK..Twice
HAIRDRESSER..Leonard
FAVE FOOD..Simple
FAVE DRINK..Orange juice
HOURS OF SLEEP PER NIGHT..9 hours min.
PRIORITY..To get as much sleep as possible. When and where you can

SANDIE

- HAIR COLOUR.. Dark brown
- EYES..Blue
- BUST..33"
- WAIST..24"
- HIPS..35"
- THIGH..18"
- CALF..12"
- ANKLE..7"
- SHOE SIZE..6

REAL NAME..Sandra Anne Goodrich
STAGE NAME..Sandie Shaw
AGE..21 years old
PROFESSION..Singer
HEIGHT..5' 8"
WEIGHT..Approx. 8 st.
DRESS SIZE..10
DRESS DESIGNER..The Sandie Shaw range of dresses
SHAMPOO USED.. Leonard's own mixture
TIMES HAIR WASHED.. Twice a week
HAIRDRESSER..Leonard
FAVE FOOD..Curry and rice
FAVE DRINK..A cup of tea
HOURS OF SLEEP PER NIGHT At least 8

LYNN

- HAIR COLOUR..Gold
- EYES..Blue
- BUST..36"
- WAIST..26"
- HIPS..38"
- THIGH..She says "No idea"
- CALF..She says "No idea"
- ANKLE..She says "No idea"
- SHOE SIZE..9b

REAL NAME..Lynn Redgrave
AGE..25
PROFESSION..Actress
HEIGHT..5' 10"
WEIGHT..10 st. 8 lbs.
DRESS SIZE..12 or 14 depending on where bought
DRESS DESIGNER..None
SHAMPOO USED..Different each time
TIMES HAIR WASHED..Every two days when working
HAIRDRESSER..Paul at Gianni-Paul, 27 Basil Street, London, S.W.1
FAVE FOOD..Yoghourt
FAVE DRINK..Alouette Rose
HOURS OF SLEEP PER NIGHT..8
PRIORITY..Baby oil gets rid of dandruff if rubbed into the scalp

IT OUT

A model, an actress and two pop girls make up our four famous dollies below. If you admire their looks see how your statistics compare with theirs when you fill in all your details in the column on the right.

LULU

HAIR COLOUR..Red

EYES..Blue

BUST..34"

WAIST..23"

HIPS..34"

* **REAL NAME..** Marie Lawrie
  STAGE NAME.. Lulu
  AGE.. 19 years old
  PROFESSION.. Singer
  HEIGHT.. 5' 1"
  WEIGHT.. 7 st. 10 lb.
  DRESS SIZE.. 8
  DRESS DESIGNER.. Lenbry Fashions
  SHAMPOO USED.. Egg with lemon
  TIMES HAIR WASHED.. Twice a week
  HAIRDRESSER.. Ricci at Vidal Sassoon
  FAVE FOOD.. Most
  FAVE DRINK.. Bitter lemon with Dubonnet (alcoholic). Orange juice (non-alcoholic)
  HOURS OF SLEEP PER NIGHT.. Average 8 hours
  PRIORITY.. Take off all make-up before going to bed at night

THIGH..19"

CALF..12"

ANKLE..6"

SHOE SIZE..4

Here's where you put down all your own statistics. Don't cheat—but when you've filled in your details turn the page ▶

Real Name Carole Parker
Nickname "Tich"
Age 16 yrs
Profession Punch Card Op.

Height 5ft 2
Weight 8 st.
Colour of Eyes
Bust
Waist
Hips
Thigh
Calf
Ankle
Shoe Size
Dress Size
Dress Designer
Shampoo Used
Times Hair Washed Per Week 2
Hairdresser
FAVE FOOD
FAVE DRINK
PRIORITY
HOURS OF SLEEP PER NIGHT

THE MINISKIRT

The steady rise of the hemline was the result of many designers working independently but all aware of each other. Mary Quant had certainly seen André Courrèges' "space-age" collections of 1964–65, but it was her own short skirts and dresses that came to be known as miniskirts in London. She named them after her favorite car, the Mini. By the fall of 1965, the term was in wide usage in the British press but still only referred to a hemline just above the knee. Top sixties model Twiggy remembered the dress she wore to her sister's wedding in October 1965: "It was an A-line with a tight top and little arm holes, and short for the time, two inches above the knee." Then Quant came up with the short "micro-mini" which outraged the press and was even banned in some countries. However, the miniskirt was unstoppable and soon it was just as ubiquitous on Fifth Avenue as it was on Bond Street, though in America the hemline was usually a little lower.

JEAN SHRIMPTON

Before Twiggy there was "The Shrimp." While the Beatles were still trying to impress the citizens of Hamburg, Jean Shrimpton was a world-famous British face, having graced the covers of Vogue, Harper's Bazaar, and Vanity Fair, wearing the fashions of 1960. However, after the Beatles had spread the word on British fashion to America the Shrimp became a more prominent face. As the girlfriend of photographer David Bailey (the inspiration for the David Hemmings character in Blowup!) and then actor Terence Stamp, her leisure time was recorded by gossip columnists and captured by paparazzi with zeal. Her perfect model body, English Rose-face, and endless legs greatly suited the miniskirt fashions and Op Art designs of the day, and she was in constant demand among the high fashion magazines. In 1967 she starred opposite Paul Jones (of Manfred Mann) to critical acclaim in an interesting but unsuccessful movie, Privilege. Despite being a clothes model, the Shrimp had a womanly figure, and her appeal was largely to women beyond their teenage years. Teens would have another, far less voluptuous clothes model of their own in the form of Twiggy.

Op Art

Not everyone was pleased with the American interest in all things British. When British optical art painter Bridget Riley had her work included in the Responsive Eye exhibition at the Museum of Modern Art in New York in 1965, one of her works was used as the cover of the exhibition catalog. The exhibition launched an Op Art craze: *Women's Wear Daily*, *Harpers*, *Vogue*, and all the design and art magazines carried articles. The windows in all the big New York stores—Lord and Taylor, Bonwit Teller, B. Altman, I. Miller, and Elizabeth Arden among them— were filled with British-style fashions displayed against eye-jolting, black-and-white optical backdrops. When Bridget Riley arrived in New York to hang the show she was introduced to Larry Aldrich at the Museum of Modern Art. Aldrich, a dress manufacturer for B. Altman, owned one of the Riley paintings in the show. He was an important collector and known as very supportive of young artists so she was pleased to meet him. He invited her to his 7th Avenue studio for a "surprise." But the surprise was regarded by Riley as more of an insult. Altman had taken the pattern of her painting *Hesitate* and had Maxwell Industries make a mass-produced textile out of it, which was then made into dresses. "I was shocked," Riley said afterwards. "In England there are laws that take care of things like that." Her design was even on the Altman's shopping bags. She had been totally ripped off: the use of her design was unauthorized and she made nothing from it. Meanwhile, Op Art was the next big thing. There were short-lived Op Art restaurants, Op stockings, Op fabrics, Op maternity wear, Op beachwear, and, astonishingly, Op girdles. It was another example of the attraction of all things British in America.

Left: Bridget Riley was horrified to find that American manufacturers had stolen her designs to use on their clothes.

Right: Sonny and Cher demonstrate one of the designs stolen from Riley.

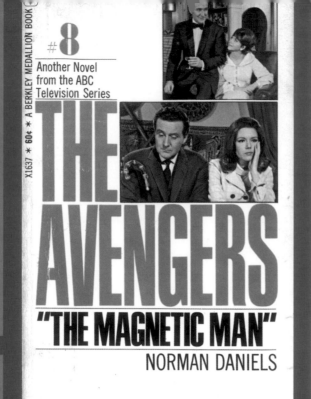

DIANA RIGG IN THE AVENGERS

The Avengers became the first British-made television series to be exported to America when it was shown by A.B.C. in 1966. The very British appeal of the series came from the leading roles of John Steed, a clichéd English gent in a Savile Row suit, bowler hat, and carrying a furled umbrella, and the lithe, athletic, cat-suited Emma Peel. There was a tension between the two, played by Patrick Macnee and Diana Rigg, which was not so much sexual (although there was a lot of flirting) as egalitarian. Mrs. Peel, who had a mysterious past (and no Mr. Peel), was a fully trained agent with excellent martial-arts skills and rarely needed rescuing by Steed. A big part of the banter between the two revolved around the fact that he was more traditional in his outlook. It was similar to the relationship that had developed between Steed and a former female companion, Mrs. Gale, played by Honor Blackman (in 1962) who had refused to cook for him or in any way succumb to traditional feminine stereotypes. She also kicked ass. Unfortunately, the first three seasons of the show were mostly broadcast live (and not taped) in black and white. By the time Diana Rigg took the role of Mrs. Peel in late 1965, the series switched to color film recording and was sold to American TV. Diana Rigg became the feminist sex symbol of the show, in which she got to wear some truly cutting-edge British fashion designs by John Bates, including black leather cat-suits which were criticized for bordering on kinky. After discovering that she was paid less for her role than a cameraman working on The Avengers, Rigg left the series in 1968. In 1969 she starred as the only woman to ever marry James Bond in the George Lazenby flick, On Her Majesty's Secret Service, sporting the high fashions for women of the upper classes of that era.

A Girl Named Twiggy

The biggest British fashion icon of all in the sixties was Twiggy. Born Lesley Hornby, the skinny supermodel took America by storm. By the time she arrived in New York in 1967, along with boyfriend and manager Justin de Villeneuve, she had only been a model for a year. However, already Mattel had released a "Twiggy" doll, like a Barbie doll but with an even smaller bust and hips. Her short-haired, androgynous look changed the world of American fashion. She was still only 17 and aside from modeling for the Paris collections she had never traveled before in her life. She loved being in America:

> It was wonderful. It was mad. I had people telling me I was gorgeous, whereas I'd always thought I was this runty little thing, and paying me money. I went out to L.A., met Sonny and Cher, and Steve McQueen. Diana Vreeland was a huge plus for me because she brought me over . . . and put me in *Vogue* . . .when she said, "This is the look, this is the girl," that was it. She put me with Richard Avedon, and the rest, as they say is history. What happened to me is a one in god-knows-how-many-million chance.

She was on the covers of *Vogue, Life, Look, Newsweek*, and *Harper's Bazaar*. Some sceptics thought she was a passing fad and the fuss would all be over in a month, but the opposite happened. She grew in fame and stature. All across the U.S.A. young women cropped their hair and painted on lower lashes in imitation of the Twiggy look. Her childlike face and body coincided with the hippie "flower children" and their love of childlike innocence, as well as the androgynous look later taken up by David Bowie and the Glam Rockers of the early seventies. The Avedon photographs treated her as a woman, not just as a bubbly teenager, and she made a successful transition into mainstream modeling. She remained at the top of her profession for four years, when she retired and moved instead into movies and records, saying "You can't be a clothes hanger for your entire life!" It was the ultimate sixties success story.

Twiggy probably did more than any other Briton to spread the minidress look across America, too. The influence of Pattie Boyd, Julie Christie, Jane Asher, and, later on, Twiggy affected the whole country. Mia Farrow, who had become a TV star in 1964 playing a long-haired teenager in *Peyton Place*, adopted the look when she left the show and married Frank Sinatra in 1966. By the time that Goldie Hawn became a regular on *Rowan & Martin's Laugh-In* in 1968, she had adopted the Twiggy look perfectly, and in turn inspired legions of middle-American women to adopt the same wide-eyed, miniskirted look. It would take the dawning of a new decade before the Twiggy look of the mid-sixties began to lose its widespread appeal in America.

Twiggy was naturally very thin but her slender figure encouraged many girls to go on crash diets and helped usher in the era of anorexically thin models.

Four straight limbs in search of a body

NEWSWEEK

FORTY CENTS

APRIL 15, 1966

LONDON: The Swinging City

TIME

THE WEEKLY NEWSMAGAZINE

VOL. 87 NO. 15

CARNABY STREET

By the time that Time magazine published their "Swinging London" issue in 1966, the one London address that every hip teenager in America knew was Carnaby Street. From 1958 the narrow West End street had begun to play host to hip boutiques selling European fashions for men. The first, His Clothes (see right), was opened by John Stephen, selling Italian-styled suits and shirts which became the staple attire of the Mods, and were ubiquitous by 1964. Stephens was the self-styled king of Carnaby Street and oversaw the expansion of his eponymous chain of shops across the UK through the 1960s. When the first women's boutique opened there, Lady Jane's in 1966, it was quickly followed by other women's wear stores. American fashion magazines sent writers to report on the latest trends shown in the windows of Carnaby Street boutiques as they popped up (one was called Pop), sold their stock, and closed, to be replaced by another hopeful. By the time this picture was taken in 1967, even young mothers were being styled by Carnaby Street, and it lost its cool appeal, becoming nothing more than a tourist attraction.

Dedicated Follower of Fashion

In Britain, the sixties marked the beginning of a wider masculine interest in fashion than had previously existed. While working-class British males had always had a dress suit for Saturday nights and Sunday mornings, it had generally been just the one (which also usually served as their wedding suit, too). But as Britain's economy improved and young men found that they had more disposable income, and that young women liked men who looked smart—witness the screaming hordes at Beatles gigs and appearances—so they began to buy more clothes in different, new styles. Because most of the new bands emerging from Britain were made up of working-class teenagers or early twenty-somethings, they cared about their "look." When Beatles' tailor Dougie Millings put the Kinks in red velvet suits, frilly-fronted shirts, and dandy-style accessories in 1964 he helped to kick-start a new interest among British males for flamboyant dressing. The flamboyance played with gender identity and sexuality, achievable at a price from the high-end retailers. By 1966, cutting-edge Chelsea dress designers like Ossie Clark and Mr. Fish found that they were beginning to attract male customers who accompanied their girlfriends to boutiques in search of something unusual for themselves. The British peacock—which had shown prior tendencies toward cross-dressing, of course—was awakening, and as it did it displayed fine tail feathers wherever it flew.

However, the biggest influence that British Invasion bands had on men's fashion in America was not on their bodies; it was on their heads. American males used to crew-cut or Tony Curtis haircuts (the latter of which had been inspired by British Teddy Boys according to Curtis) began growing their hair out in the style of the mop-tops. When the second wave of British Invasion bands started to appear in the States, sporting even longer hair than the Beatles—witness Eric

ENGLAND'S NEWEST SINGING SENSATIONS
THE HULLABALLOOS

Right: Designer Ossie Clark in 1969. He used Celia Birtwell's fabric prints to create some of the most beautiful garments of the sixties. Sadly, he had no head for business.

Below left: The Hullaballoos were a wholly British creation (and had nothing to do with the American TV show of the same name). They were managed by a peer—that's his home and staircase in the photo—and sported matching, collar-length blond hair. In 1965 that length of hair was unseen in America. Two years later every self-respecting hip teen guy had similar-length locks.

It doesn't matter how long my hair is, or what color my skin is . . .

JOHN LENNON

Clapton's very fine Jimi Hendrix-inspired Afro-style perm when fronting Cream in 1968–then American males likewise stopped using scissors altogether.

By the time that *Sgt. Pepper's Lonely Hearts Club Band* was released in 1967, the Beatles had grown out their mop-tops and added mustaches and sideburns. American bands like Roger McGuinn's Byrds had always had longer mop-tops than the Liverpudlians, but now had to out-grow their basin cuts. For them it became a symbol of their individuality and creativity, as described by David Crosby (by then with Crosby, Stills, Nash & Young) in his 1967 song Almost Cut My Hair as "I feel like letting my freak flag fly."

By 1966 the length of a man's hair had become a very visible sign of his political as well as musical and social allegiance. Anti-Vietnam War protests had grown among students and young men in fear of being drafted. In complete contrast to the closely cropped Prussian Military Academy crew-cut hair of soldiers and police officers who faced them at anti-war demonstrations, young men let their hair grow unrestricted. It became a symbol of rebellion. The Rolling Stones had begun the truly long-haired trend in America (though in Britain the Pretty Things won the prize for the longest hair), and by 1968 Mick Jagger's hair added to the androgynous look that he was beginning to favor. When he appeared live on stage at London's Hyde Park in 1968 wearing a white "dress" made by Mr. Fish (and usually wrongly credited to Ossie Clark), his hair had grown past his shoulders and his squirming antics and twirls were considered truly outlandish among the conservative older generation of Americans. The desperate attempts that were made to ban the Stones from touring the U.S.A. in 1969 were motivated as much by Jagger's look as by any supposed "revolutionary" politics expressed in one of their few politically-motivated numbers, Street Fighting Man (the single of which was banned in the greater Chicago area in August 1968).

The Beatles stopped worrying about the uniformity of the clothes they wore, but it was their decision to grow their hair that really helped to free the American and British male from the restrictions of their fashion past. Men no longer needed to buy the right suit, shoes, or shirt in order to belong to the scene; all they had to do to be a hippie was grow their hair.

It took just over five years from the arrival of the Beatles in matching suits in America to their walking (barefoot in Paul's case) in mismatched outfits across Abbey Road to bring about a real fashion revolution around the world.

The Beatles led the way in making it acceptable for men to wear their hair long. By the time they were photographed crossing Abbey Road, the Dougie Millings suits were thankfully long gone and they had each developed their own unique sartorial style, with both Harrison and Lennon sporting collarbone-length locks.

216

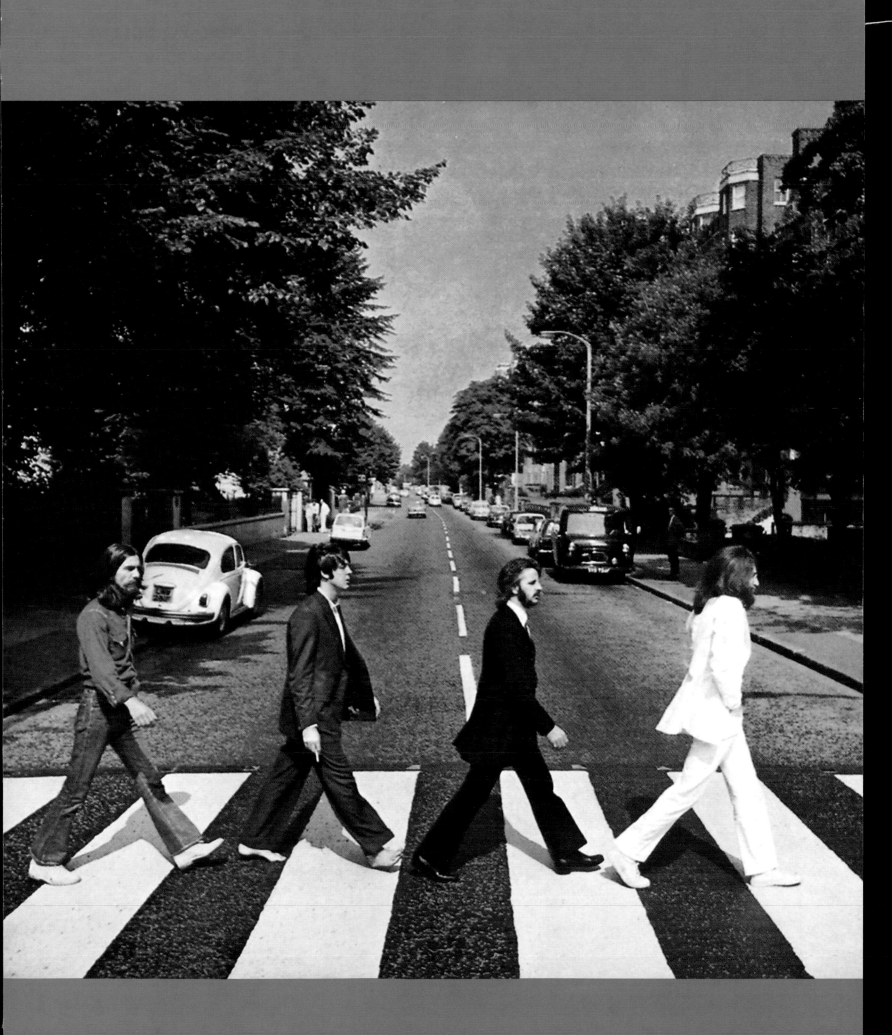

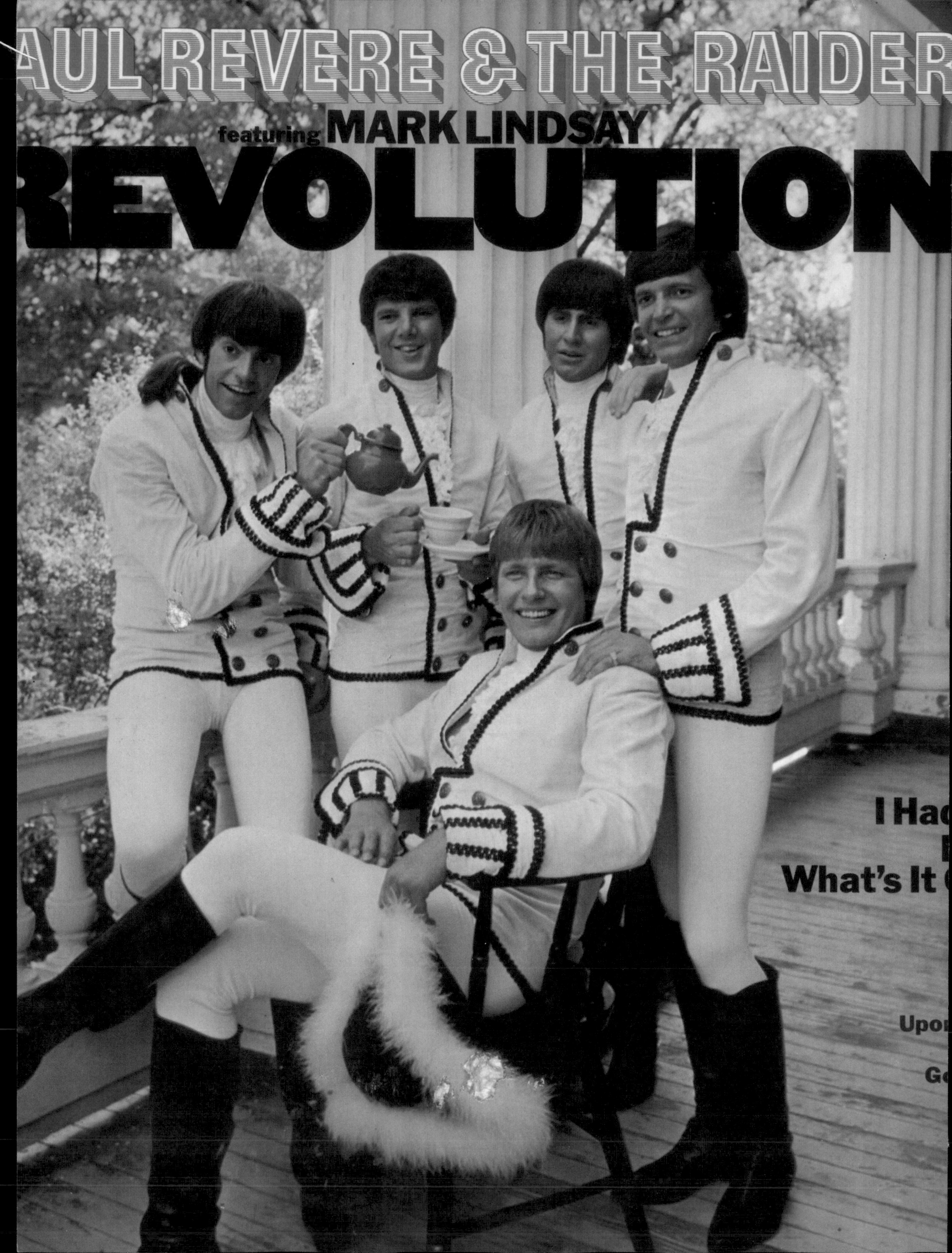

AUL REVERE & THE RAIDER

featuring **MARK LINDSAY**

REVOLUTION!

I Had

What's It

Upon

Go

6

AMERICANS FIGHT BACK

IT TOOK A LITTLE WHILE *for the American record industry to come to terms with all the new British acts who invaded its world. Initially, the response consisted largely of We Love You Beatles-type records and a mad scramble to sign up every British act that showed any sign of vital functions. At the sleazier end of the record business, executives cashed in on the interest in anything British by simply making up product. One such was Coronet Records who came up with the Buggs—not quite Beatles, but insects nonetheless. Back then, the word "Beatles" still had insects as its first meaning. The Buggs released an album called* The Beetle Beat, *which apparently had "The original Liverpool Sound, recorded in England," and featured songs with titles like: Teddy Boy Stomp, East End, Soho Mash, Swingin Thames, and Big Ben Hop. In fact, the band was from Nebraska and the album appears to have been recorded in Minneapolis.*

Everyone tried to cash in for years after the Beatles' arrival. In 1966, even Mae West, celebrated femme fatale and Hollywood screen goddess of the thirties, relaunched herself in as a rock 'n' roll singer at the age of 73, with an album that included Day Tripper and Twist and Shout. As the sleeve notes say, "Her rhythm is like no other rhythm," and it's true. Her backing quartet, featured on the sleeve, is dressed like the Beatles in black polo necks, with the guitarist, 15-year-old David Allen Clark, holding a Rickenbacker. It was as if the Beatles were backing her. Clark, who had been a serious flamenco guitarist until hearing the Beatles, and his band had begun life as the Offbeats and released one single before mutating into Somebody's Chyldren to record with Mae West. (They then released three singles before calling it a day. Clark went on to form Carmen, the world's first flamenco rock band, who toured with Jethro Tull and released three albums between 1973 and 1975. The first was memorably titled *Fandangos In Space*.)

The biggest chart casualties of the British Invasion were the manufactured pretty boys and studio groups used as vehicles for the Brill Building songwriters. When the Beatles arrived Carole King and her husband Gerry Goffin, in-house composers at Aldon Music (which formed part of the Brill Building sound), found themselves out on a limb. As she recalled:

> Then the Beatles came out and I couldn't, I don't think either of us, could quite figure out what they were doing. At first it hampered my appreciation of them because I said: "What are they doing and how am I gonna write music with those people doing that?" But then we got behind it and really loved it. It was really so good.

Meanwhile, she was happy that they chose to record some of her songs, including Boys in 1963 and Chains in 1964.

Even 73-year-old Mae West jumped on the bandwagon and attempted to launch herself as a rockstar with a backing group modeled on The Beatles.

Papa Doesn't Need a Brand New Bag

Not every American teenager and musician was positively affected by the British Invasion. Most soul and R&B acts continued to make their own music, without a Beatle-cut in sight. James Brown had hits throughout the period—Papa's Got a Brand New Bag (Part 1) reached number 8 in 1965, followed that same year by I Got You (I Feel Good) at number 3. His 1966 hit, It's a Man's Man's Man's World made number 8. By 1974 he had logged 43 *Billboard* top 40 hits.

At Atlantic Records, Wilson Pickett racked up 16 chart hits between 1965 and 1972 with songs like In the Midnight Hour (1965), Land of 1000 Dances (1966), and Funky Broadway (1967). Aretha Franklin had 14 top 40 hits between 1961 and 1976, including her 1967 number 1, Respect. (She remained a figurehead and sang at the 2009 presidential inauguration of Barack Obama.)

Over at Motown, the Four Tops had 22 top 40 hits between 1964 and 1973, the Supremes had 40 top 40 hits including 11 number 1s between 1963 and 1976, and Marvin Gaye had 30 hits between 1963 and 1974 including 1968's I Heard It Through the Grapevine. At Stax, Otis Redding had 11 hits between 1965 and 1968, including (Sitting On) the Dock of the Bay, recorded just three days before his untimely death in a plane crash on December 10, 1967. Also at Stax, Booker T and the MGs (one of the first interracial bands) got off seven hits between 1962 and 1969.

There was also safety in the charts for established, adult acts aimed at an older audience. Frank Sinatra continued to have hits throughout the sixties, including two number 1s: Strangers in the Night in May 1966 and Something Stupid with daughter Nancy in March 1967. All this proves that the British Invasion was only part of the story and plenty of American acts continued with their business, untroubled by the fact that they did not feature in every issue of *16 Magazine*.

Right: Paul McCartney gets to show how much he appreciates The Supremes.

Below left: James Brown was untroubled by the British Invasion. His audience remained solid and he continued to have hits throughout the sixties.

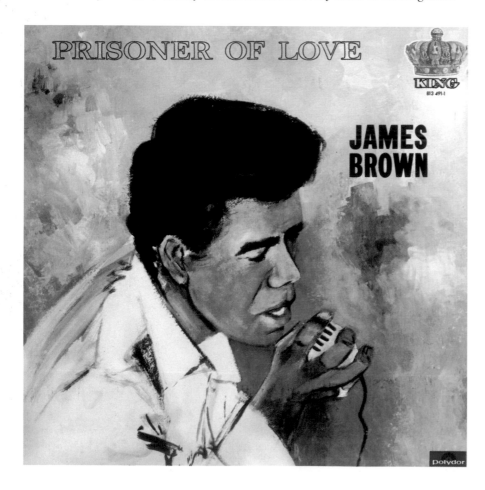

PRISONER OF LOVE

KING

JAMES BROWN

Polydor

That "English Sound"

The most obvious thing for bands in America to do was imitate the Beatles, or at least appropriate parts of their image, in order to succeed. It was very difficult for them because promoters all wanted British, or British-sounding groups. Frank Zappa recalled trying to get the Mothers of Invention hired on West Hollywood's Sunset Strip: "This was in 1965, and to get work you had to sound like the Beatles or the Rolling Stones. You also had to have long hair." Zappa had very short hair at the time, having just come out of jail for a bogus pornography rap, so the group resorted to all wearing black homburgs. Few people were fooled. According to Zappa, the Strip was filled with musicians talking in phony English accents. Being Zappa, his most obvious response to the Beatles was to answer the *Sgt. Pepper* album sleeve with an extremely clever parody, *We're Only in It for the Money*, in which both the inner and outer gatefolds imitate the original Beatles cover.

The British sound was not that hard to copy. Bands like the American Breed, whose Bend Me, Shape Me reached number 5 in December 1967, utilized a very British sound to put across this piece of pure pop and they had five chart singles in all in 1967–8. Despite their name, most people thought they were British, though it was immediately obvious that they were not just by looking at them. They adopted a psychedelic look that sat uneasily with their poppy sound. The group's core of guitarist Al Ciner and Kevin Murphy on drums took the band through numerous lineup and name changes, finishing up as Rufus, featuring the spectacular Chaka Khan on vocals. They had a top 10 hit with Tell Me Something Good in 1974.

According to the sleeve notes on the Beau Brummels' first album, *Introducing the Beau Brummels*, they were "the first American group to successfully interpret

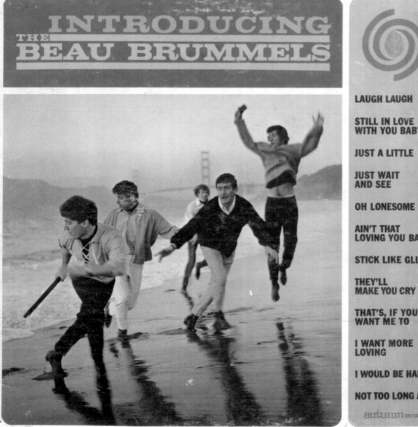

Opposite: Despite their name, many people assumed that The American Breed were British. Their move into psychedelia was particularly unfortunate.

Below left: Given that they chose a name that meant nothing to most of their audience, you would have expected The Beau Brummels to at least dress like their 19th-century English namesake, but no, they dressed like London Mods. They successfully transferred the English sound to San Francisco.

the so called 'English Sound'." The notes also, rather disparagingly, claim: "Unlike many of the other groups springing up around the country, The Beau Brummels are skilled musicians and fine singers." They were one of the first San Francisco bands to gain recognition, having three top 20 singles in 1965, beginning with Laugh, Laugh that January. Three subsequent singles reached the top 100. It was a curious choice of name as it is doubtful whether many American teenagers would have recognized the 19th-century English dandy who inspired it. The band did not dress as dandies, but affected the English Mod look, topped off with Beatles haircuts. On their first album, they even imitated photographer Dezo Hoffmann's famous pictures of the Beatles leaping in the air, albeit on the Sausalito shore with the Golden Gate Bridge in the background. They certainly imitated the English sound in their records and for the first few years of the career were often mistaken as a British band. They made six studio albums and are credited as being an influence on subsequent San Francisco bands such as the Jefferson Airplane. They were a big enough part of American popular culture to be parodied on *The Flintstones*: a 1965 episode, based on the *Shindig!* television series and entitled "Shinrock A Go Go," caricatured the band as the Beau Brummelstones, singing Laugh, Laugh.

The Chicago group, the Buckinghams (named, rather obviously, after the palace, though Chicago does also have the famous Buckingham Fountain) had a number 1 hit with Kind of a Drag in January 1967, and followed it with four more top 20 hits that same year before dropping out of the charts forever, though at the time of writing a form of the band still survives. Their name and their looks were really the only British aspect of the band, whose sound featured brass arrangements and was not very British at all. They wore tailored suits, ties, and longish Beatle haircuts, though, and certainly looked the part.

A once proudly American band was Jay and the Americans, a pre-Beatles group (founded in the late fifties) who at least displayed the Stars and Stripes at many British Invasion gigs, opening for the Beatles on their 1964 tour and for the Rolling Stones at Carnegie Hall. Their first big hit was She Cried in April 1962, which reached number 5. Come a Little Closer reached number 3 in October 1964 and Cara Mia went to number 4 in June 1965. They had ten top 40 hits in all before shifting their repertoire to become largely an oldies' band. Among the musicians in their seventies lineups were Donald Fagen and Walter Becker, who went on to form Steely Dan.

Right: The Buckinghams were unusual in that they took their image from the English groups but played a distinctly American music that really didn't need to be dressed up with Beatle haircuts.

Below left: After the success of A Hard Day's Night and the subsequent stream of British B-movies starring Brit beat acts, Hollywood began making their own versions of similarly mindless, plotless, B-movies, starring American acts.

Below right: Jay And The Americans pre-dated the Beatles, but opened for them on their first tour of the USA and adopted some of their style for themselves.

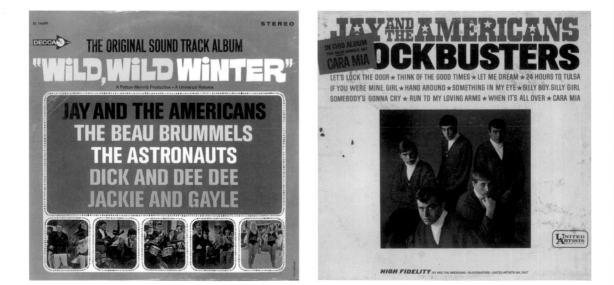

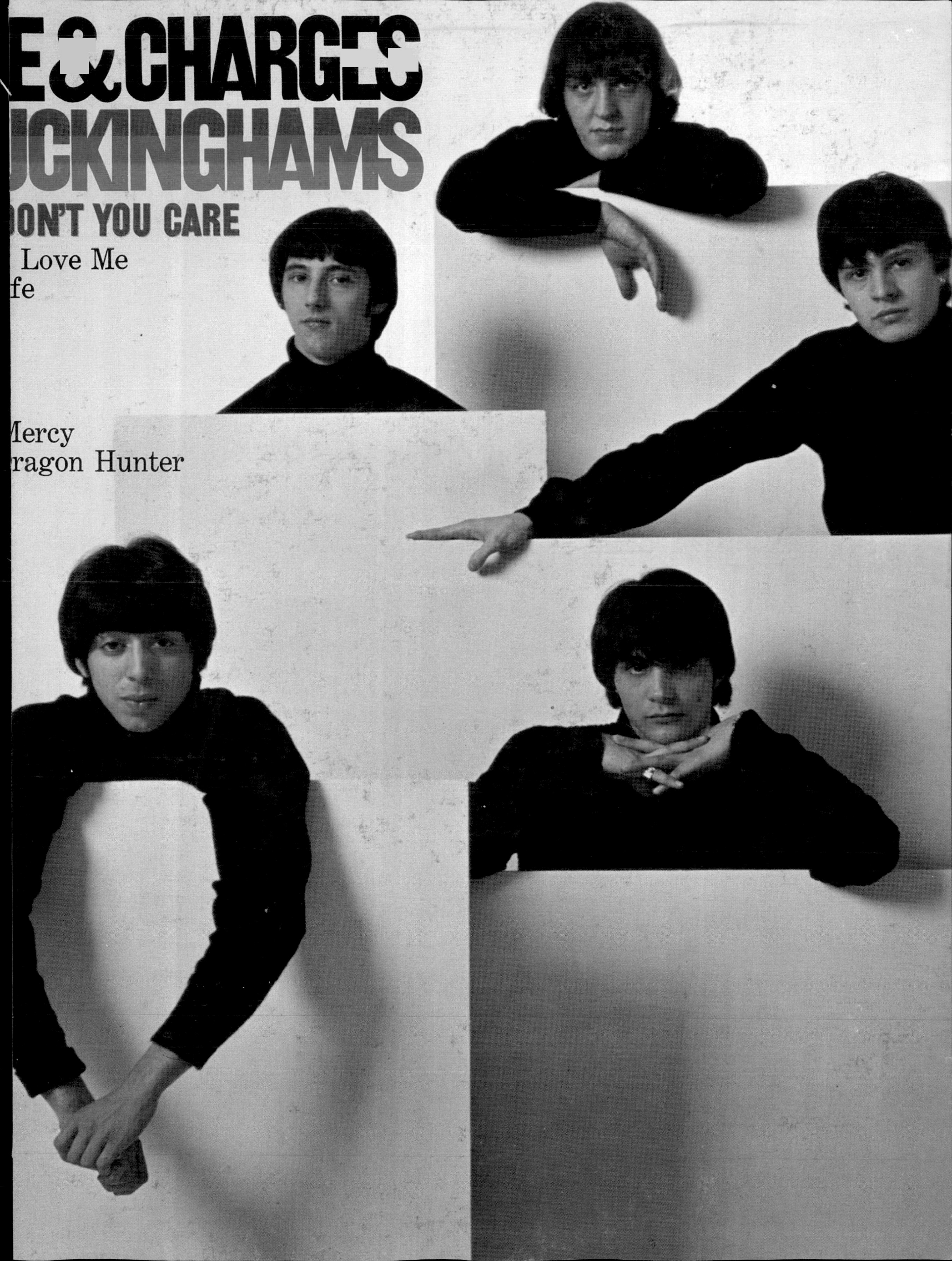
E & CHARGES
UCKINGHAMS
DON'T YOU CARE
Love Me
fe
Mercy
ragon Hunter

PAUL REVERE & THE RAIDERS

There was one band, however, who decided to re-enact the American Revolution and make a stand against the invaders: In 1965, Paul Revere & the Raiders (the band's organist's real name is Paul Revere Dick) all grew Beatles haircuts and sounded suspiciously like the British, but claimed to be resisting the invaders. They dressed in red, white, and blue American Revolutionary War soldier costumes and used a lot of slapstick in their act. The costumes and tomfoolery disguised the fact that they were actually a competent rock combo.

Vocalist Mark Lindsay recalled, "We felt like the costumes were a gimmick, like the Beatles had their look. We felt sort of like the answer to the Beatles. We were Americans, it's tied into the Revolution. 'We're gonna fight those guys.' The outfits gave us a totally unique look. Nobody, but nobody, was dressing up then like idiots."

The band had always been a bit of a novelty act, though. In April 1961, after many failures, they had pre-Beatles chart entry with Like, Long Hair, a Beatnik cash-in that reached number 38. (Their first single was Beatnik Sticks in 1960.) They reappeared as the saviors of American youth in December 1965 with Just Like Me, which reached number 11, and had their biggest hit in March 1966 with Kicks at number 4, which was the first major hit with an anti-drug message. Hungry made number 6 in 1966 and, that December, Good Thing went to number 4.

Producer Terry Melcher made them sound like a composite British Invasion band: part Beatles, part Stones, and part Animals, but with a distinctive American R&B feel. As Mark Lindsay said, it was this which got them a record contract: "[We were] a bunch of white bread kids doing our best to sound black. We got signed to Columbia on the strength of this."

In 1968 they were doing so well that they even had their own weekly Dick Clark-produced television show, Happening '68, which began in January that year, and later changed its name to just Happening. They also had a daily show called It's Happening from July to September. Both shows were co-hosted by Mark Lindsay and Paul Revere. The band toured Europe with the Beach Boys in 1969, although by then they were seen as being hopelessly out of date, appealing only to the mums and dads. They were a singles band in an album era. As their one-time publicist Derek Taylor (later the Beatles' P.A.) wrote, they were seen as "irrelevances . . . nervous citizens felt reassured that some good safe things never changed." The band went through many lineup changes and carried on in various forms for decades. Their last hit was Let Me, which reached number 20 in June 1969.

THE BYRDS
MR. TAMBOURINE MAN

Turn! Turn! Turn!

Perhaps the most significant impact that the Beatles and their fellow countrymen had on American music was to inspire the formation of hundreds of bands. David Crosby pinpoints the formation of the Byrds to first seeing the Beatles' movie, *A Hard Day's Night*. Crosby, Roger McGuinn (then called Jim), and Gene Clark saw the film together. As Crosby recalled, "I can remember coming out of that movie so jazzed that I was swinging around stop-sign poles at arm's length. The Beatles were cool and we said: 'Yeah, that's it. We have to be a band.'" They even bought the same instruments as the Beatles: Rickenbacker and Gretsch guitars, and a set of Ludwig drums for Clark, in order to be as like their heroes as possible. As McGuinn candidly puts it: "We started out as Beatles imitators."

According to Chris Hillman of the Byrds, the arrival of the Beatles just three months after the assassination of President Kennedy actually transformed the country: "I feel the Beatles actually healed us. It was almost God-sent that they came over." The Byrds signed with Columbia Records who, perhaps unfortunately, dubbed them "America's Beatles," an inappropriate label because they had quickly developed their own sound: they made their mark by playing electric versions of Bob Dylan's songs rather than anything to do with the Beatles. Their first hit, Mr. Tambourine Man, which reached number 1 in June 1965, is the epitome of the laid back, soft, Los Angeles rock sound, characterized by McGuinn's ringing 12-string Rickenbacker. This formula was repeated with All I Really Want to Do, but it only reached number 40 in the charts. However, a clever, and beautiful, arrangement of Turn! Turn! Turn! (To Everything There Is a Season), with lyrics adopted by Pete Seeger from the Bible's Book of Ecclesiastes, returned them to number 1 position in November of that year.

The cleverest response of American musicians to the Invasion was to use what the Beatles were doing and develop upon it. Paul Simon had broken from his partner Art Garfunkel to spend a year as a solo folk singer in London in 1963–4

Dubbed "America's Beatles" by their record company, The Byrds actually helped transform American rock by setting Bob Dylan to an electric "Beatle" beat.

You can see the Beatle influences which show up much more vividly on that than they do on our first Columbia album.

ROGER MCGUINN ON THE BYRDS' 1964 RECORDINGS *PREFLYTE*

before returning to New York, primed with brilliant ideas. He took the story-telling element in Lennon and McCartney's lyrics and developed it into exquisite little biographical fragments, mini-short stories, which he arranged for the re-formed Simon and Garfunkel duo. This gave him 13 top 40 hits between 1965 and 1970 with Simon and Garfunkel before he went solo again. Together form-ing an intelligent counterpoint to the Beatles, songs such as The Sound of Silence (number 1 in December 1965), Homeward Bound (number 5 in February 1966), I Am a Rock (number 3 in May 1966), and so on were well made, beautifully arranged, and took the notion of the singer-songwriter to a new level that would not be bettered until the seventies. If McCartney's Eleanor Rigby is taken as a template, Simon extended the form, using the traditional song format to paint word pictures and to explore philosophical areas never before tackled in pop.

Typical of the American response to the Beatles was The Lovin' Spoonful. In 1965, inspired by the Beatles, rockers Steve Boone and Joe Butler teamed up with a couple of folk singers from Greenwich Village, John Sebastian and Zal Yanovsky, to create an American Beatles-style band. They brushed their hair for-ward into Beatle cuts and had a couple of "good time" top 10 hits: Do You Believe in Magic? and You Didn't Have to Be So Nice. 1966 was even better for them: Daydream and Did You Ever Have to Make Up Your Mind? both reached number 2 while Summer in the City—their big summer hit, naturally—made number 1. This was followed by seven more top 20 hits, ending when they dis-banded in 1968 with the departure of John Sebastian to pursue a solo career. The Spoonful were unusual in that they not only played all the instruments on their records but wrote virtually all of their material. They are credited with inspiring the members of the originally acoustic folk act the Grateful Dead to "go electric" after seeing a Spoonful concert.

The Beatles versus the Beach Boys

Whereas Paul Simon looked to the Beatles' lyrics for a new direction, the Beach Boys' composer Brian Wilson looked to their sonic activities for his (Beach Boys lyrics continued to be about girls and the beach). As a bass player he studied the work of Paul McCartney and carefully noted all the melodic figures that were buried deep in the mix. However, both these musicians recognized the third master bass player on the scene, the virtually unknown Motown session man James Jamerson, whose work they followed assiduously. Jamerson is thought to have played on 95 percent of Motown records made between 1962 and 1968, including most of their greatest hits, but he remained unknown because Motown never credited their studio musicians on their singles and albums. Jamerson's melodic, syncopated bass-lines were a great inspiration to both McCartney and Wilson, who used the instrument in a way that no one else making pop—or rock—did at the time.

Like an old-fashioned "Battle of the Bands," The Beatles and the Beach Boys slugged it out with a series of responses and counter responses.

Wouldn't It Be Nice/You Still Believe In Me
That's Not Me/Don't Talk (Put Your Head on My Shoulder)
I'm Waiting For The Day/Let's Go Away For Awhile/Sloop John B.
God Only Knows/I Know There's An Answer/Here Today
I Just Wasn't Made For These Times/Pet Sounds/Caroline No
Plus Bonus Tracks
Unreleased Backgrounds/ Hang On To Your Ego/Trombone Dixie

Something of a competition grew up between the Beach Boys and the Beatles, with each trying to better the other in terms of innovation, sonic experimentation, odd time-signatures, and transcendent melodies. It soon posed something of a problem for Brian Wilson because some of the more commercial members of the Beach Boys wanted to stick to their old formula. Mike Love, in particular, saw no reason to change when the old surfing sound of the Beach Boys continued to sell. He was openly contemptuous of some of Wilson's most beautiful work, calling it "Brian's ego music."

One reason the Beatles stopped touring was that their work had become too complex to perform live: they had become a studio band. They had also managed the tricky feat of releasing commercial singles while developing as an album band. Hey Jude was their biggest selling single, staying at number 1 in the U.S. charts for nine weeks from September 1968. Wilson, however, had to keep it simple: the Beach Boys were a touring band and Mike Love wanted to keep it that way.

This literal interpretation of the album title disguised the fact that there were some astonishing sonic experiments going on in the grooves.

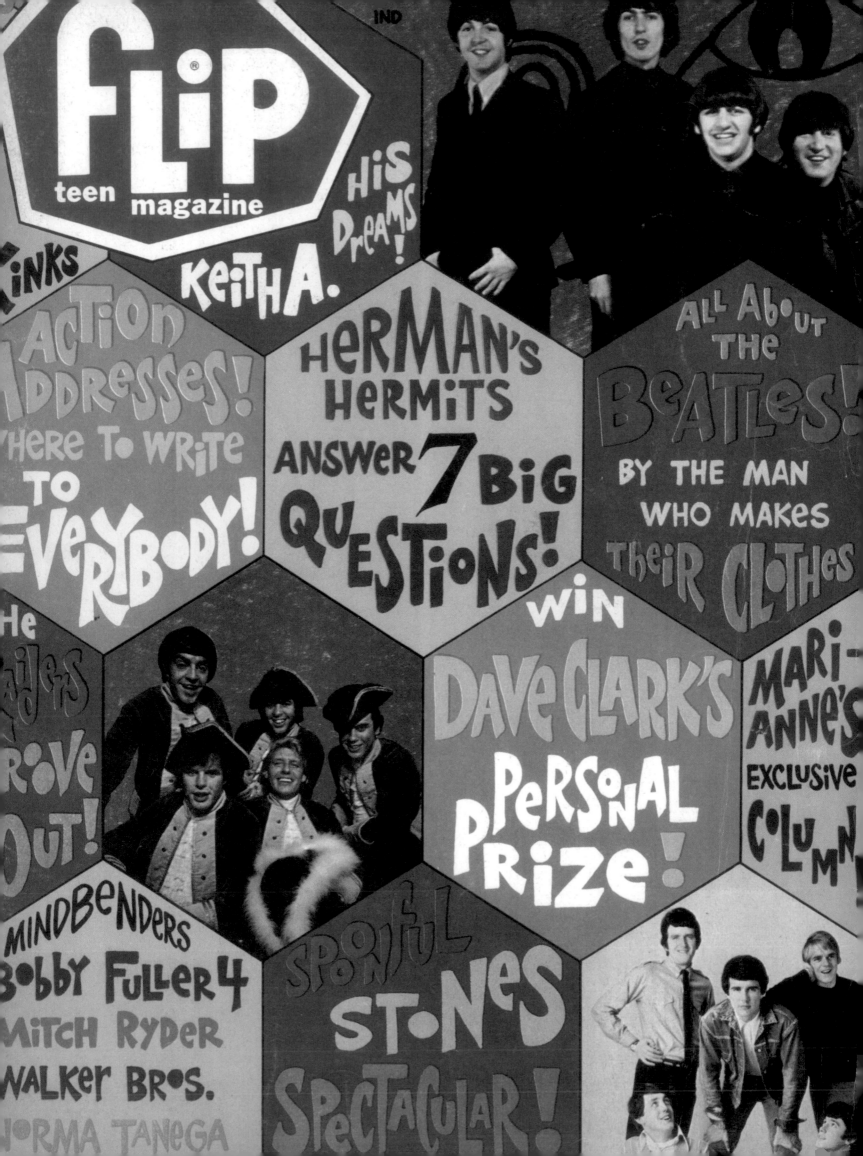

The competition between the two bands seems to have started informally as far back as 1965. The Beatles' *A Hard Day's Night*, released in August 1964 in the U.S.A., was matched in March 1965 by the release of *The Beach Boys Today*. It featured Brian Wilson's complex arrangements and is regarded by most people as the beginning of his mature period as a composer, with tracks like Help Me, Rhonda and When I Grow Up (to Be a Man). It is not known if John Lennon's title track on the *Help!* album, released in the U.S.A. on August 6, 1965, was inspired by tracks like these, but the Beatles were listening hard to the Beach Boys at the time.

The Beatles' *Rubber Soul*, released in the U.S.A. on December 6, 1965, was much more complex. It featured fuzz bass and a sitar, and contained songs like Norwegian Wood (This Bird Has Flown), You Won't See Me, and McCartney's Michelle. It is possible that Wilson had the British version of the album, which had a much stronger track selection, including Lennon's poignant Nowhere Man. Wilson was astonished and claimed that the album had "no poor tracks," which was unusual in the days when half the tracks on albums were fillers, and he said that the songs "went together like no album ever made before." He vowed to respond, telling his wife, "Marilyn, I'm going to make the greatest album, the greatest album ever made!"

He answered *Rubber Soul* with *Pet Sounds*, released May 16, 1966, an album that came as a bombshell to the Beatles. They were astonished, particularly by the robust instrumentation and beautiful harmonies. Tracks like Wouldn't It Be Nice and God Only Knows proved that rock was indeed an art form, capable of carrying the most subtle and delicate nuances of mood. McCartney has always cited it as his favorite album of all time, with God Only Knows as his all-time favorite song. The American public, however, was not interested: to them, the Beach Boys were a good-time surfer band.

When the Beatles' released *Revolver* in the U.S.A. on August 5, 1966, it included several references to the Beach Boys: Good Day Sunshine imitates their vocal style and For No One has a distinct Beach Boys feel to it. *Revolver* is regarded by many fans as the Beatles greatest album, better even than *Sgt. Pepper*, containing some complex tracks, such as Tomorrow Never Knows, which could only have been made in the studio. Wilson's Beach Boys then released the single Good Vibrations on October 10, 1966. It had originally been intended for *Pet Sounds* but was not ready in time. Supposedly including 35 edits, its masterful use of cello and theremin, its complex time changes, and its beautiful harmonies made it a million-seller in America, reaching number 1 in the *Billboard* charts in December 1966. Late in that year, Wilson began working on *Smile*, which was to be his masterwork, but mental problems intervened and the ambitious project had to be abandoned despite the fact that Capitol printed up 400,000 copies of the sleeve.

It is said that the turning point for *Smile* came when Wilson was driving in his car and Strawberry Fields Forever came on the radio. He pulled over to the side of the road to listen, and then went to tell the other Beach Boys, "You know what, guys, let's just forget it." A watered down version of the album was released as *Smiley Smile*, with none of the more ambitious tracks that Wilson had planned. An approximation of the original album was finally released in 2004.

When *Sgt. Pepper* was released in June 1967, Wilson retired to his indoor sand-pit as a beaten man, knowing that Beach Boys could never do anything as sophisticated. He recognized that even if he could envision something as good, he did not have the support of the rest of his band to create it.

THE MONKEES

The Monkees were not a musical act. We had very little to do with the music business and absolutely nothing to do with rock 'n' roll.
Michael Nesmith

Luv,
David Jones

WRITE TO DAVID AT COLPIX RECORDS, 1347 N. CAHUENGA BLVD., HOLLYWOOD, CALIF.

Here They Come

While the arrival of the Beatles and first wave of British bands prompted legions of imitators in America to spring up almost overnight, it wasn't until August 1966 that an act appeared who would seriously rival the Fab Four in the hearts, minds, and pockets of America's youth. When Last Train to Clarksville reached the number 1 slot on the *Billboard* Hot 100 it was still a month before the television show named after the "band" credited with the hit was to air. The Monkees owed a lot to the inspiration of the Beatles, although one of the show's creators, producer Bob Rafelson, claimed he had the original idea of putting together a TV show around a goofy rock band back in 1962. However, he "had a hard time selling it until The Beatles came along." More specifically, until the movie of *A Hard Day's Night* had been a huge success. Then Bob had his friend, producer Bert Schneider, sell the idea to Bert's dad, who happened to be the president of Columbia Pictures. Abe Schneider bought the idea from Bert and Bob's production company, Raybert, for Columbia's TV division, Screen Gems, to make.

In the fall of 1965, advertisements appeared in Hollywood papers for casting calls and by October Raybert had their band. They were: former child actor

Micky Dolenz (who had starred in the TV series *Circus Boy*); former child actor Davy Jones, by then a mildly successful singer after being inspired by witnessing the Beatles on *The Ed Sullivan Show* at first hand; Peter Thorkelson (known as Peter Tork), a member of Buffalo Fish whose Stephen Stills had suggested Thorkelson when he failed the audition himself; and Mike Nesmith, a Texan singer-songwriter suggested by Buffalo Springfield's manager, Barry Friedman.

Screen Gems had its own music production company, Screen Gems Music, which was run out of New York by Don Kirshner. He set two young songwriters the task of creating the songs and then recording the backing tracks for the Monkees' shows and debut album. They were Tommy Boyce and Bobby Hart and they came up with Last Train to Clarksville on being hired. "We knew this thing was going to be the American Beatles visually," Hart recalled, "and we assumed it made the most sense to do a Beatles-influenced sound—not a rip-off—musically." Hart was inspired to write the Monkees' first hit single when he heard the fade-out of the Beatles' Paperback Writer on the radio and thought it sounded as if they were singing about taking a train to somewhere. When he realized it had nothing to do with trains he came up with Last Train to Clarksville and by November 5, 1966, it was sitting at number 1 in the American singles chart.

The TV show had debuted by the time Clarksville hit the top, and it too was an immediate success. Each of the band members exuded a different personality, the storylines of the show made little sense but offered opportunity for laughs and physical fun. The band got to mime along to the songs, which were chosen for them and recorded with minimal input from them. Peter Noone of Herman's Hermits recalled, "I would say, 'My God, they've even got an English guy with the same accent as me. He's doing Herman better than Herman does it.'"

The Monkees meet Sammy Davis Jr., one of the old-style Hollywood all-singing, all-dancing, acting stars, as he moves with the times.

Not Your Steppin' Stone

The first eponymous Monkees album had been created by Kirshner in July 1966 using session players, with Jones, Dolenz, Tork, and Nesmith only providing the vocals for the recordings. It made number 1 in November 1966 and the Monkees were officially the first, true American challengers to the Beatles' supremacy. While Nesmith's contract had stipulated that he got to write and produce two songs for every album release, and that did indeed happen, it wasn't long before Tork also wanted to contribute songs to the show and recordings. Don Kirshner, who not only chose Clarksville as the band's first single but also picked Neil Diamond's I'm a Believer as the second (which also got to number 1) thought that he knew best what would succeed musically. He resisted Tork and Nesmith's requests to write and perform their own songs with the Monkees, and when he sanctioned the release of the Diamond-written A Little Bit Me, A Little Bit You in February 1967 (it reached number 2) instead of Nesmith's The Girl I Knew Somewhere (which was on the B-side), he was fired. The band had already shown dissent at Kirshner's level of control: when he released their second album, *More of The Monkees*, on which they had again only contributed vocals (the tracks were left over from the July 1966 sessions), they had threatened to quit. Obviously, since the TV show and record sales were only just beginning to take off, Screen Gems did not want to lose their stars and so got rid of Kirshner instead.

The Monkees number 1 hit; and they played all their own instruments!

From then on the Monkees played their own instruments and recorded with Chip Douglas—a bassist on many of their first recordings. Even Davy Jones got to shake a tambourine and maracas on some numbers. They hit number 1 on the charts with the third album, *Headquarters*, in June 1967 and toured America (with Jimi Hendrix as the opening act, of all people!). During breaks in the tour the band recorded songs for a new album and one, Pleasant Valley Sunday (written by Goffin and King), was released as a single in July 1967, reaching number 3. The album *Pisces, Aquarius, Capricorn & Jones Ltd.* hit the top of the album charts in December 1967 in what was to prove to be the high point of the Monkees' career.

In 1968, with ratings for the TV show failing and the band exerting more control over their activities, *The Monkees* television show was canceled. The band did not mind: they were putting all their creative energy into making a movie with Raybert and Jack Nicholson, the provocatively titled *Head*. A celluloid version of a psychedelic trip and representative of the burgeoning hippie scene of the day, the movie has no discernible plot or device to link disparate scenes that make

The Monkees was a straight sitcom. We weren't threatening.

PETER TORK

little sense. The film was a commercial failure (just as the Beatles' *Magical Mystery Tour* had been the same year). The year had begun well, however, with Daydream Believer (composed by John Stewart) topping the singles charts in December 1967, making it their third (and last) number 1 hit. The band began recording more songs for a new album in January 1968—but they took to recording their own songs with their own chosen musicians and not each other. *The Birds, The Bees and The Monkees* was released in April 1968 and became the first Monkees album to miss the top slot in the charts, reaching only third place, the same position that the single Valleri (Boyce-Hart), taken from the album, had reached in March. The soundtrack to *Head*, released six months later, only reached number 45. In December 1968, Peter Tork left the Monkees, and they never recovered.

In February 1969 the remaining three Monkees released their seventh album, *Instant Replay*, and it failed to make the top 30. In the same month, the single

With **Pisces, Aquarius, Capricorn, & Jones Ltd.** *the Monkees embraced flower power and produced what many regard as their finest album.*

Tear Drop City (Boyce-Hart) struggled to 56 in the charts. A year later Mike Nesmith left the Monkees and while Dolenz and Jones struggled on, producing another unheralded album (*Changes*, in June 1970), the band was over. For two-and-a-half years though, the Monkees had been almost as big as the Beatles even if their musical impact was negligible.

Other American Beatles-inspired bands proved to be far less successful. In an attempt to have it both ways, the Beatles manager Brian Epstein took to managing his own American band, an outfit called the Cyrkle in 1965 (the eccentric spelling was courtesy of John Lennon). They were discovered by Epstein's American partner, Nat Weiss, and they opened for the Beatles on their 1966 American tour along with the Ronettes. They had two chart singles on the strength of it: Red Rubber Ball, which made number 2 in June 1966, and Turn Down Day, which reached number 16 two months later. However, after a few flops they disbanded in 1967.

The Young Rascals

The Young Rascals also enjoyed the Beatles' patronage, although in a slightly less direct way than the Cyrkle. They formed out of Joey Dee and the Starliters in 1964 when Felix Cavaliere, Gene Cornish, and Eddie Brigati returned from a tour of Europe having played Dee's hit Peppermint Twist a few times too often, and decided to form their own band. Along with drummer Dino Danelli, they became the Young Rascals. They always admitted the Fab Four's influence on their peculiar look and raw R&B sound. "We always admired the Beatles because they proved that you could write great songs as well as play and sing them," said Gene Cornish.

At Shea Stadium in August 1965 the Young Rascals got to witness the Beatles playing their songs first-hand when they won a support slot, via their manager—also the gig's promoter—Sid Bernstein. Sid knew what made a great pop band and clothes were part of it, so he had the Young Rascals dress in knickerbocker trousers with matching pageboy-style, round-collared shirts worn with identical ties. They certainly looked original. "Before people remembered the name, they remembered the kids with the knickers," recalled Cornish.

However, before long people knew the name because of their hit singles. Their debut release for Atlantic Records, I Ain't Gonna Eat Out My Heart Anymore, had not troubled the top 40 in 1965, but their second release, Good Lovin', reached number 1 in February 1966 and was followed by two more hits, You Better Run (number 20 in May 1966) and I've Been Lonely Too Long (number 16 in February 1967). Once they were established, Cavaliere and Brigati, the band's songwriters, allowed their love of soul and R&B music, plus their growing social conscience, to dictate their sound and they became more original. By the time Groovin' became an international number 1 hit in April 1967 they had developed a uniquely soulful sound. In 1968, they had their third (and final) number 1 single, People Got To Be Free, dropped the 'Young' from their name (inserted previously because there was another band called the Rascals), and lost the knickers. The single hits dried up, but after the critically acclaimed hit–albums, *Groovin'* (number 5 in July 1967) and *Once Upon a Dream* (number 9 in February 1968), a greatest hits compilation called *Time Peace* made the number 1 slot on the *Billboard* albums chart in June 1968. The following year's *Freedom Suite*, full of anti-war protest soul, made number 17, but the band's last four albums failed to trouble the top 40 and they disbanded after Brigati and Cornish left (in 1970 and 1971 respectively).

ARE YOU FOR OR AGAINST?

Mick Jagger took the magazine and threw it against the wall. Keith Richard looked on with surprise. "Those bloody reporters," he sneered, "When are they going to run out of things to say about us!"

"Never," chortled Andrew Loog Oldham, smiling in the background. "You're stars now. You've got to take the bad with the good."

The good up to now has been the success the Stones have received internationally for their unbeatable talents in the record world.

The bad has been the unfair way the Stones have sometimes been treated by the press and outraged adults who insist on labeling these English wonders as the 'Bad Boys of the Music Business.'

It all started years ago when someone picked up the phrase, "Would you let your daughter go out with a Rolling Stone?" Since this time the Stones have not been regarded in the best circles as "those most likely to be honored by the Queen." And this is a far different case than their famous friends, The Beatles.

Nevertheless, The Stones have managed to gain the friendship of Ed Sullivan, who's notoriously hard on misbehaved singers. Their last concert tour in the United States was a smashing success. And according to a few hotels where the Stones stayed on their tour, their after hours performances were also smashing successes with hundreds of dollars in bills to be paid for property breakage.

Whether or not any of the stories told about the Stones' misbehavior is true, the boys still manage to have more Pro and Con statements hurled their way than any other group.

Here at TiGER BEAT, our daily mail is always flooded with them. Reprinted, without the names of course, are some of the more candid comments from our readers.

THOSE FOR THEM:

1. "The Stones are the one group in England with the true Soul Sound. They, alone, have captured the magic of the old-time Southern rhythm."

2. "I met Mick Jagger only once. He was as interested in me as I was in him. He took the time to not only sign my autograph book, but also he asked me questions about myself and what I was like as a person. At all times he was polite and a gentleman. His clothes were off-beat, but very neat and clean."

3. "If you've ever seen the Stones in person, you'll never forget them. They don't just come out and sing a few songs and then go back behind the curtains. They put on a real show. Each and everyone of them is a true professional. To see them is even better than to hear them, and you can't say that about most of the other groups who just come out and sing for 20 minutes and don't even move around."

8

4. "Keith Richard and Mick Jagger are as talented a songwriting team as Lennon and McCartney. This year will prove that they have a talent that is unbeatable in every respect. Just listen to their new recordings and you'll discover what I mean."

5. 'The Stones are current. They're up-to-date about every subject. When they're questioned on anything from religion to music, they have a good answer. They are informed."

6. *"They don't brag about it, but the Stones are very good to their parents. I know for a fact that each of them conducts themselves in a well-behaved way toward adults."*

7. "Mick Jagger gives pleasure to so many people by really giving everything he has to a song. True, he's sexy, but that's just Mick putting his all into his work so that audiences will enjoy themselves and for a little while forget the troubles of the world."

8. "This isn't something that the Stones brag about, but I happen to know that the last time they were here in town, Keith personally phoned an invalid girl who had been sick for years. After she heard his voice, the girl began to improve. Now, she's almost well. Don't tell me the Stones are Godless boys."

9. **"Someone who's gifted with rhythm like Mick just can't help himself. Anyone who has natural rhythm like this is fortunate. There's nothing wrong with his movements."**

10. **"Charlie Watts doesn't brag about it, but he's a wonderful husband. I know a girl who is friends with his wife and she tells me about all the sweet things Charlie does for his wife while he's on tour. He calls her every day without fail no matter where they are and talks for as long as he wants. When he gets home he always brings the most beautiful gifts. I wonder how many girls have husbands as thoughtful as Charlie."**

11. "At a concert in California, I saw a fan throw a medal that hit Brian in the face. Though it cut him, Brian simply laughed this off and picked the medal up and put it in his pocket saying 'thank you.' I've seen this happen to other groups and they aren't nearly as polite about it. Some, whom I could mention by name, get furious and throw things back at the fans. I say, hooray, for the Stones."

12. "My girlfriend and I were in Florida when the Stones were there and we went to their hotel to try to meet them. We met Andrew Loog Oldham in the lobby and we asked him if we could see the Stones. He was wonderful to us and said they were up in their room. He not only told us we could meet them, but he took us up to the room and personally introduced us. They were all charming to us and I can truthfully say I've never had a better time."

Well, that's just a sampling of controversy over the Stones. As far as we're concerned, any group which stirs up this much comment must have talent and a lot to offer. Otherwise, they'd be totally overlooked. What's your opinion of the Stones? Are you For or Against?

9

Get Off Of My Cloud

To the relief of many American bands the Beatles stopped touring in 1966, but their place was then taken by the Rolling Stones. After recovering from the death of Brian Jones on July 3, 1969, they made the American stadium circuit their own after reasserting their position in the charts with a number 3 and a pair of number 1s: Jumpin' Jack Flash from 1968, Honky Tonk Women in 1969.

After touring the U.S.A. in June and July 1966, the Stones stayed away from the circuit until November and December 1969, when they played 24 concerts in 15 cities, culminating with the disastrous free concert on December 6, 1969, at the Altamont Speedway in Livermore, California, where an estimated 300,000 to 500,000 fans attended what was hoped would be a new Woodstock West. The lineup included Santana, Jefferson Airplane, the Flying Burrito Brothers, and Crosby, Stills, Nash & Young. The Grateful Dead were supposed to play but left, appalled at the violence precipitated by the Hells Angels who had parked their bikes next to the stage and then outraged when one got knocked over.

The Stones had hired the Angels as security on the recommendation of the Grateful Dead and assumed all would be well. This was not the case: sporadic violence flared up, egos were bruised, and Marty Balin from Jefferson Airplane was knocked unconscious while onstage by one of the Angels. During the Stones' set, one of the fans, 18-year-old Meredith Hunter, got involved in a fight with the Angels and drew a gun. He was stabbed and then kicked to death by them. The Stones did not realize that anyone had been killed and continued with their set, even though they were interrupted several times. Subsequently, Hells Angel Sonny Barger boasted that he held a gun to Keith Richards and told him to, "Keep playing or you're dead." Keith Richards recalled:

> It felt great and sounded great. Then there's a big ruckus about one of the Angels' bikes being knocked over in front of the stage. Oh dear, a bike's got knocked over. I'm not used to bein' upstaged by Hells Angels—over somebody's motorbike. Yes, I perfectly understand that your bike's got knocked over, can we carry on with the concert? But they're not like that. They have a whole thing going with their bikes, as we all know now.

The alleged murderer, Alan Passaro, was acquitted by the jury as acting in self defense, though none of the violence would have even happened had the

Opposite: After their first couple of hit singles the Stones were treated by teen mags and merchandisers as the second Beatles. It didn't last as long as it did for the Fab Four, though.

Above: After losing Brian Jones, The Rolling Stones played a string of American shows in 1969 with a new guitarist, having shed their teen following along with their deceased founder member. From left: Charlie Watts, Mick Taylor, Mick Jagger, Keith Richards, and Bill Wyman.

Hells Angels not been at the concert. The Stones did not return to the States again to perform until 1971.

The Stones' influence on American bands was less obvious than their Liverpudlian rivals, but no less strong. Their influence was also brought to bear later, with bands such as Aerosmith, the New York Dolls, and Spirit all beginning in the shadow of the golden-era Stones, between 1969 and 1973. Later, artists like Steely Dan, Guns n' Roses, and Foo Fighters would acknowledge the impact of the Stones on their sound and look: "elegantly wasted."

Perhaps because Jagger and Richards' songwriting remained true to their R&B, blues, country, and rock 'n' roll roots—becoming darker, more explicit, and flirting with occult imagery—they did not influence as many mainstream artists as the Beatles. However, because of their longevity and adherence to the "rebel" stance that they began with, they have become an enduring part of the great rock 'n' roll mythology.

As long as both the Beatles' and Stones' music is played on radios around the world, it's likely that they'll continue to influence young musicians—that is, for as long as there are young musicians with electric guitars and drums.

Below left: Hells Angels, acting as "security" at the Rolling Stones Altamont show, quieted some troublemakers in the crowd.

Right: Recorded in New York in 1969, the Rolling Stones' second live album release captures the band almost as they were, with new guitarist Mick Taylor—although some overdubs cleaned up the odd bum note for the record. That's drummer Charlie Watts with the donkey, in a photograph taken by David Bailey.

'GET YER YA-YA'S OUT!'
The Rolling Stones in concert

LOVE OR CONFUSION

AFTER THE BEATLES RELEASED Sgt. Pepper's Lonely Hearts Club Band *in 1967, a clear division took place in the world of pop music. While many of the songs on the album could have been released as singles, it was not just a collection of songs put together on a 33 1/3 r.p.m. disc. There was a theme to the album that prompted buyers to listen to it all the way through, rather than just cut to the songs they liked best. As already mentioned, the Beatles had a policy—not adhered to by their American record company—of never including singles on albums because they reckoned, accurately, that the fans already had them. This allowed them the freedom to develop their albums as a separate form, segueing tracks into one another, including tracks that would have been too long to issue as a single and, in the case of Sgt. Pepper, even adding a reprise.*

The album stopped everyone in their tracks. For weeks the music drifted through the doors of boutiques and shops, from apartment windows, and from students' rooms. It was impossible to avoid it at parties and it gave British musicians food for thought. Within days of its release, Jimi Hendrix had worked up his own arrangement of the title track which he premiered at Brian Epstein's Saville Theatre, to the great pride and satisfaction of Paul McCartney who was in the audience. More importantly, it represented rock's coming of age.

OFFICIAL BEATLES FAN CLUB

A DIVISION OF APPLE MUSIC INC.

For membership, send your $2.50 annual dues to THE OFFICIAL BEATLES FAN CLUB, P.O. Box 505, Radio City Station, New York, N.Y. 10019. If you wish information on how to start your own chapter, send a stamped self-addressed envelope to the same address, writing CHAPTER INFO on the outside, or a stamped self-addressed envelope writing PHOTOS AND SPECIALS INFO, if that is your interest.

DEAR BEATLE PEOPLE:

I would like to start off this newsletter by saying that I do hope you all had a very Merry Christmas and Happy New Year. I know I am a bit late with these wishes, but since we had no newsletter in the last issue please accept these wishes from all of us here at headquarters at this late date. As you can see from our new logo, we have changed our policy at headquarters by bringing the fan club to new heights and bringing you the "1970 BEATLES". We have received hundreds upon hundreds of letters saying how groovy the new X-Mas is and we are again proud that we could bring it to all of you. We are sorry that there was a delay in mailing the records out, but with all our fans eager to receive it, we truly did our best. We are now mailing out the 1970 OFFICIAL BEATLES FAN CLUB book to all new members and renewed members. We hope you dig it along with the groovy, out-of-sight new 1970 membership card and offers for great new pics, posters and goodies for the new year. We still have plenty of X-Mas records left and if you are not a member of the fan club, we ask that you mail in your annual $2.50 to us and we will send you your record, the new book and everything else you would be entitled to as a member.

BEATLE PICS: For the new year we now have in addition to our regulars Superpix, an additional six great new photos. They are numbered #19 through 24 . . . You can get all six of these new photos by ordering #25 on our photo list, which is a complete combination of numbers 19 through 24. You can also order #1 INDIA, #2 THE McCARTNEYS, #3 HELLO GOODBYE, #4 STRAWBERRY FIELDS — PENNY LANE, #5 RELAXATION TIME, #6 THE COMPOSERS, #7 GONE WITH THE WIND, #8 THE INVADERS, #9A PAUL, #9B PAUL, #10A JOHN, #10B JOHN, #11A GEORGE, #11B GEORGE, #12A RINGO, #12B RINGO, #13 REVOLUTION,, #14 THE FAB FOUR, #15 NEW TWO-SOME, #16 HEY JUDE, #17 GARDEN MEDITATION, #18 GROUP INSPIRATION as well as our PAUL SPECIAL and JOHN SPECIAL and brand new RINGO SPECIAL. We are also still selling our GROOVY COUPLE PIC, George and his wife Pattie. The APPLE POSTER is still going strong as well as our MAGICAL MYSTERY TOUR photo and the CONCERT

BOOKS from 1964, 65 and 66. We are selling in addition to the above the 1969 BEATLES USA LTD. booklet, which we gave out to all members and the 1969 Spring "REVOLUTION" POSTER. Just send a self-addressed, stamped envelope to us at headquarters requesting "PHOTO INFO" and we will send you ALL the advertisements and coupons so that you can obtain these groovy photos. I suggest though that you order your photos NOW so you don't miss out on anything!! Photo info is sent upon request to members and non-members alike. Prices differ for members and non-members. We will soon be discontinuing the sale of photos to non-members as we feel that only fans who are members of the club should be entitled to these groovy we offer.

FAN CLUB NOTES: One thing that hasn't changed is that we have asked before and are still asking that you PLEASE PLEASE always place your membership number in the top left hand corner of your envelope when you write to the club. If you don't abide by our wishes we might not reply to your letter. We have over 40,000 fans and cannot stop and check to see if someone who writes has a membership number or not, so if you would like a reply, please help us here at headquarters by abiding by our policy and wishes. Many of you have either been putting your number inside or on the back of your envelope or omitting it altogether and we find it extremely difficult when sorting the mail. It is absolutely imperative that your membership number ALWAYS appears in the proper place!!

REMEMBER, we have an area secretary for the following states and if you live in any of these states please write to your area secretary instead of to headquarters. YOU WILL RECEIVE A MUCH MORE PROMPT REPLY. BE SURE TO SEND ALL PHOTO ORDERS TO HEADQUARTERS ONLY! Our Area Secretaries to help you are:

ALABAMA: Mr. Bobby Hudgins—3612 Kingshill Rd.; Birmingham 35223
ARIZONA: Patti Porcaro—939 E. Rose Lane; Phoenix 85014
CALIF. (NORTH): Joann Maloney—Freeborn Hall; Room 212; University of California; 2650 Durant Ave.; Berkeley, Calif. 94720
CALIF. (SOUTH): Patti O'Neil—5360 Oceanview Blvd.; La Canada 91011
CANADA: Joan Thompson—36 Scotia Avenue; Scarborough; Ontario; Canada
COLORADO: Eve Birgen—8031 Stuart Place; Westminster 80030
CONNECTICUT: Fran Tilewick—545 River Road; Hamden 06518

Just as opera, cinema, and photography all started as popular forms of entertainment before developing into "fine art" (or at least developing a fine-art arm), so rock 'n' roll now ranged across the spectrum from bubblegum music to A Day in the Life. A whole raft of musicians seized this new freedom to experiment and develop new forms, and explored new directions in rock. These were the bands of the so-called second wave of British groups to "invade" the U.S.A., made up of musicians empowered by the Beatles but not copying them in any way except in intention. Some bands, of course, were part of the transitional phase. One such was the Hollies.

Can't Let Go

The year preceding *Sgt. Pepper* had introduced the Hollies to America. They were the second most successful singles band in Britain throughout the sixties, with 22 top 40 records between 1964 and 1970. Their career in the U.S.A. took longer to get off the ground but they still managed 13 in the top 100 singles during the same period.

Although part of the original invasion, the Hollies were never just Beatles imitators: they produced exciting, beautifully crafted pop songs with skillfully layered sound and changes of texture, which were most of all characterized by their innovative use of high three-part harmonies that were much copied by other groups—and by many newly emerging heavy-metal bands in particular. Their U.S.A. breakthrough came with Bus Stop, which made number 3 on both sides of the Atlantic in 1966.

By concentrating so much on the singles market though, the Hollies never developed the parallel album market that the Beatles were to achieve. This was, as usual, not helped by the commercial attitudes of their American label, Capitol, who removed tracks and mixed up material so that the American L.P. releases bore little relation to the British originals. Their second American single, Stop, Stop, Stop, made number 7, followed by Look Through Any Window at 32, and I Can't Let Go at 42, all in 1966. Carrie Anne was released in 1967 and reached number 9.

At the time of writing the Hollies are one of the few British Invasion bands still in existence—although there was a major lineup change in 1968. Unlike the other band members, singer Graham Nash had developed a deep interest in the hippie counter-culture then emerging on the West Coast and in London, which was having a massive affect on the British music scene from the Beatles and Stones to the Animals and Donovan. And, though he was proud of his well-made songs, Nash wanted to produce something more serious. No one ever listened to Hollies songs for their meaningful lyrics and he wanted to change that. Tensions grew within the group and came to a head over plans to release an entire album

The plan to record an entire album of Dylan songs was the breaking point for Graham Nash who left the Hollies to join Crosby, Stills & Nash.

I don't feel like a superstar at all.

GRAHAM NASH

of Dylan covers (it was released as *Words & Music by Bob Dylan* in the States; their versions managed to sound both pointless and terrific). The break came in December 1968 when Nash was made an offer he could not refuse by his friend David Crosby of the Byrds, who invited him to join a new group he was putting together. The other group member was Stephen Stills from Buffalo Springfield. Crosby, Stills & Nash is generally regarded as the first true supergroup in that all three members had previously been in very successful bands. The trio represented the paradigm shift that had occurred within the music business by the end of the decade (they were joined by Neil Young in late 1969, just in time for the four of them to play only their second gig together at Woodstock).

The Hollies continued without Nash. In 1969 Sorry Suzanne reached number 56 in the American charts, and the follow-up, 1970's He Ain't Heavy, He's My Brother, once more put them in the top 10, peaking at number 7. They continued to find American success in the seventies with Long Cool Woman in a Black Dress and The Air That I Breathe both reaching the top 10.

The Hollies, photographed just before Graham Nash (center) left the band. The remaining members carried on performing and recording without him, enjoying some success.

IAN WHITCOMB

Ian Whitcomb was yet another of the British public school boys (meaning private schools) who had a hit in America and liked the country so much he stayed there, settling in Los Angeles. He reached number 8 in the Billboard charts in July 1965 with You Turn Me On but turned from rock 'n' roll to a career as a writer, producer and ukulele player. He never charted in Britain.

PLAYABLE ON **STEREO** & MONO PHONOGRAPHS

SOCK ME SOME ROCK | IAN WHITCOMB

Hound Dog
Sock the Rock
Louie, Louie
High Blood Pressure
Rockin' Pneumonia
Bye, Bye
The Noteable Yacht Club of Staines
The Naked Ape
The Star
Heroes of the Rocker Pack

tower

MEET

IAN WHITCOMB

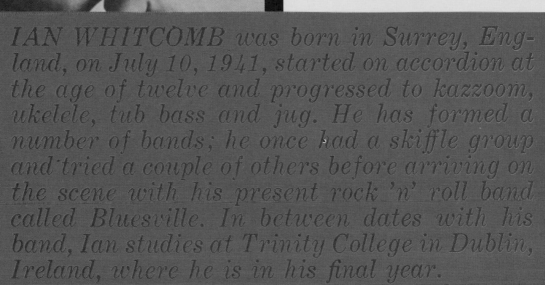

IAN WHITCOMB was born in Surrey, England, on July 10, 1941, started on accordion at the age of twelve and progressed to kazzoom, ukelele, tub bass and jug. He has formed a number of bands; he once had a skiffle group and tried a couple of others before arriving on the scene with his present rock 'n' roll band called Bluesville. In between dates with his band, Ian studies at Trinity College in Dublin, Ireland, where he is in his final year.

Personal facts: Ian's hair is long and mouse-colored, his weight is 170 pounds, his favorite recording artists include Max Morath, Bob Darch, George Formby, Roy Orbison, the Beatles and Chuck Berry, the people he admires include Groucho Marx, and his ambition is to play music the way he likes it.

Cream Rises to the Top

Though Cream, the first of the power trios in rock, lasted only from July 1966 to November 1968, they were of enormous influence, particularly on all the heavy-metal bands that followed in their substantial wake: forty years later, posters of grimacing groups with ultra long hair who sing in high falsetto vocals could still be found in teenage bedrooms throughout the world, though the protagonists could as easily be Scandinavian or British as American.

Predating Crosby, Stills & Nash, Cream can also lay claim to being the first supergroup. The lineup was guitarist Eric Clapton from the Yardbirds and John Mayall's Bluesbreakers; bass player Jack Bruce, also from the Bluesbreakers and previously from Alexis Korner's Blues Incorporated and the Graham Bond Organization; and drummer Ginger Baker, who was also from Blues Incorporated and the Graham Bond Organization.

The Cream rose to the top. Their powerhouse, improvisational heavy-rock sound, incorporating absurdly long, self-indulgent solos, appealed to a mass audience and their first album, *Fresh Cream*, found success on both sides of the Atlantic, reaching number 39 in America in 1967, followed later that year by

The Cream are a threesome which is surely aptly named, for when they formed themselves together in July, 1966, it was widely recognised that each member was an outstanding performer. Ginger Baker had played drums with many top outfits on the scene. Eric Clapton was a guitar ace who had been with the Yardbirds and John Mayall. Jack Bruce—bass player, singer and harmonica expert—had shown his talents with the Manfreds, John Mayall and the Graham Bond Organisation.

First public performance by The Cream was a week or two after their formation. It was at the sixth National Jazz and Blues Festival at Windsor, Berks. They received a wonderful ovation from a discerning audience. Their first disc didn't come out till the following October—on the Reaction label. It was called "Wrapping Paper". It hit the charts only three weeks later.

To prove this was no fluke, The Cream also had a long chart run with their follow-up, "I Feel Free." Talent had triumphed for sure!

Now for some personal details about the boys.

Ginger Baker: Born August 19, 1939, in Lewisham, London. Is a gifted painter and sculptor. His main hobby is stamp collecting. His tastes in music are "the widest possible".

Jack Bruce: Born May 14, 1943, in Glasgow. Spent some of his childhood in Canada, some in Italy. Studied at Royal Scottish Academy of Music. Says he wouldn't mind playing Hamlet!

Eric Clapton: Born October 8, 1944, in Ripley, Surrey. Went to Kingston Art School, Surrey. Says if ever his career as musician falters, he would like to become a painter.

The Cream

The last year with Cream was just agony. It's damaged my hearing permanently.

GINGER BAKER

Disraeli Gears which made number 4 and became one of the top-selling albums of 1968. This was a period of transition, before the full impact of *Sgt. Pepper*, when singles were still regarded by the industry as the only possible way to break an album. 1968 saw two American top 10 singles for the band: Sunshine of Your Love, which got to number 5, and White Room, which reached number 6.

Unfortunately, their management toured them endlessly, which exacerbated the personal differences between Bruce and Baker. Bruce later claimed: "They just worked us too hard. By the time we were a success, we were all fed up with each other." Baker said: "Eric said to me, 'I've had enough of this,' and I said, 'So have I.' I couldn't stand it." They played a farewell concert at the Royal Albert Hall on November 26, 1968, a live recording of which reached number 2 in the *Billboard* charts in 1969. Their greatest American success, however, was 1968's *Wheels of Fire*, a double album with a sumptuous silver and black psychedelic sleeve designed by Eric Clapton's King's Road roommate Martin Sharp, the designer of *Oz* magazine who was also responsible for the colorful collage sleeve of *Disraeli Gears*. Despite being a double album, and therefore more expensive, *Wheels of Fire* made number 1.

By that time Clapton and Baker had already moved on from Cream, joining Ric Grech from Family and Stevie Winwood from Traffic to form Blind Faith. They lasted less than a year, broken, as before, by the rigors of an extensive American tour. Before they had even officially split, Clapton had already flown off to join John Lennon in Toronto for his impromptu Plastic Ono Band concert of June 1969, and then to join the American group Delaney & Bonnie and Friends on tour as one of the friends.

The differences between British and American acts were breaking down. Jimi Hendrix was playing with two British musicians, Graham Nash was in a band with two Americans: "rock," as it was now known, was seen more and more as a transatlantic community of like-minded musicians, their families, and friends. As the decade grew to a close, hundreds of British musicians moved to Los Angeles, mostly to Laurel Canyon and its surrounding wooded lanes, and a good number of Americans settled in Britain.

Cream at the beginning of their time together, and before they adopted more colorful outfits. From left: Eric Clapton, Jack Bruce, Ginger Baker.

Shades of Deep Purple

Deep Purple was the first of the British heavy-metal bands to profit from the breakup of Cream. They had toured America as a support act for Cream on the trio's "Goodbye" tour, establishing their connection with the band and their natural right of succession with Cream's audiences. In October 1968, while still touring with Cream, they had an American number 4 hit with a cover version of Joe South's Hush, which helped to lift their debut album, *Shades of Deep Purple*, to number 24 in the *Billboard* album chart. In 1969 they released two more albums in the U.S.A: *The Book of Taliesyn* (number 54) and *Deep Purple* (number 162), but then their record label, comedian Bill Cosby's Tetragrammaton, went bankrupt and the group were left stranded until Warner Brothers took over their contract. Deep Purple went through many lineup changes—for a while featuring the classic lineup of Ritchie Blackmore (guitar), Jon Lord (keyboards), Roger Glover (bass), Ian Paice (drums), and Ian Gillan on vocals—which meant that they never had the immediate recognition enjoyed by the Beatles or Stones.

Primarily thought of as heavy-metal pioneers, they were also at the forefront of British progressive rock. They recorded with orchestras and incorporated many classical elements into their work, usually courtesy of Jon Lord who composed their *Concerto for Group and Orchestra,* which was performed at the Royal Albert Hall in September 1969 with the Royal Philharmonic Orchestra. (It was released in the U.S.A. in December 1969 but made little impact on the Christmas album market, reaching only number 149 in the *Billboard* charts.)

Below: Deep Purple experienced an unusually large number of lineup changes. Perhaps because, as singer Ian Gillan said: "You can only be Ritchie Blackmore's backing group for so long."

Right: Three months to record with a string section: The Book of Taliesyn was at the forefront of prog rock.

In Rock

Many acts, usually those who did not write their own material, were unable to convert to becoming album bands and fell by the wayside as fans of rock music abandoned the pop market, perceiving it as being only for female teenage fans. Rock 'n' roll, which used to be largely entertainment and fun, now became the voice of a generation, dealing with the issues of the day, exploring relationships in ways unknown to the brigade of early sixties songwriters. By the late sixties, songs written by young bands in both Britain and America dealt with drugs, alienation, loneliness, and taking a stand against the Vietnam War and all wars—the everyday experiences of the sixties generation. This trend was to culminate in the

Jimmy Page, Robert Plant, and John Paul Jones of Led Zeppelin provide the signature long-hair look that was to dominate heavy metal bands from their time on.

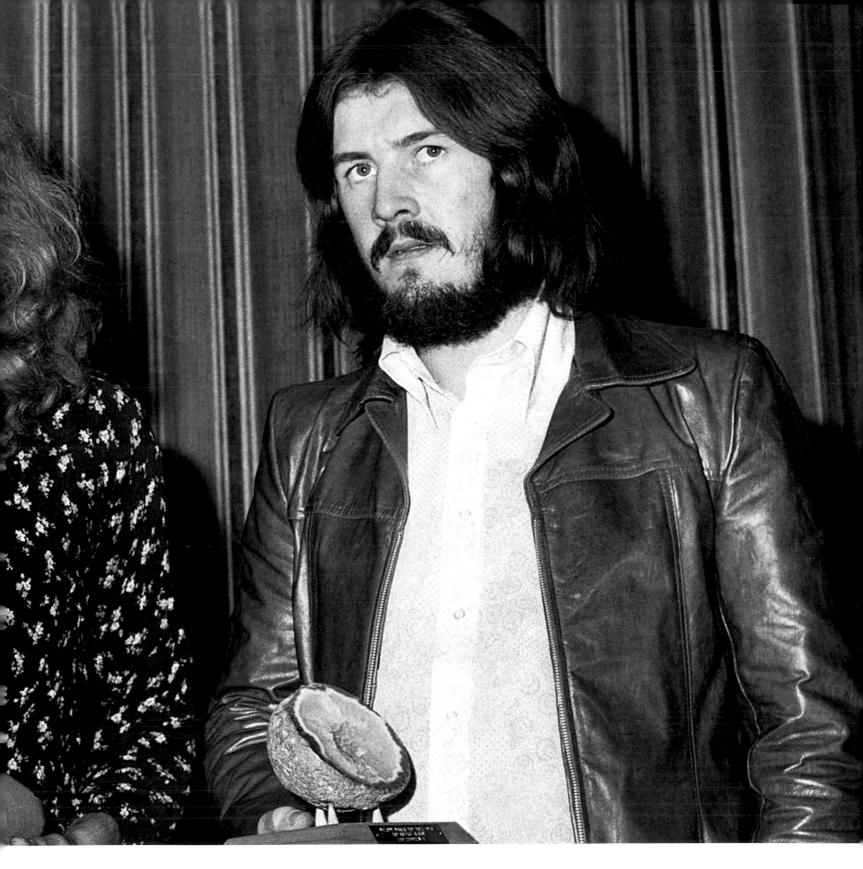

singer-songwriter movement of the early seventies which saw rock 'n' roll as a fully formed art form of its own. Whereas Phil Spector had attempted—sometimes successfully—to create an entire opera in three minutes, bands like the Who now stretched their opera out over an entire album, exploring different aspects of a theme, sometimes using a symphony orchestra or unusual instrumentation to assist them.

After *Sgt. Pepper*, any band hoping to sell to the white middle-class college kids had to make albums. Some groups, such as Pink Floyd or Led Zeppelin, refused to release singles as a way of distancing themselves from the pop market and of declaring themselves as something altogether more serious. Led Zeppelin

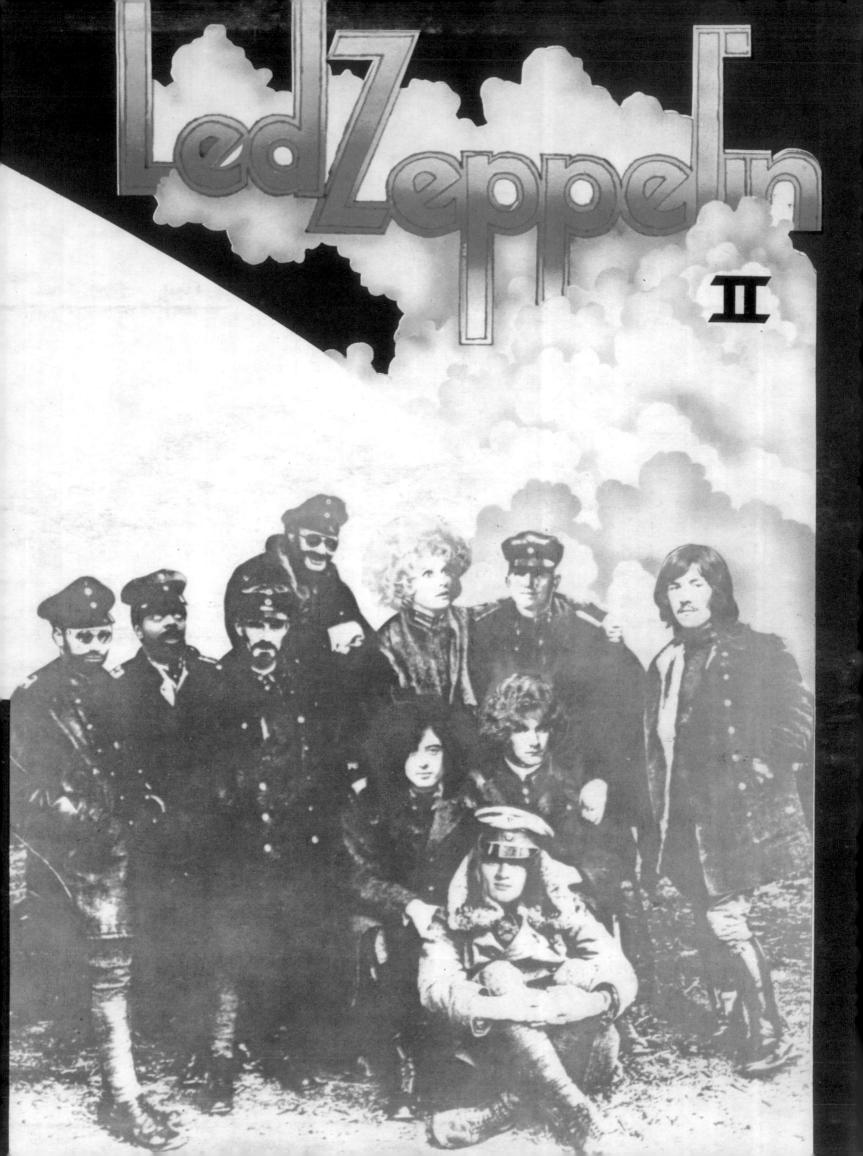

resisted tremendous pressure from their record company to release Stairway to Heaven, from their *Led Zeppelin IV* album, as a single in 1971, and were vindicated by the fact that the album went on to sell more than 23 million copies in the U.S.A. alone (and more than 37 million worldwide). That success was in part because it was the only way for fans to get their hands on the song, which was receiving massive airplay on college and FM stations (and it still does).

Led Zeppelin were among the first of the heavy-metal bands and though they had most of their success during the period from 1972 to 1977 when they dubbed themselves "The biggest band in the world," a title the Rolling Stones no doubt disputed—they began as a second-wave British Invasion act. Their name came from the Who's Keith Moon and John Entwistle who, together with Jimmy Page and Jeff Beck, were discussing the idea of putting together a group when Moon commented, "It would probably go over like a lead balloon," which was amended by Entwistle to "a lead Zeppelin." Formed in 1968 by Jimmy Page on guitar (having left the Yardbirds), singer Robert Plant, John Paul Jones on bass and keyboards, and drummer John Bonham, Led Zeppelin typified the self-indulgent, guitar-oriented, blues-influenced, heavy-rock bands of the seventies.

Their first American concert was on December 26, 1968, in Denver, Colorado, designed to promote their first, eponymous album, released two weeks later. Led Zeppelin's appeal was very much aimed at the underground counter-culture and college kids. They had the longest hair, the most groupies, the nastiest manager, their solos were the longest—one drum solo is rumored to have lasted more than a quarter-hour—and their private lives were rumored to be a bit sinister. They were perfect role models for the new anti-war, pro-pot, free-loving generation. *Led Zeppelin II*, released in October 1969, gave them their first American number 1 and sold half-a-million copies in its first year of release.

Opposite: Led Zeppelin's second album went to number 1, thereby establishing them as the leaders of blues-based heavy metal.

Below: Led Zeppelin's first album sleeve, showing the crash of the LZ129 Hindenburg Zeppelin on May 6, 1936, in New Jersey. It caused controversy when the Zeppelin family objected.

Which One's Pink?

Perhaps even more of an album band than Led Zeppelin, Pink Floyd tended to perform whole albums at concerts and seamlessly joined up their songs so that people would often relate to entire sides of albums rather than individual songs. Pink Floyd rejected the cult of personality, preferring to remain relatively anonymous, despite their fame, developing the idea of the band rather than its individual members, something which these days would be seen as branding but which was then seen as more of an artistic impulse.

Though very much a part of the second wave of British bands, Pink Floyd did not really have much impact on the American market until 1973 when *Dark Side of the Moon* shot up the album charts, staying in the *Billboard* charts for more than 400 weeks, longer than any other album in rock history. Their 1967 debut album release *The Piper at the Gates of Dawn* reached only number 131 on the

The album cover for Piper at the Gates of Dawn. Pink Floyd's first album did not trouble the American Top 100 but it became something of a cult album among American fans of psychedelia.

charts, but a small band of aficionados of psychedelic pop gave them some American support. Sales were not helped by the fact that Capitol left off three of the best tracks: Flaming, Bike, and Astronomy Domine.

The Floyd flew to America to promote the album, opening their tour at the Fillmore West in San Francisco on October 26, 1967. Sadly, by this time, the combination of schizophrenia and a prodigious intake of L.S.D. and other drugs had rendered their main songwriter, singer, and lead guitarist, Syd Barrett, very unstable. As Roger Waters later commented: "That tour was an amazing disaster. Syd by this time was completely off his head." They appeared on Dick Clark's *American Bandstand* but "Syd wasn't into moving his lips that day." After he refused to speak a word to the host on *The Pat Boone Show*, their management canceled the rest of the tour. Even celebrated sixties' "anti-psychiatrist" R. D. Laing pronounced Syd as "incurable." On March 2, 1968 he left the band and, after a couple of solo albums, returned to his old love, painting. He was replaced by his old school friend from Cambridge, David Gilmore, and the new lineup went on to conquer the world of prog rock.

The Pink Floyd in archetypal psychedelic pose. From left: Roger Waters, Syd Barrett, Nick Mason, and Rick Wright.

Mellow Troubadour

When Donovan (Donovan Leitch) first appeared on the scene he was unfairly compared with Bob Dylan, largely because they had both developed their style from the same influences: Woody Guthrie and Ramblin' Jack Elliott. However, even though he was clearly influenced by Dylan's first two albums, Donovan was far from being a Dylan clone. In 1965 he had three chart singles in the U.S.A: Catch the Wind (number 23), Colours (number 61), and Universal Soldier (number 53), which established the strong anti-war message that would feature in all his later work. In 1966, after escaping his original management contract, he teamed up with record producer Mickie Most, the man responsible for the success of the Animals and Herman's Hermits.

Donovan was one of the first British musicians to incorporate the hippie/flower-power message into his music and his first collaboration with Most, Sunshine Superman, is sometimes referred to as the first psychedelic record, with its overt reference to L.S.D. and its spacey atmosphere. The single

English rock 'n' rollers, and even folk musicians, liked to raid the dressing-up box. A rare picture of Donovan in Byronic mode.

went to number 1 in America in 1966, proof of Mickie Most's commercial acumen and of Donovan's prescient understanding of the way the mood of moment was changing. That year's follow-up, Mellow Yellow, rose to number 2, and the *Sunshine Superman* album had advance orders of a quarter-million copies, reaching number 11 in the charts. It became known as one of the most enduring albums of the psychedelic era, combining an eclectic range of instruments, including the first extensive use of a sitar on a pop album, as well as other Indian instruments such as the tablas. The album, which blended elements of folk music, jazz, and chamber music, contained the song Season of the Witch, inspiring producer Joe Boyd to name his record company Witchseason (the label featured Incredible String Band, Fairport Convention, and Nick Drake).

In 1967 Donovan released the first rock box-set, *A Gift from a Flower to a Garden*, which reached 19 on the charts and eventually went gold even though Columbia chief Clive Davies had insisted that the two albums also be available separately. It was a classic work of psychedelia, with a sleeve featuring Donovan dressed in flowing velvet robes and holding flowers and peacock feathers. The back sleeve showed him holding hands with the Maharishi Mahesh Yogi, and early in 1968 he joined the Beatles, their wives and girlfriends, as well as Mike Love from the Beach Boys, on a meditation retreat at the Maharishi's ashram in Rishikesh. It was here that Donovan taught McCartney and Lennon the claw-hammer pluck method of guitar-picking and also where he wrote his 1968 hit Jennifer Juniper about Pattie Boyd's sister, who was also on the trip. The single reached number 26 in the U.S.A. and number 2 in Britain.

Donovan continued to make gentle folk-rock hippie records throughout the sixties: Susan on the West Coast Waiting made number 35 in 1969 and the even more hippie ballad Atlantis reached number 7. In late 1969 the growing antagonism between Donovan and Mickie Most resulted in a split—Most objected to "too many hangers on" in the studio—and Donovan never again achieved such commercial success. His innocent, peaceful folk ballads helped define the hippie scene in the U.S.A. and Britain, and helped pave the way for other solo-performing artists to play in front of audiences more used to seeing and hearing full electric bands.

Below left: Donovan in Concert, *released in August 1968, reached the Top 20 partly for its live version of his hit Mellow Yellow.*

Below right: **A Gift From a Flower to a Garden** *was the first rock 'n' roll box set and reached the Top 20, to the great surprise of Columbia Records.*

ARTHUR BROWN

Donovan and Eric Burdon and the Animals of the San Franciscan Nights period were the two main British psychedelic acts to impact on America in the late sixties, but there was a third act to successfully transfer to the States: the Crazy World of Arthur Brown, albeit for only one single and album. Brown, a psychology graduate from the University of Reading, came to fame at the London underground club U.F.O., where Pink Floyd and Soft Machine were the other house bands. He was a precursor of Kiss, painting his face into a black-and-white mask. He wore flowing robes and a flaming head-dress that sometimes had to be extinguished by pouring beer over him if his hair caught fire (below).

His showstopper was a number appropriately called Fire, and Pete Townshend, a regular visitor to the U.F.O. club, persuaded his record company to release it, with Townshend producing. Fire reached number 2 in the American charts in 1968, and the subsequent album, The Crazy World of Arthur Brown, got to number 7. However, Brown was never able to follow up on his success. His band disintegrated during their 1969 tour of America for the usual reasons of stress and over-indulgence in the rock 'n' roll lifestyle, and by the time he put another act together a year later, the momentum had been lost. The sight of Arthur doing his "Egyptian" dancing, with head-dress aflame and robes thrashing, made the band a surefire hit on the live circuit, but they never were able to regain the moment.

THE CRAZY
WORLD
OF ARTHUR
BROWN

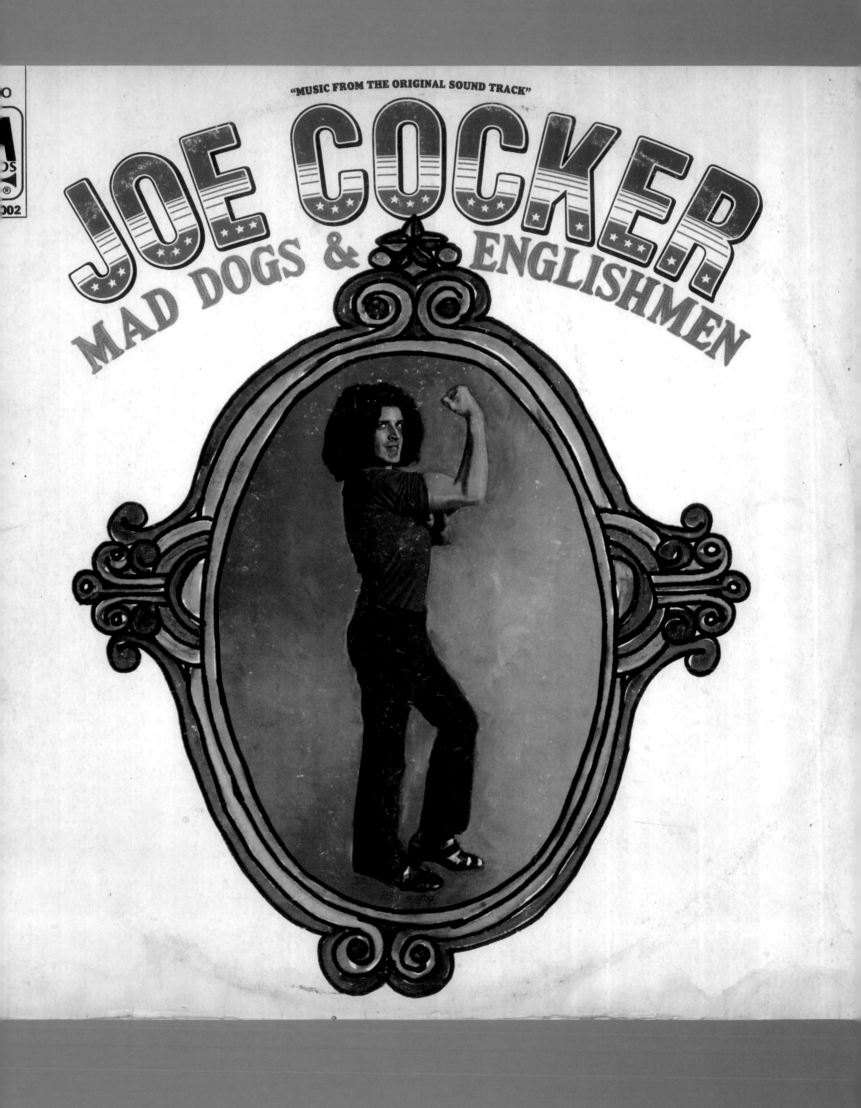

With a Little Help

The biggest second-wave British Invasion solo artist to hit America was arguably Joe Cocker, whose work during the late sixties and early seventies typified the notion of a rock 'n' roll community, with the music holding together a whole generation of young people. A huge fan of the Beatles, Cocker built his career around cover versions of their songs. His first single was I'll Cry Instead back in 1964, with Jimmy Page on lead guitar, but it went nowhere. Page also played guitar on Cocker's first hit, a slow blues rearrangement of Lennon and McCartney's With a Little Help from My Friends, taken from the *Sgt. Pepper* album and released in October 1968. It only reached number 68 in the U.S.A. but many people noticed his distinctive, raw, Sheffield blues shout and it was played by the hip underground rock stations and student stations.

The album of the same name reached number 35 in the charts, helping to establish him as part of the counter-cultural "rock as a lifestyle" community that was later defined as the Woodstock Generation. (Cocker gave a powerful performance of With a Little Help from My Friends at the Woodstock Festival which was included in the 1970 documentary film of the event, *Woodstock: Three Days of Peace and Music*.) Cocker recalled, "Those early tours of the States were the greatest. Like the gig at the Atlanta Raceway with Spirit and Janis Joplin and Hendrix. I remember going on at like, six in the morning, and all these kids acid blazed. It was a very warm occasion."

He combined forces with ex-Phil Spector sideman Leon Russell to make a follow up album, *Joe Cocker!*, which reached number 11 in 1968. Russell was good friends with Delaney & Bonnie and together they all came up with the idea for the legendary "Mad Dogs and Englishmen" tour that swung across America from March through May, 1970, with 43 musicians plus an enormous entourage of road crew, friends, groupies, and drug dealers. It showcased Cocker's soulful, uninhibited vocals (as well as his well-known air-guitar playing–later imitated by John Belushi on *Saturday Night Live* to hilarious effect), and gave rise to Cocker's two biggest American singles of the period: The Letter (which reached number 7) and Cry Me a River (number 11), both in 1970. It also spawned one of the better rock documentary films ever made, *Mad Dogs and Englishmen*, and a bestselling double album soundtrack of the same name (it reached number 2). However, the tour was too much for Cocker who came off the road in terrible shape, leaving Leon Russell to use the tour as a vehicle for his own, albeit temporary, stardom. Cocker left the tour broke: "I thought I could give it away." Sadly the tax men thought otherwise.

The distinctive, hand-colored cover of Mad Dogs *was released as the soundtrack to the movie. It was made while on the road and was an homage to traveling sideshow posters of the late 19th century.*

We ran around in the nude and had some pretty wild times.

JOE COCKER

MOODY BLUES

The Moody Blues had their greatest success in the U.S.A. in the seventies, but they were originally a British Invasion band, getting off to a good start in 1965 with Go Now, which reached number 10 in the American charts and topped the charts back home in Britain. It was a very catchy number that instantly lodged in the memory of the listener. It spent six weeks in the U.S. top 20 and established the group's name. They could have been just another invasion group but instead they chose to withdraw. Two members left (one of them, Denny Laine, showed up again six years later in Paul McCartney's Wings) and, with the addition of Justin Hayward and John Lodge, they went into seclusion to get their heads together in proper sixties style.

They re-emerged in late 1967 with a magnificent concept album, Days of Future Passed, a song cycle taking place over the course of a single day. The album fitted the zeitgeist perfectly with cosmic mystical references as far out as Donovan, strong classical themes realized with the help of the London Festival Orchestra, and even the seemingly obligatory weird new instrument (in this case the Mellotron). Days of Future Passed was perfect for underground rock stations and college radio. It reached number 3 in the American album charts, their best showing until 1972's Seventh Sojourn which got to number 1.

Days of Future Passed became the template for all the Moody Blues future albums, which sometimes even had a bit of doggerel between songs on a par with the poems of William McGonagall (a 19th-century Scot often referred to as the world's worst poet). Their follow-up, In Search of the Lost Chord (1968), contained Legend of a Mind, a track written by Ray Thomas in tribute to Timothy Leary, showing their current interests. Ever up to date, 1969's To Our Children's Children's Children was a concept album inspired by the first moon-landing. By skillfully moving from psychedelic rock to progressive rock, the band developed a cult following of devoted fans, which, at the time of writing, is still in existence.

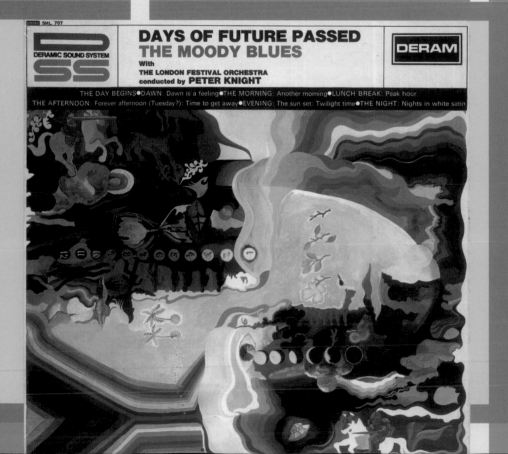

SML. 707

DERAMIC SOUND SYSTEM

DAYS OF FUTURE PASSED
THE MOODY BLUES
With
THE LONDON FESTIVAL ORCHESTRA
conducted by **PETER KNIGHT**

DERAM

THE DAY BEGINS●DAWN: Dawn is a feeling●THE MORNING: Another morning●LUNCH BREAK: Peak hour
THE AFTERNOON: Forever afternoon (Tuesday?): Time to get away●EVENING: The sun set: Twilight time●THE NIGHT: Nights in white satin

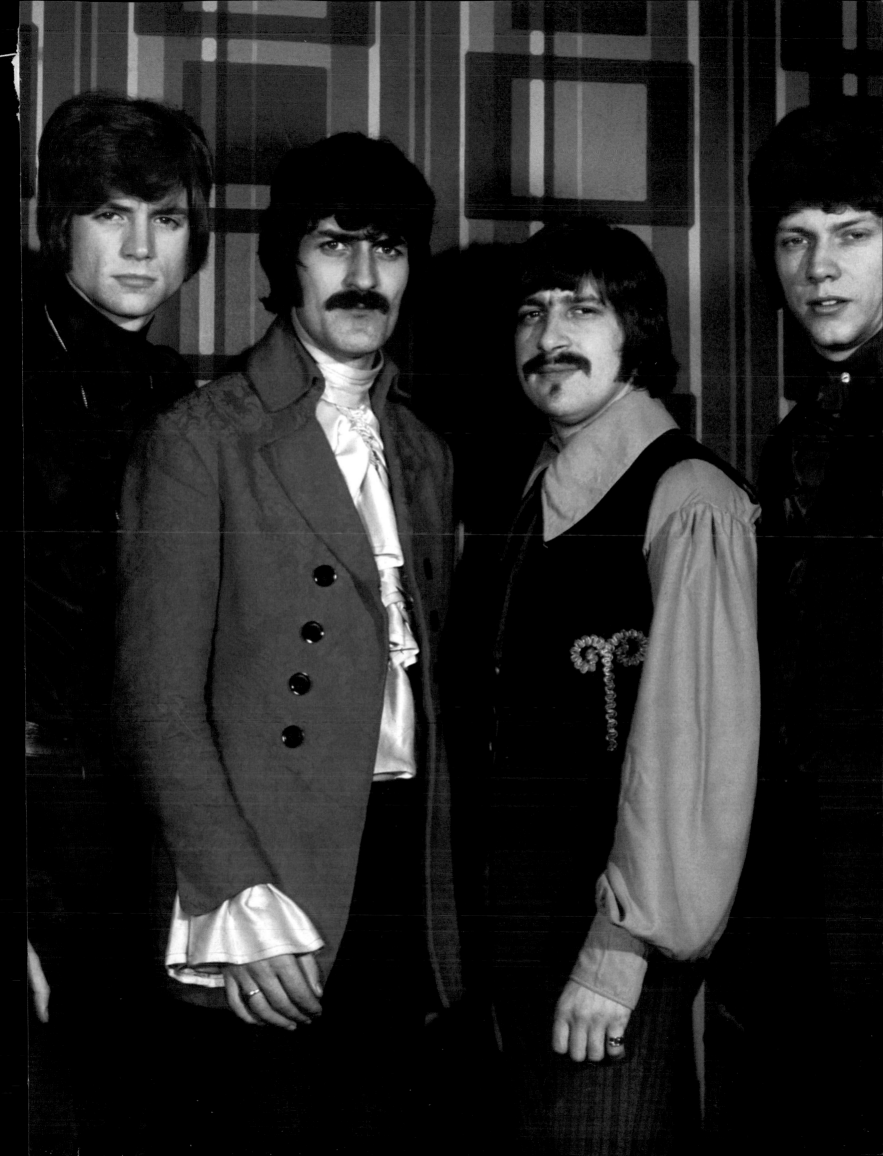

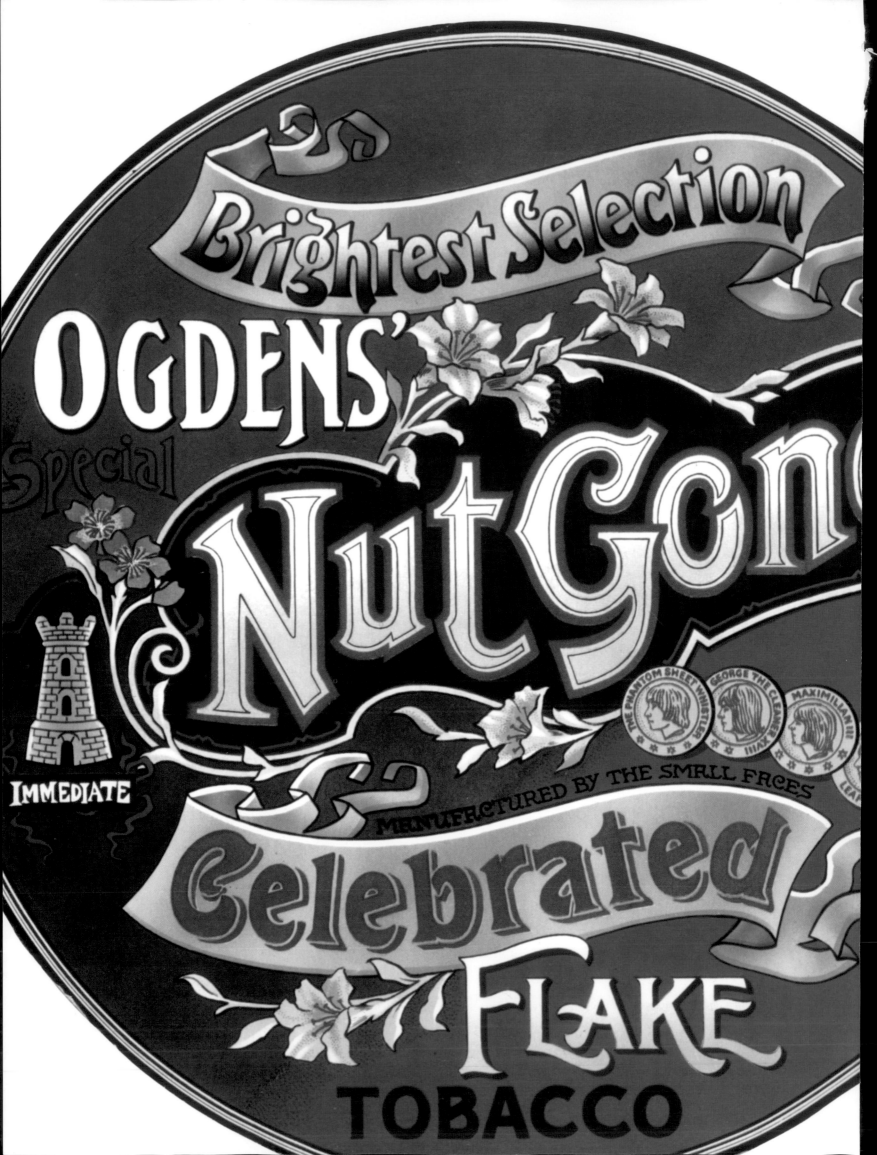

Small Faces

The Small Faces' name said it all: a "face" was Mod-speak for someone of importance, even if it was self-importance. They had all the Mod gear: sharp Italian boxy jackets and perfectly tailored suits with neatly brushed haircuts. They were filled with energy and Cockney enthusiasm. The Small Faces were essentially a singles band originally, but despite having four top 10 hits in Britain in 1966, they made no impact in America. It was not until 1967, with the overpowering influence of psychedelia, that they turned hippie with a vengeance, dressing in flowery shirts, velvet, and Nehru jackets, and releasing Itchycoo Park, with its lines about getting high. It worked and in America they were seen as part of the British psychedelic movement rather than as Mods, and thanks to the massive counter-cultural youth movement, Itchycoo Park got as high as number 16 in the *Billboard* charts.

The Small Faces refused to tailor their act to the American market though, and their next album, 1968's *Ogdens' Nut Gone Flake*, was named after a brand of British pipe tobacco and used the tobacco tin as an inspiration for an elaborate fold-out, circular record sleeve. Best described as a psychedelic Cockney knees-up, it combined music hall with heavy rock. The B-side featured an inter-song narration by British comedian Stanley Unwin, whose act consisted of talking in a surreal language which sounded like English but wasn't. To make it even more unintelligible to Americans, he incorporated modern slang words fed to

him by the band. The album was regarded as a triumph in Britain (where Unwin was just as unintelligible) and it stayed at number 1 in the British album charts for six weeks. In America the record company did not know what to do with it, and in the end marketed it purely on the strength of its amazing sleeve. It only reached 159 on the charts.

In early 1969 Steve Marriott quit the band to form Humble Pie with Peter Frampton. The remaining Small Faces—Kenney Jones (drums), Ian McLagan (keyboards), and Ronnie Lane (bass)—teamed up with singer Rod Stewart and guitarist Ronnie Wood from the Jeff Beck Group to become the Faces and finally Rod Stewart and the Faces. They became one of the greatest live acts to tour America between 1970 and 1973. By joining up with "Rod the Mod" they returned to their roots.

Trafficking

Traffic emerged from the British R&B and rock 'n' roll community of musicians. They were led by Stevie Winwood, an astonishing singer and guitarist who first began his career with the Spencer Davis Group when he was only sixteen. The story of Traffic could have been written by a P.R. man (and probably was): Stevie Winwood, Chris Wood (flute and sax), drummer Jim Capaldi, and guitarist Dave Mason spent six months in a remote country cottage in Aston Tirrold in Berkshire "getting their act together"—or, as Stevie Winwood recalled it: "four blokes not even out of their teens, shoved together and living in squalor." It worked and gave rise to their critically acclaimed first album, *Mr. Fantasy*. Released in the U.S.A. in December 1967, it reached number 88 in the charts and was the source of the single Paper Sun, which also made the U.S. charts, creeping in at 94.

Their next album did much better in the U.S.A. *Traffic* (1968) reached number 17 and was followed in 1969 by *Last Exit* at number 19. Then came four top 10 studio albums, making Traffic one of the biggest bands of the early

Above: Traffic's major international hit single, Hole In My Shoe.

Right: As an organist and guitarist, Steve Winwood backed visiting blues singers Muddy Waters, John Lee Hooker, Howlin' Wolf, B. B. King, Chuck Berry, Bo Diddley, and many others, which gave him a thorough grounding in rhythm and blues.

The moment of truth for Steve Winwood came in April, 1967. He had risen to fame as lead singer with the highly popular Spencer Davis group. Now he decided to leave and launch a group of his own. He was still only 18 years old.

He was young, but in a way a showbiz veteran. He first started making music at six—picking out tunes on the family piano. At nine, he appeared in the band run by his father—a professional sax player. Later he added to this experience by performing in a jazz group run by his brother, Muff. That was in Birmingham, his home city.

Spencer Davis had been asked to perform regularly at an R. & B.club which had opened in Birmingham. He had already met Steve, Muff and Pete York on the local scene. He asked them to form a group with him, and they agreed. They achieved much together till the time Steve decided he wanted to form his own group and give his own ideas about music a chance of full expression.

Traffic . . . the name for the new group was the idea of drummer Jim Capaldi. It came to him one night as he left a Birmingham cinema and saw the traffic hopelessly jammed up. Steve had formed the group with him and Dave Mason (guitar, percussion, harp, sitar) and Chris Wood (tenor sax, flute, percussion).

First Traffic disc was "Paper Sun". It was about a girl who had gone to Guernsey, in the Channel Islands, to look for work. It hit the charts in June, 1967—and Traffic had credit not only for having recorded it but for having written it. The group were talked about, not just for their disc but for the fact that they worked in a country hideaway on the Berkshire Downs.

How and why did they come to pick on this hideaway? Explains Steve: "Our basic thought was that we wanted somewhere to concentrate on our songwriting and on our recording ideas. It had to be away from all the rush and tear of showbusiness. We heard about this cottage from a friend. It proved to be just the job. True, there were snags. When we moved in, we found there was no phone, no hot water and no electricity. The last snag was the greatest problem. We needed electricity for our instruments. We solved the problem by arranging for a cable to be run from the house next door, which had electricity."

Traffic improved their lot in other ways. They contacted a girl in a local cafe who was ready, willing and able to bring hot meals to the cottage. They rigged up an outdoor stage for rehearsals. The weather was cold, so they played their instruments wearing gloves with the fingers cut away.

For relaxation from their work Traffic hired horses and went riding through the Berkshire countryside.

"Paper Sun" was followed by another chart success, "Hole in my Shoe". It was put out with a coloured sleeve showing Traffic in a field of buttercups.

Then in the early weeks of 1968 the group scored a double success. In the LP charts they scored with their first album, "Mr. Fantasy". In the singles charts, they registered a profitable run with "Here We Go Round the Mulberry Bush".

The latter disc was, of course, linked with the film of the same name—starring Barry Evans, Judy Geeson and Adrienne Posta. Traffic had been asked to write some of the music for the film back in the summer of 1967. They had worked on it at their Berkshire cottage—at one time planning "Here We Go Round the Mulberry Bush" as their first single. Later they decided to delay its release until somewhere near the date of the film's premiere.

Late in 1967 it was announced that Dave Mason was leaving the group for a solo career. Steve declared Traffic would be carrying on as a trio. What seemed sure was that the musical talents of the group would keep them busy on the scene, whatever their number. Dave re-joined in May, 1968.

Steve Winwood!
Chris Wood!
Jim Capaldi!
Dave Mason!

seventies. The band was troubled by constant lineup changes, though, with Dave Mason leaving and then returning, followed by Winwood leaving to join Blind Faith and also make a solo album before eventually also returning. Traffic's great value was to extend rock 'n' roll to include jazz, folk, and Indian influences and to use a multi-instrumental lineup to introduce textures and layers previously unknown in rock.

Procol Harum

Procol Harum are one of those progressive rock peculiarities: a cult band whose members remain virtually anonymous. They grew out of the Paramounts, one of Brian Epstein's less successful signings, who made six singles and an extended player for Parlophone before calling it quits. Then their vocalist Gary Brooker met Keith Reid at a party. Reid had just written some vaguely surrealist lyrics that

Their first single made Procul Harum internationally famous and instantly successful.

he called Procol Harum, which is cod Latin for "beyond these things" (correctly, it would be *procul his*) and the name of a Burmese cat owned by one of his friends, the legendary producer Guy Stevens. Brooker set the lyrics to music by appropriating themes from Bach's Air on a G String and Sleepers Awake, though there are no direct quotes. They called it A Whiter Shade of Pale and knew the song was a winner.

Having advertised in the music press and assembled a band called Procol Harum, they signed to Deram Records and recorded the song at Olympic Studios in London, with Denny Cordell producing. It was released on May 12, 1967, and premiered at the U.F.O. Club that same night. The band played U.F.O. again on June 9, by which time the single was already number 1 in Britain. Whiter Shade of Pale later reaching number 5 in the American charts, with the album *Procol Harum* climbing to number 47 (their best American album chart position was a live album in 1972, which reached number 5).

When performing live the band would often be dressed as medieval knights and courtiers, though that was as exciting as it got; their act consisted largely of standing immobile on stage throughout their set, barely moving a muscle. Nonetheless, they still toured hard, partied hard, and quickly succumbed to the rock 'n' roll illness: "too much too soon." Tours were canceled and band members hospitalized for "exhaustion."

Their second and third albums both did well in America, though: *Shine On Brightly* reached number 24 in 1968 and *A Salty Dog*, a particular favorite of their fans, reached 32 the following year.

Procol Harum Mk II in superhero capes perform for TV in 1968. From left: Gary Brooker, Dave Knights, Robin Trower, B. J. Wilson and Mathew Fisher.

Jethro Tull

There were just so many bands around by the late sixties that in order to attract attention you had to have a gimmick: a flaming head-dress, a lightshow, or a charismatic frontman or woman. Jethro Tull appeared on the scene with a wild-haired flute player, standing on one leg like the Pied Piper of Hamlin, taking center stage. His demonic playing dominated their sound. The American public first saw them on a television special in 1970 called *Switched on Symphony* in which the Los Angeles Philharmonic attempted to work with various pop groups. Jethro Tull wiped the floor with the other bands and their Bourée was the best thing on the program. The *Los Angeles Times*' classical music critic wrote: "A clever fellow named Ian Anderson does marvelously obscene things to Bach, to a bourrée, and to a flute in one brief episode." Their album *This Was* reached number 62 in 1969 but it was not until the seventies that they had their real American success with albums such as *Thick As a Brick* and *A Passion Play*, both of which went to number 1 (in 1972 and 1973).

Jethro Tull was formed by the amalgam of two British blues band: The John Evan Band and McGregor's Engine. In addition to being the first British invader to wear tights and a codpiece like a medieval court jester, Ian Anderson can be credited with introducing the flute to rock 'n' roll, and he subsequently utilized ethnic flutes and whistles to vary the acoustic textures in Tull's music. He later added mandolin, Balalaika and other less well known stringed instruments to the band's repertoire.

Above: From left: Glen Cornick, Ian Anderson, Clive Bunker, and Mick Abrahams pose for the back cover of their debut album This Was.

Right: The cover of This Was *featured the band disguised as aged backwoods men. They didn't explain why.*

Are You Experienced?

Were it not for the British Invasion, rock might have been denied one of its greatest ever acts: the Jimi Hendrix Experience. Hendrix, born in Seattle, moved to New York City in January 1964 and got by playing with acts like the Isley Brothers and Little Richard in their backing bands. Little Richard was to remain an influence, with Hendrix saying, "I want to do with my guitar what Little Richard does with his voice." It was thanks to Linda Keith—then Keith Richards' girlfriend—that Hendrix was discovered. She first recommended him to Andrew Loog Oldham and producer Seymour Stein, both of whom decided they were not interested. She next approached Chas Chandler, the bassist who was fed up with the Animals and looking for a band of his own to manage and produce. He heard Hendrix play Hey Joe and thought he could make it into a hit single. He signed him up and flew with him to London in September 1966 where he paired him with two British musicians, bass player Noel Redding and drummer Mitch Mitchell. (Hendrix could not decide between Mitchell and Aynsley Dunbar; the result was decided by the flip of a coin. Dunbar went on to play with Zappa, Journey, and many other American bands.)

Chandler was right about Hey Joe, and Hendrix was quickly taken up by Eric Clapton, Pete Townshend, Paul McCartney, and the other rock aristocracy in London. He became a fixture on the "in club" rock 'n' roll night life, jamming at the Speakeasy and the Bag O' Nails. His new group, dubbed the Jimi Hendrix Experience, quickly established themselves in the British charts and on television. Their first three singles all went top 10 in the UK: Hey Joe in December 1966, Purple Haze in March 1967, and The Wind Cries Mary in May of the same year. Meanwhile, the only thing stopping their debut album, *Are You Experienced?*, from being number 1 was *Sgt. Pepper*. Hendrix famously learned the title song and played it days after the album's release at the Saville Theater to the Beatles.

Paul McCartney was on the board of the Monterey Festival in 1967 and suggested that Hendrix should be asked to perform at it. Hendrix blew the crowd away and Jimi's American record company finally readied his debut album for release, as usual leaving out tracks and adding singles. It sold well, causing his follow-up, *Axis: Bold As Love*, to be delayed in the U.S.A. because the first album was still "shifting units." Eventually, *Axis: Bold As Love* went on to reach number 3 in the American album charts. The album had been hard to make, having been beset by problems including Hendrix leaving the original master tape of side one in a London taxi, and it was never seen again.

The third Jimi Hendrix Experience album, *Electric Ladyland*, was released in the U.S.A. in September 1968 and went to number 1, his only album to hit the top. It is thought by some to be the greatest rock album of all time. It certainly sums up the period and has to be the greatest psychedelic guitar album. Hendrix's insistence at having loads of friends and hangers on in the studio during recording, and his perfectionism—there were 43 takes of Gypsy Eyes—precipitated a falling out with Chas Chandler, meant that they severed their management ties in May 1968. Chandler sold his management share to his partner Mike Jeffery. Relations were also strained between Noel Redding and Hendrix during the recording of the album and *Electric Ladyland* was the last album the Jimi Hendrix Experience made. Hendrix went on to form the Band of Gypsies with Americans Buddy Miles and Billy Cox, so from this point on can no longer be regarded as a member of the British Invasion. He remained in love with London and his English girlfriend Kathy Etchingham, and it was in London that he died on September 18, 1970.

AND IN
THE END . . .

WHAT WAS THE LEGACY OF THE BRITISH INVASION? *Rock 'n' Roll had died in 1958, was resurrected in 1963 in Britain and returned to the States in a different form. It had the same youthful energy and teen spirit, only this time it had a British accent.*

The ephemera of the first era of rock 'n' roll—hot rods, leather jackets, pony tails, jelly-roll hairdos, jukeboxes, drive-ins, James Dean, and Marlon Brando—has become identified with the music to form an image of a distinct youth movement that is now looked back on with nostalgia as representative of a golden age of American popular culture. This is why there is such a strong interest in "oldies" with radio stations such as WCBS-FM devoted entirely to fifties music and a proliferation of vintage clothing and vintage record shops in the big cities. The era is a source of imagery that is constantly raided by advertisers and designers, and never seems to lose its fascination.

The second era of rock 'n' roll, that of the British Invasion, brought in long hair and Carnaby Street fashions for men, and Mary Quant and Mod clothes for women. The British Invasion should be restricted to the period 1964–7, but the central role played by the Beatles, the Rolling Stones, and other bands that dominated the sixties means that it is inexorably bound up with the whole counterculture of the decade and beyond: with hippies, drugs, and the anti-war movement. What began with girls throwing away their hairspray ended with them throwing away their bras (though that was largely a myth) and the movement for sexual freedom and demands for personal freedom helped to pave the way towards equality for blacks, gays, and women.

The second rock 'n' roll era was bigger and had more products than the first. The Beatles transformed the world of pop merchandising, which up until then had consisted largely of Colonel Tom Parker touting signed photographs of Elvis

American Beatles albums were not released in Britain. Those that bore some resemblance to UK releases had different tracks and often fewer of them. The Beatles reinstated the original formats when they released their records on CD but many Americans were nostalgic for the playlists of their youth. **Meet the Beatles** *was released in January 1964 in the U.S.A.*

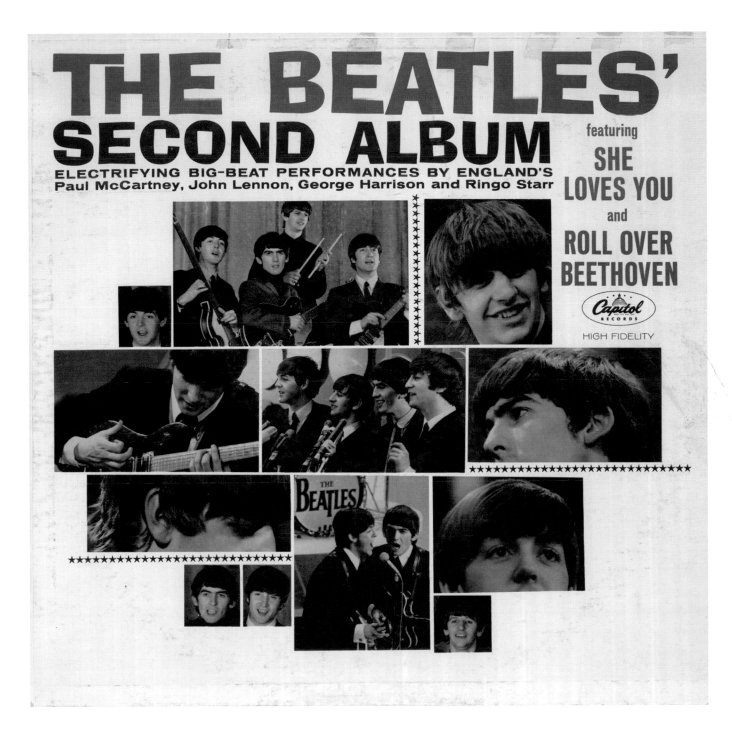

in the aisles at gigs. With the Beatles came Beatles wigs, wallpaper, posters, post-cards, trays, stockings, dolls, pencil cases, bags, notebooks, and in fact just about any product that had a surface on it big enough for the word "Beatles" to be printed on it with, if there was room, four tiny stylized heads. The Beatles lost control of their merchandising when it quickly got out of hand, but subsequent bands realized its potential and now merchandising is a major part of the income stream of any major working band.

As Jimmy Horton (and Lonnic Doncgan) sang in The Battle of New Orleans: "the British kept a-coming." These days people refer to the peacock boys and girls with funny hair such as A Flock of Seagulls, Adam Ant, Duran Duran, Psychedelic Furs, New Order, and so on as the "Second British Invasion," but surely that title should go to the great wave of British acts who dominated the American stadiums in the seventies: Elton John, Pink Floyd, Wings, David Bowie, Rod Stewart, Rolling Stones, and so on. The fact is, once British acts got a

There was no Beatles Second Album (April 1964) released in Britain— instead it was With The Beatles (November 1963) which contained only five of the songs included here.

IGINAL MOTION PICTURE SOUND TRAC

THE BEATLES

A HARD DAY'S NIGHT

gh fidelity   THE BEATLES · A HARD DAY'S NIGHT · UNITED ARTISTS UAL 3366

foothold, they never really went away. Though the traffic has slowed somewhat, there is usually a good showing of British acts in the American charts.

The Beatles grew up with the same fantasy of the first rock 'n' roll era that people have today, only it was viewed from a distant, poverty-stricken country where everything in America seemed larger than life: the U.S.A. was more highly colored, brighter, more romantic, more wonderful, and freer than Britain. The British did not see the conformity, the endless mindless suburbs, the poverty, or the segregation in the South; they only saw the American promise, Abe Lincoln's American Dream, where it seemed human potential could be fulfilled. The Beatles did seem to hold a mirror to America and in their endless press conferences—one before each concert as well as many on radio and TV—they constantly praised America.

The U.S.A. was still in a state of shock at the time; the death of President Kennedy appeared to have dented its spirit. The arrival of the Beatles reminded them of Kennedy's speeches: how an American would walk on the Moon, how there would be full integration of schools in the South, how America would lead the world in science and the humanities. The sense of purpose—and destiny—had seemed all but wiped away by Oswald and whoever was behind the assassination.

More than that, the Beatles helped to show to Americans aspects of the nation that they had not previously noticed properly: the great R&B artists of the north, the rich blues tradition of the south, and the black vocal groups—great American music just waiting to be rediscovered. Sometimes it takes an outsider to show you the obvious. The music might have originated in the American South, the industrial cities of America's North, and the honky tonks of the Midwest, but it was finessed and played by the British; the fashion may have been Italian and French-influenced, but it was shipped across the Atlantic by the British; the movies may have taken their lead from Hollywood and Paris, but they were made in England. The attitude and accents, at least, were all British. And it was acceptable because it was coming from Britain, the country with which the U.S.A. has its greatest historical ties. Millions of Americans have British ancestors; it is the home of the language and much of the legal system; innumerable place names east of the Mississippi have British origins; and less than 20 years before the Beatles arrived, Brits had fought alongside Americans in the Second World War. So, it was more like cousins coming to visit than a real invasion.

And once the British found they were welcome, more and more of them came. In the 1970s, in addition to Elton John, Rod the Mod, and the big stadium acts, the British gave heavy metal to America. Black Sabbath, Judas Priest, and

The American cover for the soundtrack to A Hard Day's Night was different to the UK release, as was the track listing. It was released in July 1964 in the UK and June the same year in the U.S.A.

It was like being in the eye of a hurricane.

JOHN LENNON

Led Zeppelin were all formed in 1968 and hailed originally from the industrial Midlands of Britain, but they struck a chord, particularly in Rust Belt America. Heavy metal also gave American musicians the opportunity to grow their hair really long and sing in Minnie Mouse voices so that in the end there were dozens of heavy rock bands doing the rounds.

Then Britain came up with Glam Rock, taking dressing up to a new level of subversiveness. Singers like David Bowie influenced kids like the Ramones to started their own bands; Patti Smith, the Ramones, and Blondie, who in turn crossed the Atlantic and inspired Britain's homegrown punks to start their own. The Sex Pistols were the first to go to America—which killed them—and then came the Clash, who reintroduced America once again to the beauty of the original rock 'n' roll music of the fifties, complete with all the appropriate stage moves taken from the classic rock 'n' roll pose handbook from Elvis Presley to Pete Townshend.

In the early eighties, Boy George and Culture Club had a string of top 10 hits in the U.S.A. with Do You Really Want to Hurt Me?, Time (Clock of the Heart), Karma Chameleon, Miss Me Blind, and so on. America responded by giving the world Madonna who had also received more coverage in Britain than in the U.S.A. in the early days of her career—Sire Records boss Seymour Stein realized the importance of the British rock press after seeing how British press coverage of the Ramones and Talking Heads had helped break the bands in America. Then came a wholly African-American music, hip-hop and rap, which would be particularly hard for the British to appropriate.

In the late eighties, American Kurt Cobain and Nirvana were well received in Britain, where the Seattle-based Sub Pop label groups were given enormous coverage by the British music weeklies such as *Sounds* and the *NME*. Cobain was

Right: In Britain Beatles For Sale, from which 8 of the 11 tracks on Beatles '65 are taken, was released in the same month, December 1964.

Below left: Beatles VI was released in June 1965 and collected together tracks from various UK releases that hadn't been issued in the States.

apparently singing Beatles songs by the age of two and wrote About a Girl after listening to *Meet the Beatles* for three hours straight. He named Led Zeppelin, Black Sabbath, and Queen as early influences and loved the British seventies punk bands. British media coverage helped Nirvana to be taken on in a big way back in America, where they inspired the whole grunge movement. Grunge bands played the kind of guitar music that the Beatles had brought to America 30 years earlier, just louder and faster, and with their shirts untucked.

Not everything transfers easily both ways and there have certainly been some blips along the way. There was a period in the middle of the nineties when both countries went nationalistic. The British spawned some Beatles impersonators and called it Brit Pop, which made little impact outside of the country, while America embraced Garth Brooks and country music in a way that no other nation could.

In the 21st century pop music has seemingly lost its power to influence whole sections of culture and society in the way that it had back in 1964. In the sixties, the Beatles were like a huge roadblock that bands had to somehow deal with, one way or another. Since then, popular music has fragmented into endless, ever smaller sub-divisions, and those in turn have become globalized. There are no longer obvious national differences in music: it has been commoditized and homogenized. Britain's Leona Lewis could almost be the sister of American Beyoncé Knowles; Radiohead could hail from Chicago as easily as Oxford; Nickelback could be from London, England, instead of Alberta, Canada; the Fray could have formed in Grantham, Lincolnshire, instead of Greeley, Colorado. Only rap and country stars seem more authentic if they are American (though some Europeans would argue about rap).

We were all on this ship in the sixties, our generation, a ship going to discover the new world. And the Beatles were in the crow's nest.

JOHN LENNON

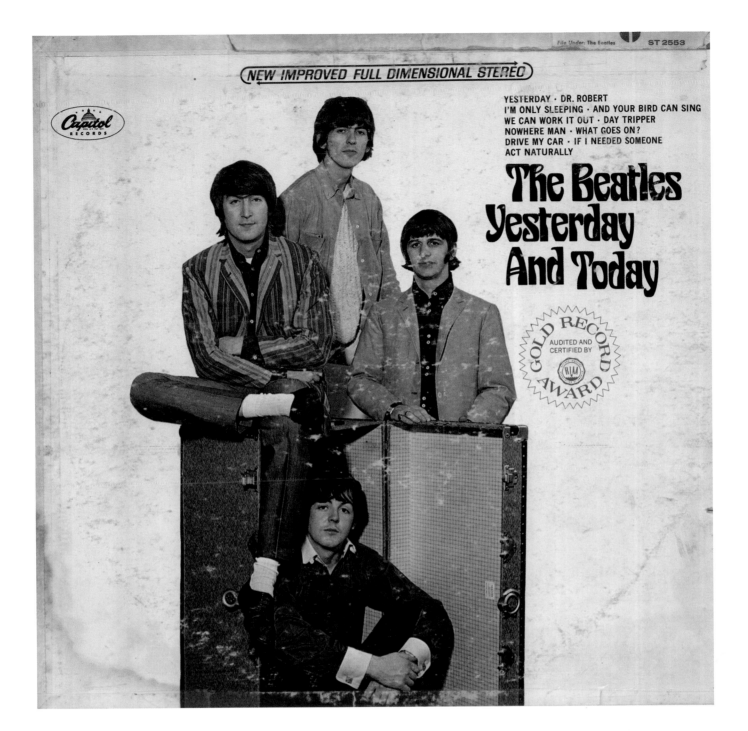

Pop, rock, R&B, metal, and even jazz musicians can and do hail from all around the world in the 21st century. There will never be another British Invasion because we all wear clothes from Gap (made in India), drink coffee in Starbucks (grown in South America), get insurance from A.I.G., use Visa credit cards, talk via Motorola cell phones, communicate via the internet using Apple computers, and listen to our music on iPods.

There are no more social or cultural borders to cross (though many political borders remain). There are no differences to celebrate between kids who watch the same videos on YouTube, illegally download the same tracks from websites, twitter to each other about the same mundane inanities, and have crushes on the same actors in the lucrative, worldwide smash movies and T.V. franchises.

It's doubtful that JFK airport will ever again see scenes of teen mania like those witnessed on February 9, 1964, and certainly not for something as unimportant and marginal as a "pop band" has become.

John Lennon disliked this sleeve, taken when he was in what he called his "Fat Elvis" phase. The first Beatles-approved cover image had the band wearing butcher's aprons, slabs of raw meat, and broken dolls. The record company didn't approve, though.

Index

Picture credits

The author and publishers have made every reasonable effort to contact all copyright holders. Any errors that may have occurred are inadvertent and anyone who for any reason has not been contacted is invited to write to the publishers so that a full acknowledgement may be made in subsequent editions of this work.

2 courtesy of *16* magazine, 6 Bettmann/Corbis, 9 Corbis, 10 Swim Ink 2 LLC/Corbis, 12 Michael Ochs Archives/Corbis, 14 courtesy of NIXA/UK, 16 courtesy of *Life* magazine, 17 courtesy of *Life* magazine, 18 Michael Ochs Archives/Corbis, 21 courtesy of London records, 22 Michael Ochs Archives/Corbis, 23 courtesy of Columbia records, 24 courtesy of Columbia records, 26 courtesy of World Distributors, 28 courtesy of Ace records, 29 courtesy of Summit records, 30 courtesy of *Tiger Beat* magazine, 31 courtesy of Chess records, 32 courtesy of *Tiger Beat* magazine, 33 Michael Ochs Archives/Getty Images, 35 Bettmann/Corbis, 36 Michael Ochs Archives/Corbis, 37 courtesy of Checker records, 38 Bettmann/Corbis, 39 courtesy of *Photoplay* magazine, 40 Michael Levin/Corbis, 43 Michael Ochs Archives/Corbis, 45 courtesy of MXA records, 46 Keystone/Getty Images, 48 Bettmann/Corbis, 50 courtesy of *Talking Pictures* magazine, 51 courtesy of CBS records, 52 Michael Ochs Archives/Corbis, 53 courtesy of Reprise records, 54 Bettmann/Corbis, 55 courtesy of Fontana records, 56 (top) courtesy of Penguin Books, 56 (bottom) courtesy of Apple Corps Ltd., 57 courtesy of *Shindig* magazine, 58 Bettmann/Corbis, 60 courtesy of Lancer Books, 61 Popperfoto/Getty Images, 63 courtesy of *Tiger Beat* magazine, 66 courtesy of *Teen Circle* magazine, 67 CA/Redferns, 68 courtesy of Apple Corps Ltd., 69 John Springer Collection/Corbis, 70 courtesy of Marvel Comics, 71 courtesy of Marvel Comics, 72 Michael Ochs Archives/Getty Images, 75 courtesy of *Teen Life* magazine, 76 Bettmann/Corbis, 77 courtesy of *Photoplay* magazine, 78 courtesy of Apple Corps Ltd., 80 courtesy of Epic records, 81 courtesy of Columbia records, 82 Bettmann/Corbis, 84 courtesy of *16* magazine, 86 courtesy of Columbia records, 87 courtesy of Barry Miles, 88 courtesy of *Shindig* magazine, 89 CA/Redferns, 91 courtesy of MGM records, 92 courtesy of MGM records, 93 Hulton-Deutsch Collection/Corbis, 94 courtesy of *Tiger Beat* magazine, 96 Hulton-Deutsch Collection/Corbis, 98 courtesy of Philips records, 99 Michael Ochs Archives/Corbis, 100 Bettmann/Corbis, 103 Bettmann/Corbis, 104 Bettmann/Corbis, 105 courtesy of Magnum Publications, 107 CAT'S/Corbis KIPA, 108 Bettmann/Corbis, 110 Bettmann/Corbis, 112 courtesy of Apple Corps Ltd., 113 Bettmann/Corbis, 114 courtesy of *Photoplay* magazine, 116 courtesy of Vogue records, 117 courtesy of Fontana records, 118 courtesy of CBS records, 119 courtesy of Deram records, 120 John Hoppy Hopkins *www.hoppy.be*, 122 John Hoppy Hopkins *www.hoppy.be*, 123 Terry Cryer/Corbis, 124 courtesy of *Photoplay* magazine, 127 courtesy of *Photoplay* magazine, 129 courtesy of EMI records, 130 courtesy of EMI records, 131 courtesy of EMI records, 134 Tony Frank/Sygma/Corbis, 137 courtesy of Reprise records, 138 CinemaPhoto/Corbis, 141 courtesy of Sphere Books, 145 courtesy of Magnum Publications, 146 courtesy of Columbia records, 148 courtesy of United Artists, 150 courtesy of *Tiger Beat* magazine, 151 courtesy of MGM records, 152 Hulton-Deutsch Collection/Corbis, 153 courtesy of the Rank Organisation, 154 Paul Guglielmo/Apis/Sygma/Corbis, 156 John Springer Collection/Corbis, 158 courtesy of United Artists, 159 Bettmann/Corbis, 160 courtesy of Colpix records, 161 Bettmann/Corbis, 162 Bettmann/Corbis, 163 courtesy of CBS records, 164 courtesy of RCA records, 165 Hulton-Deutsch Collection/Corbis, 166 courtesy of United Artists, 168 courtesy of *Photoplay* magazine, 170 Bettmann/Corbis, 171 courtesy of Allegro records, 172 courtesy of *16* magazine, 175 CinemaPhoto/Corbis, 176 Hulton-Deutsch Collection/Corbis, 177 courtesy of Panther Books, 179 Sunset Boulevard/Corbis, 181 courtesy of Buena Vista records, 182 courtesy of New English Library, 183 courtesy of Pyramid Publication and King Features, 184 Bettmann/Corbis, 186 Hulton-Deutsch Collection/Corbis, 187 Bettmann/Corbis, 188 Maurice Rougemont/Sygma/Corbis, 190 courtesy of *16* magazine, 191 Bettmann/Corbis, 192 Bettmann/Corbis, 193 courtesy of Cassell Books, 195 courtesy of Archie Comic Publications, 196 courtesy of *16* magazine, 197 courtesy of *Datebook* magazine, 198 Hulton-Deutsch Collection/Corbis, 199 courtesy of Columbia records, 200 Ted West/Central Press/Getty Images, 202 courtesy of Fleetway Publications, 204 Hulton-Deutsch Collection/Corbis, 206 Hulton-Deutsch Collection/Corbis, 207 Bettmann/Corbis, 208 courtesy of Berkley Publishing, 209 R. Viner/Express/Getty Images, 210 Bettmann/Corbis, 212 courtesy of *Time* magazine, 213 Bettmann/Corbis, 214 courtesy of Roulette records, 215 Hulton-Deutsch Collection/Corbis, 217 courtesy of Apple Corps Ltd., 218 courtesy of CBS records, 220 courtesy of Premier Albums, 221 courtesy of EMI records, 222 courtesy of Polydor records, 223 Bettmann/Corbis, 224 courtesy of Paramount, 225 courtesy of Autumn records, 226 (left) courtesy of Decca records, 226 (right) courtesy of United Artists, 227 courtesy of CBS records, 230 courtesy of CBS records, 232 courtesy of Kama Sutra records, 233 Bettmann/Corbis, 234 courtesy of Apple Corps Ltd., 235 courtesy of Capitol records, 236 courtesy of Kahn Communications, 238 Bettmann/Corbis, 241 Bettmann/Corbis, 242 courtesy of RCA records, 243 courtesy of RCA records, 244 Bettmann/Corbis, 245 courtesy of Columbia records, 246 courtesy of *Tiger Beat* magazine, 249 Hulton-Deutsch Collection/Corbis, 250 John Springer Collection/Corbis, 251 courtesy of EMI records, 252 BIPs/Getty Images, 255 courtesy of Apple Corps Ltd., 256 courtesy of Epic records, 257 Henry Diltz/Corbis, 258 courtesy of Tower records, 260 courtesy of Reaction records, 261 courtesy of Purnell and Sons Ltd., 263 Jan Olofsson/Redferns, 264 Hulton-Deutsch Collection/Corbis, 265 courtesy of EMI records, 266 Hulton-Deutsch Collection/Corbis, 268 courtesy of Atlantic records, 269 courtesy of Atlantic records, 270 courtesy of EMI records, 271 Andrew Whittuck/Redferns, 272 Michael Ochs Archives/Corbis, 273 (left) courtesy of Epic records, 273 (right) courtesy of Pye records, 274 Ron Howard/Redferns, 275 courtesy of Track records, 276 courtesy of A&M records, 278 courtesy of Deram records, 279 Hulton-Deutsch Collection/Corbis, 280 courtesy of Immediate/UK/Sanctuary records, 281 Petra Niemeier – K & K/Redferns, 282 (top) courtesy of Island records, 282 (bottom) courtesy of Purnell Books, 283 Neal Preston/Corbis, 284 courtesy of Deram records, 285 Michael Ochs Archives/Getty Images, 286 Michael Ochs Archives/Getty Images, 287 courtesy of Chrysalis records, 288 Douglas Kent Hall/ZUMA/Corbis, 290 Bettmann/Corbis, 292 courtesy of Apple Corps Ltd., 293 courtesy of Apple Corps Ltd., 294 courtesy of Apple Corps Ltd., 296 courtesy of Apple Corps Ltd., 297 courtesy of Apple Corps Ltd., 299 courtesy of Apple Corps Ltd.

Where T...
All Beg...

Ever wondered wher... the great names of to... day started from? I did... so I went and found ou...

Ireland

Peter O'Toole . .
Connemara,
2nd August, 1933.

Richard Harris . .
Limerick,
1st October, 1933.

United States of America

Bob Random . .
Chilliwack (B. Columbia),
29th January, 1945.

Simon Dee . . Ontario,
Canada, 28th July, 1936.

Bob Dylan . . Duluth,
Minnesota,
24th May, 1941.

NEW YORK
James Drury
18th April, 1934.
John Walker
12th November, 1943.
Felix Cavaliere (Young
Rascals)
19th November, 1942.

CHICAGO
Raymond Manzarek
(Doors)
2nd December, 1942.
Bruce Johnston (Beach
Boys)
27th June, 1944.
Raquel Welch . .
5th September, 1942.

Al Jardine (Beach Boys)
Lima, Ohio,
3rd September, 1942.

Eddie Brigati (You...
Rascals) . . Garfiel...
22nd October, 194...

Michael Parks . .
Corona (Calif.),
24th April, 1938.

Scott Walker . .
Hamilton, Ohio,
9th January, 1944.

Peter Tork . .
Washington,
13th February, 19...
Jimi Hendrix . .
Washington, 27th
November, 1945.

LOS ANGELES
Robert Krieger (Doors),
1st August, 1946.
4th December, 1944.
Mike Love (Beach Boys)
15th March, 1941.
Burt Ward
6th July, 1945.
Ryan O'Neal
20th April, 1941.
Micky Dolenz
8th March, 1945.

...ian Wilson (Beach
...ys) . . Hawthorne,
...lifornia, 20th June,
...42.

Carl Wilson (Beach
Boys) . . Hawthorne,
California,
21st December, 1946.

Dennis Wilson (Beach
Boys) . . Hawthorne,
California,

David Janssen . .
Naponee (Nebraska),
27th March, 1930.

Lee Majors . .
Middlesboro (Kentucky),
24th April, 1941.

James Coburn . .
Laurel (Nebraska),
31st August, 1928.

Elvis Presley . . Tupelo,
Mississippi,
8th January, 1935.

John Phillip Law . .
Hollywood,
7th September, 1937.

Roy Orbison . .
Vernon, Texas,
23rd April, 1936.

Tony Bill . .
San Diego (Calif.),
23rd August, 1942.

Julie Felix . . Santa
Barbara, California,
14th June, 1941.

...hn Densmore (Doors)
...nta Monica,
...lifornia,
...t December, 1944.

Mike Nesmith . . Dallas,
30th December, 1942.

James Morrison
(Doors) . . Melbourn...
Florida,
8th December, 1943.